SECURITY MANAGEMENT:

BUSINESS STRATEGIES FOR SUCCESS

SECURITY MANAGEMENT:
BUSINESS STRATEGIES FOR SUCCESS

Dennis R. Dalton

Butterworth–Heinemann
Boston • Oxford • Melbourne • Singapore • Toronto • Munich • New Delhi • Tokyo

Copyright © 1995 by Butterworth–Heinemann

ℝ A member of the Reed Elsevier group.

All rights reserved.

 Recognizing the importance of preserving what has been written, it is the policy of Butterworth-Heinemann to have the books it publishes printed on acid-free paper, and we exert our best efforts to that end.

Library of Congress Cataloging-in-Publication Data

Dalton, Dennis R.
    Security management : business strategies for success / Dennis R. Dalton.
       p.   cm.
    Includes bibliographical references and index.
    ISBN 0-7506-9492-0
    1. Industries—Security measures—Management.   I. Title.
    HV8290.D34   1995
    658.4'7—dc20
                                      94-38942
                                        CIP

British Library Cataloguing-in-Publication Data
A catalogue record for this book is available from the British Library.

Butterworth-Heinemann
313 Washington Street
Newton, MA 02158

10 9 8 7 6 5 4 3 2
Printed in the United States of America

*This book is dedicated to my friend, business partner
and loving wife of 25 years, Linda. Simply put,
without you this would not have been possible.*

Contents

Acknowledgments

As with any first time publication, the end result is a reflection of the efforts of a lot of different people. And like so many authors, for many years I talked about "the book in me." I'd like to begin by thanking Bob Champion. A former boss and now client, but more importantly a friend and advisor. Without your support and guidance, many of the concepts in this book would not have been experienced and tested. The encouragement that Doug Griffin, a friend and colleague gave me certainly kept my dream alive. The soft, but strong support given by Bill Zalud deserves special acknowledgment as well; not to mention his kind Foreword for this book. Making this a reality is also dependent on someone's ability to get it typed. For this I thank Linda Miller. Without your timely assistance, I dare say this would still be rolling around in my mind. I want to especially thank Karen Speerstra, Laurel DeWolf, Maura Kelly, and Marcia Ledwith at Butterworth-Heinemann. Your confidence, support, copy editing, and continuous professional "checking-in" kept me on target and focused. I want to thank my reviewers, John Fay and J.T. Roberts. Your insights are greatly appreciated as evidenced by your suggestions being reflected in the book. Finally, a very personal thanks to Walter Stone, my father-in-law. A proven executive, for the past 25 years his ideas and approach to business management have proven invaluable to me. Dad you'll no doubt see a lot of your mentoring scattered throughout the book. Thank you everyone.

Foreword

This book helps you see the big picture while simultaneously making you feel like a genuine and successful part of it. That's what Dennis Dalton is all about.

New ways of doing business. Complex threats. Global competition. In big and small ways, change itself has taken on added, critical dimensions. And Dennis charts a course through the myriad transitions facing security.

Since first meeting him, I've gained a better understanding of value, accountability, flexibility, emerging knowledge, and how each impacts the security operation. Like Dalton's advice, this book, what Dennis calls "perceptions and prescriptions," provides something else—confidence to not only survive but succeed.

That dose of confidence today is more important than ever for doing business today, let alone security work, is more difficult than before. But not impossible.

Which is another concept that deserves attention: goals are reachable—especially lofty ones. Key to this accomplishment is mastering a changeable organizational fit from a narrow, fixed perspective of security.

What sounds a bit bizarre is really the first glimmer of exciting changes coming in the security field. Dennis maintains a positive and hard-nosed edge even when describing the bumpy evolution of downsizing to employee empowerment and outsourcing to strategic alliances.

By eschewing faddist gloom, we all can view these periods of sluggish business acceptance of change as a time personally and professionally to shift gears and recharge our batteries. Things, it turns out, aren't so bad.

Just as our fear of crime is both perception and reality, so too is our confusion over changes in the ways businesses and security departments operate.

For example, security workers, and especially middle managers, overwhelmingly view jobs and employment as unstable today. But career jobs, and especially asset protection jobs, haven't vanished.

Of course, throughout the 1980s, companies "downsized." The American Management Association reports that downsizing has, in fact, been institutionalized today into many organizations as a "lean and mean" cost-containment structure.

Still, most middle-aged workers have settled into jobs that last. A recent U.S. Labor Department survey found that half of all security workers between 45 and 54 had been with their present employer at least 10 years, down only slightly from 10.3 years in 1983.

And technology—an investment hot button—hasn't triggered massive career upheavals either. Most people still change their jobs for better-paying or more satisfying work, not because they have been replaced by computer software or a CCTV-equipped robot. In 1991, about 10 percent of workers shifted occupations—not much different from 1978 (12 percent) or 1966 (9 percent). New technologies may alter job content, but most of us adapt.

Part-time work hasn't exploded either. The myth that companies have substituted hordes of part-timers for career workers is less dramatic than perceived. According to the Employee Benefit Research Institute, between 1969 and 1992 the share of part-time workers in the labor force only rose from 15.5 percent to 18.9 percent. Most of this work is voluntary: parents balancing jobs and child-rearing; students mixing school and an after-class job.

So some things aren't so bad. But there's still a lot to accomplish; still a lot of changes to face. Today's rallying-cry: customer-driven reengineering. It's good to listen to Dalton's reengineering tales: like any sweet risk, business process redesign can be more failure than success, whether you're building cars or securing a warehouse. No matter what the label, however, the beliefs underlying reengineering are not fads. They're a lifetime exercise that leads to dramatic performance improvements in cost, quality, service, and speed.

Pioneer organizations have already forcefully moved away from yesterday's assembly line but only now are catching up in terms of human resources, communications, responsibilities and structure.

Littering the transition to a future of virtual corporations and borderless territories are such relics as the "functional silo," which can address security as well as sales concerns—where everyone in the silo looks inward toward themselves and upward to the boss; but no one's looking outward.

Successful reengineering of the security function, no doubt, is more than avoiding silos. It can produce quantum leaps in performance in the best ways. People aren't forced to work harder or faster. Some may have a lot more time to do their work. But they *must* know more than their jobs. They must know their context within the company.

There's simple commonality on our new bottom line:

Get paid for the value you create.

Accept ownership of problems and solve them.

Be a versatile team player.

Bill Zalud
Security Magazine

Preface

"Despite all the evidence to the contrary, we continue to believe that somewhere there are adults who know what they are doing."

Anonymous

A few years ago I was asked to address one of the sessions for the American Society for Industrial Security's annual conference. My topic was business management strategies. I began by putting up a slide that generically listed six Fortune 100 companies; e.g., A Fortune 100 Retailer, A Fortune 100 Financial Firm, A Fortune 100 Manufacturer, etc. I then asked the attendees to tell me what each had in common. The attendees expected that this was a typical workshop opening, the traditional icebreaker exercise designed to elicit a laugh and relax the audience. As a consequence, some played along with me and suggested that the commonality was their inclusion in the Fortune 100. True enough, but they were pressed for another answer. Others responded by saying that they all engage in the business of satisfying customers. Also true, but I pushed them further.

After a few more suggestions, I informed them that within the past 12 months all had released their security directors for failure to meet the business objectives of the firms. In other words, they had failed to demonstrate their ability as business managers first and security professionals second. More importantly, they had failed to show the added value their programs brought to the companies' bottom-lines. I was challenged by a Fortune 100 security director in attendance who claimed to know most of his peer group and did not believe my representation. He was shown the names of the companies and affected security directors. After pausing a moment, he admitted that he had not taken the time to actually make such a count. He was surprised that so many had, in fact, been released.

Since becoming a management consultant, I have been asked by many senior executives to assist them in assessing the "business" aptitude of their asset protection manager. Many times it has been to evaluate whether the time is right to make a change. For others, it might be a review of their workload or the organizational readiness to appoint someone to the role of full-time asset protection manager. Regardless of the reasoning, the purpose is generally the same—security is an essential service therefore, how should it be managed to achieve its objectives within the context of proven business management strategies?

One client told me that he would never hire a former law enforcement officer because they "don't understand corporate life." Another characterized her security decision-maker as being professionally competent, but lacking in basic management skills. It is a result of these experiences that I felt the need to write this book. Our industry has traditionally shied away from dealing with the need to see ourselves as part of the corporate team. Executives have likewise defined our contribution along some narrowly defined roles. Together, these issues spell a formula for something less than success. This book is a deliberate attempt to reverse the cycle. Not everyone will agree with my observations, comments, suggestions and success formulas, but seeking universal agreement is not my intent. On the other hand, if I can push the debate to a new level and get policy makers and program initiators assigned the responsibility of asset protection thinking anew, then I will have accomplished what I set out to do.

As noted in the opening chapter, our success is not tied to an ability to demonstrate competence in security matters. To do so is to achieve only half of our mission. The second part—and the more significant aspect—is an ability to demonstrate business acumen. Gone are the days of selling security as though it is a necessary evil. Rather, we should be willing to embrace a new approach, one based on showing that security of people and assets is directly related to an organization's profitability. This does not require a reliance on esoteric economic theory or complicated financial formulas. To the contrary—success is an end result, an outcome. It is the measure of doing things right, even the small and everyday things we are asked to carry out.

To realize success we must understand that it begins with speaking the language of the business we serve. This means we must first understand the business and know how our programs complement the overall plan. This requires developing and consistently implementing practices that others can relate to, e.g., strategies defined in business terms. As both a practitioner and a consultant, I have seen many security managers engage in a "smoke and mirrors" approach to defining what is needed. This type of management can lead managers to become their own Wizards of Oz.

Is it any wonder that our profession suffers some measure of credibility? Does this book contain a formula for guaranteed success? Not really, but I believe that it charts a course that certainly increases the odds. This book is about executives and for executives—both those that serve as a customer for security services and those that provide the service. It is designed to help decision-makers make smart, business oriented decisions and is set against the backdrop of today's dynamic environments. This book recognizes that the rules of yesterday can be helpful today, if they are applied in new ways. It also requires the reader to push the envelope in defining what security services are and how they are to be pursued.

For me, this book is about doing. It is intended to offer some guidance. There's a plaque that hangs on my wall. It's author is unknown, but the message is clear:

> "The man who decides
> what he wants to achieve
> And works till his dreams come true,
> The man who will alter his course
> when he must
> And bravely begin something anew,
> The man who's determined

to make his world better,
Who's willing to learn and to lead,
The man who keeps trying
and doing his best
Is the man who knows how to succeed."

Charting new courses, being bold enough to take measured risks—that is what this book is all about.

Setting the Stage

1

Recently a client asked for help assessing the feasibility of outsourcing his security force. He said that he was seeking a strategic alliance with a third party supplier. When asked what he meant by the term "strategic alliance," he explained that he wanted to create a "lean and mean" organization. Since he was already outsourcing part of his organization, he went on to tell me that the staff reductions would allow him to achieve an even lower billing rate based on the increased volume of hours possible with contract workers. On the surface this sounds like a proven business manager familiar with carrying out some of today's organizational tactics for achieving a competitive advantage. After questioning him a little further, his understanding of strategic alliances and outsourcing became suspect since they were not grounded in fact. It was apparent that his pursuit of this course would likely backfire, resulting in serious consequences. (We'll talk about the specifics in Chapter Seven.) For now, suffice it to say this experience underscores the very reason why I've decided to write this book.

Today, corporate security is going through challenging transitions. Historically, senior management paid little attention to how their asset protection programs were administered. Leadership was drawn largely from the public sector. Typically these security directors were not equipped to develop fiscally prudent plans or other business-oriented performance measures. Compounding these frustrations was that most security company owners were driven from a pure profit motive, nothing else. Guard companies were large "cash cows" with low overhead, cheap labor costs, and billing rates left unchecked because of client indifference.

Over the past several years, however, this has begun to change. Corporate management has been asking serious questions about the value of security versus bottom-line performance. In today's competitive world difficult decisions are being made about all aspects of a company's infrastructure, including security. Lacking an ability to answer client inquiries based on sound business rationales, security managers are discovering that their programs are in deep trouble. Whether such programs are necessary or not, security managers' inability to demonstrate a thought process based on solid decision-making criteria is causing them to fail. Gone are the days when a director can merely rely on "gut feelings" or conclusions that cannot be empirically measured.

Likewise, there is a growing movement by security providers to set aside "business as usual" routines. A week doesn't go by when I come across another solidly managed local or regional security company. Even the big boys are redefining their approach and developing policies, compensation strategies, billing rates, and marketing approaches that rival even some of their Fortune 100 clients. Pinkerton chairman Tom Wathen once said shortly after his company, California Plant Protection, acquired Pinkerton, "I can no longer afford to be a security man. While I must admit that I miss it at times, now I'm a corporate executive. And, if my company is going to survive, a lot of others around here are going to have to become corporate executives as well."

Although many security directors are in step with business management thinking, most are still struggling or have yet to awaken to the need. Likewise, evidence abounds that most security providers are still driven by a low-bid mentality that works against both quality service and the perceived professionalism of the industry. This book promotes the need for better management on both sides of the security fence:

THE SUCCESS CYCLE

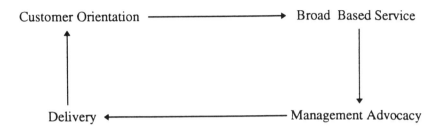

Figure 1.1: The Success Cycle

those charged with protecting a company's assets and those who assist by providing external support.

One view is that the security field is evolving. Decades ago the field was largely defined as a night watch against fire and unwanted intrusions. Security guards today provide other services, not all of which are security related. The profession has slowly developed as a business-oriented approach requiring a faster and more deliberate pace. Executives today look for managers schooled in disciplined thinking that reflects the needs of the company and their employees. Hopefully this book will serve as a tool that can help them respond accordingly.

As successful managers can attest, achievements are linked to hard work, staff support, timing, and a sprinkle of luck. Organizational achievement also comes in understanding what the role of security is and how it can contribute to your company's profit plan. As the former director of security for Continental Illinois Bank (now in merger talks with Bank of America), I saw the security budget shrink by 23 percent without reductions in quality of service and deliverables. Reworking one program alone netted a reduction of more than $1.3 million annually. As corporate security manager at Montgomery Ward, I saw similar savings achieved. Even dating back to my first days at Crocker National Bank (now part of Wells Fargo Bank) in California, success was measured by business-oriented attitudes from the security function. Success was not then, nor is it today, measured by the size of the security force or the number of recoveries made in a given year. The single, most common thread for achieving success is understanding the playing field of Corporate America and responding in business-oriented ways.

In consulting and other referral-based careers, one quickly learns the meaning of "results beget referrals." It's as simple as that. And, the same can be said for the asset protection field. Results beget requests for more help. Why? Because the requester knows that results will follow, creating the proverbial win-win situation for both parties—a phenomenon I call "The Success Cycle."

It looks simple, doesn't it? Conceptually, it is. The challenge is in doing it.

This cycle involves the interaction of dynamics beginning with a demonstrated commitment to serving others. A department's mission reflects service to both internal and external customers followed by a desire to define service in broad terms, expanding beyond traditional definitions of asset protection. It is then followed by an understanding that widespread advocacy is needed and that such advocacy requires nurturing. Finally, the success cycle requires an ability to deliver what has been promised.

This book is all about the cycle of success for security decision-makers. I've chosen to write it because there is a dimension to our profession that has not been fully capitalized on by those who profess to know what security is all about. Namely, our contributions are measured within the context of defining ourselves as business managers and less as professional security people. Those who have heard me speak at conferences and seminars around the country know my theme well: individual success is defined within a framework of showing senior management your business acumen and less on your ability as a security professional.

There is the inevitable career fork in the road that each of us encounters. For some it comes early, for others later. Regardless, if you are a security manager, you will inevitably encounter the fork. The trick is choosing the right path. Actually, it is fairly easy to do. Even if you choose the wrong path, there are plenty of warning signs telling you that you're on the wrong path. (We'll explore this in more detail in Chapter Six.) For now, you're cautioned to take heed and watch for the signs. If you see them, run as fast as you can back to the fork and go down the other path. Failure to do so will only lead to disaster.

Conversely, choosing the right career path doesn't automatically guarantee success. You might elect to take the business path, but without certain skill sets you won't go far. Acquiring the skills necessary for success requires experience and the ability to listen—not skills that typically are learned in the classroom. Most professional seminars focus on developing technical skills. Sadly, many seminar leaders chosen by professional associations often have little or no actual business management experience. Associations will commonly defer to those from the public sector, the halls of academia, or technical specialists, a limiting choice since these people may lack an experiential base in business management.

Colleges and universities have fallen into a similar trap. Almost consistently you will find that they house Security Administration within the School of Criminal Justice. Here students learn the ways of law and order and little about business administration. Most CJ professors have little experience in the world of corporate management, yet they are charged with the responsibility of instructing tomorrow's asset protection leaders.

To achieve balance, there is a need to aggressively recruit security managers who have "lived the corporate life." As we shall discuss in the chapters ahead, business management experience is an essential ingredient in understanding asset protection and how to survive in today's corporate world. Drawing exclusively on experiences from the public sector falls short. With a doctorate in public administration and years of experience as a business manager, it is my conclusion that there is a distinct difference between the profit motive and the service motive.

Conversely, business schools generally neglect, as part of their required core curriculum, basic course work in asset protection management. They dedicate time and effort to developing theories and formulae aimed at achieving profitability, yet they typically overlook a critical factor in any organization's success—its profitability is directly related to protecting existing assets, new concepts, employees, and customers.

Those who have succeeded in the security profession need to extend a hand to those contemporaries still struggling to find the "secret formula" for success.

Before we begin, another critical point must be made. Recently, an interesting development has taken hold in large corporations: the notion of operating in a "lean and mean" environment to remain competitive. The end result has been the downsizing of many operating units, including security departments. Many have been outsourced and others have been eliminated altogether. (We'll explore these new management modes as well.) For now, it is important to point out that this trend can have dangerous side effects if not judiciously managed. Although the concept has considerable validity, without proper oversight and administration, serious exposures and unacceptable levels of risk can slip in unnoticed. As loss events occur, adverse consequences arise for everyone, including the security manager.

Stuart Feldman, writing for *Management Review* notes: "Restructuring. Getting lean and mean. Downsizing. Whatever a company calls it, letting employees go has become an all too common tactic for organizations desperate to cut costs in the face of recession, heated competition, mergers and acquisitions. The list of U.S. companies that have cut heads reads like a who's who of American business: IBM, Sears, General Motors, American Express, and AT&T to name a few. Recent studies have begun to make it clear, however, that rashly giving employees the ax may be akin to cutting off your nose to spite your face. The success of numerous alternative cost-cutting strategies suggests there is an alternative."(1) We will examine this phenomenon in-depth and lay out strategies that can mitigate risk and/or losses while reducing operating expenses.

John Swearingen, the former chairman of Amoco and Continental Illinois, once told a group of his executives that there are only two ways to remain profitable: increase sales and reduce costs. While not particularly profound, it is a dead-on observation. The problem is that many junior executives misinterpret this perspective, believing that cost reduction is a justification for wholesale elimination.

Recent studies and warnings from such leading organizational gurus as Warren Bennis, Peter Drucker, and Tom Peters are beginning to suggest that widespread elimination of middle management positions needs to be reexamined. Corporate powerhouses such as Travelers, Kodak, and Compaq are suggesting that outsourcing and strategic alliances are appropriate sometimes but should not be the primary way of doing business.

My own experience with outsourcing demonstrates that a great deal can be said for maintaining a proprietary staff—this from someone who has managed over 200 workforce conversions! As will be discussed, cost reduction is more than elimination or trimming back. Successful companies are distinguished from "wannabes" by their ability to differentiate between organizational fat and bone marrow. Perhaps another way of viewing this is to heed a lesson learned from our Japanese counterparts—an understanding of the value of *balance*. Cost cutting is valuable only when it is balanced against the need to protect profitability.

What follows in this book, then, is a series of perceptions and prescriptions intended to serve as a guide. We will explore several basic business principles, ideas, and strategies that are typically found only in the classroom of life. We will explore how you, as a security manager, full-time or part-time, can deliver greater impact by simply redirecting your focus. I don't know how many pearls of wisdom will flow, if any. That's not my purpose. Rather, I hope reading this book will help you discover a way to approach your business responsibilities and duties more effectively.

This book, then, is about the management of security, or stated another way, asset protection. While use of the terms "security" and "asset protection" will be interchangeable throughout the book, use of the latter is not intended to serve as a euphemistic term for the former. The term is carefully chosen because it broadens the perceived role of traditional security management and better integrates it into the business mainstream.

In the following pages you will *not* learn how to close out criminal cases more effectively, deploy personnel, monitor alarms, or design better surveillance systems. There are plenty of other texts that provide such information. You will be exposed to a variety of management issues and strategies—basic axioms that I believe hold true for success in today's corporate world. What you will learn are ways that can lead to better management of your company's security program from a business perspective.

Chapter Two begins with a look at a model developed to help non-security decision-makers better understand the dynamics of asset protection, an important consideration since it initiates the advocacy we identified above as part of the Success Cycle. It lays the foundation for another concept I call "Success Acquisition," a term used to explain the dynamics associated with senior management seeing you as a smart business person. This model has been so effective in setting the proper management mindset that nearly every one of my consulting reports begins with a discussion of it.

Leveraging on a discussion of defining the dynamics of asset protection, we then examine the four types of advocacy you are likely to encounter. You will see that not all advocates are fully supportive of your aims. Some will proclaim their support until confronted with a choice between their interests and your interests. Others will limit, or bracket, your credibility in narrow terms. Finally, there are those that simply reject you and your ideas for a variety of reasons, some of which are blatantly unjustified.

Chapter Two also outlines the three basic types of corporate security programs found in the U.S. and explains how you can counterbalance each to better define your role. As with any model, there are exceptions that support a blend of any two. This means that your particular program may reflect the advantages, or disadvantages, of any combination of types. Nevertheless, this can benefit you, provided you know your type and how to maximize your position.

Chapter Three shifts to a more directed focus and concentrates on the critical management task of internal marketing, one of the most challenging aspects of our profession. This chapter begins by exploring one of the most powerful management methodologies available: value added contribution (VAC). You will see how it can redefine your most routine operations in ways that senior management can easily relate to and support. We then shift to an analysis of more than 20 strategies for "getting the message out" and interpreting clear signals that test whether it is being positively received or not. Examined next is how one corporate security department tackled this issue head-on and developed one of the most progressive and effective marketing programs in the country.

The fourth chapter is an analysis of achieving cost reductions without suffering a loss in quality service. Discussed are simplistic ways to reduce current costs, such as taking a line-item approach. Since security is largely a people-intensive business, the most direct way to reduce costs is to attack those areas associated with personnel expense. Yet, this is typically not the wisest approach. What can you do then, especially if you are not a creative person by nature?

In this chapter we also examine 10 proven strategies that can lead you to creative ways to manage the business of asset protection. An examination follows of nine ways to reduce your operating budget without losing quality of service. Each strategy has been tried and proven successful in one or more organizations. The end result is a view of cost reduction as an opportunity for redefining your program and broadening your scope of responsibility. Absent in the discussion is a low road perspective that defines security in such quantitative terms as the size of full-time staff, number of alarm points monitored, access levels and cardholders, and escorts. Rather, a higher road approach is presented that introduces more significant measures, such as performance contributions based on the fewest number of traditional security indicators—terms understood by executives.

Chapter Five looks at several creative, but practical, ways to demonstrate your department's VAC. As a part of this discussion we take a close look at several of the latest management trends now pursued by corporate executives: Continuous Quality Improvement Strategies (CQIS, which includes Total Quality Management (TQM), The Baldrige Process, and Re-Engineering). We also examine other management tools such as benchmarking and defining security activities in terms of the business you purport to serve. You will be shown, for example, how loss recoveries can be restated in terms of annual sales for retailers, how lower operating expense can be presented in terms of enhanced revenues for bankers, and how a drug testing program can be expressed in terms of new revenue accounts for a utility company. These tools are worth analysis—each presents an opportunity to manage an apparent security cost through to a successful contribution.

We will also examine the concept of quality in measurable terms and show why it is essential that all asset protection services operate under the umbrella of customer service. The single most worthwhile pursuit for corporate security should be to establish an environment that caters to the needs of its customers—internal and external. In so doing, the challenge for the security decision-maker is to articulate a business orientation that says: "The customer may not always be right, but our job is to make them feel as though they are." Such an orientation allows asset protection people to create a mission statement based on cooperation, not imposition.

The chapter ends with a discussion on how you can convert your most fundamental services to revenue generators without detracting from your basic mission of providing security. In pursuing these trends, security professionals can capitalize on each to become fully integrated and establish itself as a contributing partner in the overall business plan. The stage is then set for the discussion in Chapter Six dealing with third party relationships.

Chapter Six is my "fun" chapter. Here we look at 20 basic axioms for managerial success as both a security professional and a business partner. We examine five ways to "beat your internal competition" and discover ways to avoid ELVIS (Executive Level Vicious Infighting Syndrome). Also explored are various management techniques that tell you whether you are on track or not. In spite of the lighter tone, the message is serious; there are real indicators that can act as a beacon to guide you through a maze of management practices.

Chapter Seven is an examination of third party relationships, a discussion particularly helpful since one emerging corporate trend is the use of external relationships. My first private sector job in 1979 involved the management of a large operational budget. After several months of signing what seemed to be an endless number of invoices for essentially two outside maintenance contractors, I began to examine the business benefits of using proprietary workforces versus contract suppliers. As a result of this analysis I went to my boss and told him that one day organizational support units will be administered from a 3 x 5 index card file. With a puzzled look, he asked what I meant. I went on to explain that banks, retailers, and manufacturers will one day get serious about focusing on their core businesses and outsource their support functions to specialists. They will seek external expertise via contractual relationships and have them handle daily operational matters. In the most extreme circumstances, a manager would need only draw a supplier's name and telephone number from a readily accessible file and request a service. Managing a large internal resource consisting of a proprietary workforce would be passé.

In short, bankers should concern themselves with financial services, retailers with selling merchandise, and manufacturers producing commodities. None of them should be in the business of providing security, safety, fire suppression, food service, or landscaping. Yet, each does. This, I told him, seemed crazy and a diversion of valued resources.

Recently, *Business Week* reported on a new concept called the "Virtual Corporation," described as "An entity that focuses on doing what it has been charted to do. In other words, bankers banking, retailers engaging in retailing, manufacturers producing product...."(2) They went on to suggest that today's businesses will survive only if they adopt a strategy of outsourcing those support functions that diffuse needed resources away from their primary mission. Sound familiar?

Here's the irony. Such thinking is actually behind the survival curve. That's right. Contrary to what appears to be the "trend" of the 1990s as projected by my respected colleague, William Cunningham (author of the *Hallcrest Reports I* and *II*) and several other noted authors, the truth is that we have eclipsed the cycle of traditional outsourcing and are beginning to witness a new era in external relationships. Strategic alliances are now beginning to replace traditional buyer-seller relationships. Corporations are looking to develop an open and fully integrated relationship with their external partners. Third party suppliers are being looked upon to provide more than a service as defined in the conventional terms of client-vendor relations. Together, both parties recognize the reality that there is value in sharing both risks and their rewards.

Unfortunately, for security service providers, few—if any—have come to terms with this new approach. Certainly this can be said of the top 20 companies as measured in terms of sales. Even with their claims of providing quality service with a strong infrastructure to support local accounts, they simply have yet to "get it." Strategic alliances require a new orientation—a paradigm shift—in their way of thinking. Assumed is a willingness on their part to take on risks and become assertive in positive ways. It may mean they will have to walk away from certain accounts, despite the prestige associated with a particular client. An open and trusting relationship is also entailed. The supplier is forced to be accountable in new ways and open their books to demonstrate needed profit margins. In other words, it requires a new way of doing business.

Some service providers are beginning to move in this direction, while others give lip service and still others are just now asking questions about strategic alignments. Yet, the bottom-line remains the same. Unless the contract industry is willing to rapidly embrace the new approach, others will backfill the need and emerge as the new leaders. Similarly, this single largest threat is coming from established property and facility management firms. Trammell Crow, La Salle Partners, and Winthrop Management are three firms with their own security forces who are now beginning to sell their services to outsiders. Others, like venture capitalist Golder, Thoma and Cressey, are underwriting the formation of new contract security companies, such as U.S. Security Associates, whose aim is to become a top-five company through aggressive acquisitions.

The book concludes with a discussion of the merits of establishing standards for security workforces. Examined are the current legislative efforts to enforce quality measures due to a misconception that the industry is failing to police itself. While it is true that many smaller security companies, and some larger firms, are intent on generating volume to the detriment of quality, the good news is that there is a growing backlash. Many are engaging in quality improvement programs as an augmentation to a proprietary program.

We'll examine why you cannot simply legislate quality—quality is itself an end product resulting from a commitment to consistently do the best possible in spite of many challenges. The chapter examines a set of performance criteria that can be applied to any type of security staff. Even though it is an extraction from my model contract for third party relationships, the performance criteria are designed for security staffs and therefore are applicable to both in-house operations and external suppliers. As an added bonus, Appendix A is a copy of the model contract that I encourage you to use when entering into third party relationships. It has been purchased for use by more than 200 companies, including Sony, Hughes, and two dozen other Fortune 100 firms across the country. Every major professional security journal and several facility management periodicals have hailed it as the new standard. It's my gift to you.

Before beginning the text, it is important to point out a special feature developed for your ease of reference. As you will come to read, there are many "Situational Cases" used to illustrate a point. For quick reference they have been numbered and labeled consecutively. For future referencing, they are also summarized in Appendix B. Also, by now you have discovered that I have chosen an informal conversational tone for the book. I find this easier to help me "tell the story."

Two final points. First, I have attempted to present this material in a balanced perspective with regard to gender recognition. There will be times, however, when it is more appropriate to use the singular pronoun of either he or she, him or her to make a point. Use of the male gender will be more common simply because it reflects the wider audience. Secondly, throughout this book several companies will be recognized for their contributions to the industry. These will range from hardware suppliers to consulting companies to security service providers. Their mention is not an endorsement. Rather, they have been selected to serve as examples for the point under consideration. Many other equally qualified companies also can be considered. The purpose is to simply acquaint you with how certain firms are addressing one or more of today's challenges. It is the qualitative aspect of their approach that you should bear in mind when considering an application for your situation.

Finally, both the publisher and myself would like to hear from you. If at the end, you have any questions or comments, please let us know. Thank you.

2

Establishing the Business Case

INTRODUCTION

Want to be successful? Here's the first critical operational step to take. Define your mission and then seek plenty of advocates. In today's business world the simple truth is that you cannot go it alone. No matter how gifted you are as a manager or how much others need your services, without advocacy from those who make the final decisions, you don't stand a chance. That's a rather blunt way to begin any book, let alone one intended to help. On the other hand, it's exactly what is needed to be said at the outset.

Advocates are those who believe that your security services are necessary. They're convinced that without your program, theirs is somehow lessened. That's because they are either threatened with a potential loss or are concerned for their own safety and/or that of their employees. Regardless, advocates see the value you bring to the organization and are willing to state their support for you. They want you to succeed. For in doing so, they, too, stand a better chance of succeeding.

Advocates are not just limited to senior managers. They can be found at all levels and across the entire organizational sphere. Obtaining senior management's support, however, is far more meaningful when it comes to getting the necessary approval for advancing your aims. Even though this sounds fairly basic, I'm continuously amazed to find how many security directors expend a disproportionate amount of their time and effort trying to convince those below their level of security's value. It's easy to understand this tendency since it is fairly unconstrained and safer to sell those who do not control the resources. These people do not have to make the hard decisions associated with allocating limited resources. Their problems may be real enough and they, therefore, will encourage you to advance your ideas to the company's planning committee or senior executives. The bottom line, though, is that their advocacy is not as critical for the near term as those who will be required to make the ultimate go-no go decision on your programs. Here's a quick example of misdirected advocacy.

Situational Case #1: Misdirected Advocacy

A major research and development firm recently redefined its business structure. To move away from quasi-public status, the organization reorganized as a full for-profit company, which was then divided into four major units, each headed by a president who in turn reported to a chief executive officer. They appointed a new security director whose scope of responsibility extended across the entire organization. After considerable study of the corporate campus, he concluded several capital improvements were required. Total expense for a new access control system, closed circuit television configuration and control room exceeded $500,000.

He submitted his capital plan only to have it rejected due to its expense and perceptions that the changes ran counter to the organizational culture. As one unit president explained, "Now that we are a profit driven company, we have to watch our expenses and select only those deemed most critical. Besides, some of the senior staff members aren't comfortable wearing identification badges and having to use card readers. They're also asking why we need all these cameras."

Undaunted, the director persisted. He collaborated with several other department heads and formed a security task force to study his proposals. Together, they represented more than 20 different end-users. At the end of their analysis they concurred with the security director and developed a position paper endorsing his original plan. Armed with this widespread support he went forward and made a presentation to the senior group consisting of the chairman and the four unit presidents. Two days later he was told that his plan had won conceptual support but funding was held back. In other words, he had failed to gain the really important support necessary to bring his plan into action. Why? Because his efforts to gain advocacy were misdirected.

Instead of focusing on the true decision-makers and augmenting his effort with support from his peer group and below, he spent his valued resources addressing only one side of the equation. In subsequent interviews with the senior officers it became apparent that several key business criteria had been missed: a demonstration of associated liabilities for corporate officers, the opportunity to strategically align the security systems with other department needs (thereby significantly enhancing the return on investment), and an ability to offset the capital expense with ongoing labor savings. Had the security director taken the time to interview each group president and discover their individual "hot buttons," he could have probably saved a great deal of time and energy and created a true win-win situation with advocacy from the entire corporate sphere.

THE LOOPING ASSET PROTECTION MODEL

Building advocacy entails a multidirectional strategy. Key among the various efforts is achieving a clear understanding of what is meant by asset protection by those to whom you are seeking support. They can-

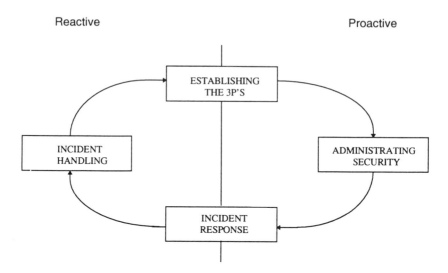

Figure 2.1: The Looping Asset Protection Model

not be relied on until you know that they are comfortable with the organizational mission of the security division.

Several years ago I devised the following conceptual model, still in use today. Its strength comes in stepping clearly and precisely through each of the major asset protection components with a non-security partner. Figure 2 illustrates the model.

As the looping model depicts, asset protection is defined within the larger, dual context of proactive and reactive service. Advocates must understand this context up front since it underscores the need for systems, staffing levels, and practices that are both preventive and reactive in nature. When security management is asked to reduce its operating or capital budget, the impact is likely to affect both interconnected spheres. Understanding the dual nature of security can also help explain why costs on the surface may appear to be high when in fact the same expenses are directed for two security operations simultaneously.

Clearly, there is abundant evidence of abuse by some asset protection managers. As we will explore in subsequent chapters, there are practical ways to hold costs or even reduce expenses without forfeiting the integrity of security's mission. For now, it is important that your advocates see the framework in which security operates.

This dual purpose is often even misunderstood by those charged with the responsibility of protecting the company's people and property. In these cases, it is little wonder that some departments have been severely trimmed or eliminated altogether. When I conduct workshops on managing asset protection I like to test my audience's level of understanding regarding the complexity and dynamics of a *relevant* security program. To do so we go through the following exercise:

I begin by asking those who believe security is, or should be, largely proactive to raise their hands. Invariably, at least 75 percent of the audience does. I thank them politely and say that their show of hands demonstrates that they are enlightened—well, half enlightened, anyway. I then ask the same question, only soliciting a response from those who believe that security is primarily reactive. Without fail there are far fewer hand-raisers. Typically, less than 10 percent agree with this proposition. To their surprise, I inform them that they, too, are only half enlightened—a true "setup" situation since security is by its very nature both proactive and reactive. Setting the fun aside, we then discuss how security, like most corporate support units, must establish their programs within the dual spheres of the business world.

The discussion then shifts to a brief overview of the profession's struggle to define its primary focus. We discuss how corporate security used to largely mimic the "Hooverian" style of security (after J. Edgar Hoover's management philosophy during the early FBI years), which essentially entails having security professionals sitting at their desks, waiting for the phone to ring, and then "jumping into action." In short, a largely reactive management style. By the 1970s there was a noticeable shift to more proactive programs. Many organizations changed names from corporate security to loss prevention in an attempt to show that their primary focus was crime *prevention*. Private security forces were not alone in this practice. Most police agencies began developing their own crime prevention programs.

Both the reactive and proactive schools of thought missed the point, however. To be truly effective, the very nature of protection requires a balance between the two. As the model shows, one feeds the other in an ever-looping process. Let's take a closer look at each of the four dynamics that make up the model, and then tie them to the need to achieve an understanding with our advocates.

Dynamic # 1: Establishing Operable Controls

The business of corporate security is about control. Since an organization's success is dependent, in part, on its ability to protect its assets, we can say that security's primary mission is to be the catalyst for control. The style of control is another matter. Controlling can, and should be, defined within the broader context of customer service (which is discussed in Chapter Five). For now, the important point is that security's role is defined within a framework of developing and administering those controls necessary to assure protection of valued assets. It is, therefore, not surprising that the beginning and ending of the loop depend on the dynamics of control.

Another way of viewing the control process is to say that asset protection begins with the establishment of policies, practices, and procedures (the 3 P's). The basic building blocks for the entire program, they spell out management's expectations regarding the movement of people and property. Policymaking sets parameters for employees, contractors, and suppliers and becomes a "public record" for investors, customers, and visitors to explain why certain practices and procedures are in place. Policies also serve to give security its license to establish corresponding operational practices and procedures.

These practices and procedures extend along the entire organizational continuum. There are those intended strictly for use by security personnel—post orders for the guard force, notification procedures for investigators, logs for console operators, and training manuals for supervisors. Similarly, adhering to access control procedures, wearing identification badges, and following parking rules and regulations are signs of employee and vendor compliance. Whatever the activity, each is governed by a set of approved guidelines and all achieve a singular result—the ability to control, and therefore protect, the company's assets.

Developing each policy and procedure need not be an expensive or time-consuming proposition. As conditions change, most policies need to evolve with a corresponding enhancement, modification, or elimination of some practices and published procedures. Occasionally, there may be a need to stop and revisit the entire set of policies and procedures to check for relevancy, a situation that typically occurs when a significant change takes place within the organization. For example, security shifts its reporting relationship from one manager to another, and the new executive wants a fresh look. Similarly, with the introduction of a new security director there is often an opportunity to reexamine existing procedures and weigh their relevance to the new boss. Regardless of how they are defined, policies, practices and procedures still serve as the primary backbone for controlling the corporation's assets.

Dynamic #2: Administration of the Security Program

Establishing an asset protection base with the introduction of written policies and procedures is only the beginning. Moving from a position of intent to reality is the focus of our looping model's second dynamic— where the written word literally comes to life. The heart of the program, this is critical for the advocate to understand. If we liken Dynamic #1, development of controls, to the brain center, then Dynamic #2 is the heart and lungs of the security program. It involves the actual staffing, equipping and deploying functions, all matters directly affected by the amount of budgetary commitment approved by senior management— those areas most in need of well-placed and influential advocates. Simply put, the ability to carry out executive management's intent is dependent on the type and degree of the security infrastructure put into place.

Implementation will require staffing, and whether they directly or indirectly report to a designated security department, a measure of accountability must be placed somewhere within the organization. Its size, style (proprietary or contract), and makeup (the number of line versus professional workers), are all issues that need to be addressed to assure compliance with the controls articulated in Dynamic #1.

Staffing is affected by the type and amount of equipment employed: radio communications, closed-circuit television monitoring, surveillance alarms, or electronic access control, for example. Each of these, when balanced with labor needs, defines the operational aspects of the program. This is the one area that trips up most security administrators. Creating an imbalance or attempting to maintain more than is necessary (failing to adjust as conditions change) is often the root cause for executive management's complaints about the "high cost of security."

Likewise, the actual layout of interior spaces, the design of the grounds, the location of the property, and type of construction all impact how security is defined within the organization. In some companies the design and use of appropriate devices and procedures can result in a security program that does not require a full-time staff commitment. This is especially so for emerging companies, professional firms in multi-tenant high-rise environments, and light manufacturing companies. Others, by the nature of their business or physical context (neighborhood, age of the property, etc.) may require a significantly higher level of security. Nevertheless, it is important to understand that preventive security is defined within the context of its officers patrolling, cameras detecting, alarms monitoring, and trainers instructing. In short, prevention is an active part of the security program.

The business of security is more than protection, however. It often involves other services such as transportation for executives, administration of first aid, visitor assistance, and concierge-type services. These duties and responsibilities also require certain levels of staff and support equipment.

It is therefore essential for the security manager to make everyone aware of the active nature of asset protection through preventive measures. The president of a major Southwest bank once commented after having this aspect of the model explained, "You know, I never stopped to associate the fact that when I see a guard walking around or all those cameras about that it is security's way of bringing to life the very policies I've endorsed. Too bad my security director has never explained it this way. When you stop and think about it, it makes very good sense." What an unfortunate admission of failure by the security director.

Dynamic #3: Incident Response

The bridge from the proactive world to the reactive world occurs when an incident occurs or a call for service is initiated. Security's measure of effectiveness is demonstrated by its ability to respond quickly and professionally. Incident response involves the support mechanism necessary to receive the call and the ability to dispatch. It also involves security's own capability to detect the occurrence of a situation and summon aid. To accomplish either requires adequate staffing, equipment and employee support.

Incident response involves the need for an effective communications system, which may include radios, pagers, and cellular telecommunications. Without these tools the case can be made that the corporation could be liable for both the asset loss and any resulting harm that might befall either a victim or the responding security officer. The same can be said if inadequate staffing prohibits an effective response. In short, the ability to offer a professional response is directly linked to the capability, e.g., people and equipment.

Defining a professional response can take many forms. One such definition may be measuring the time from when the dispatch center or security person receives the call to the time of the officer's arrival. This requires more than the necessary equipment and appropriate levels of staffing; it involves training and discipline to record receipt times and dispatch times. Automated systems are available to capture such data, unfortunately many private organizations define this as a service "add-on" as opposed to an important management system that helps determine staffing levels and scheduling. Response time in an emergency can be the literal difference between life and death. Without resorting to scare tactics or emotional appeals, this activity can be presented in straightforward business terms that build advocacy because it simply makes good business sense in today's litigious world.

Before leaving this dynamic, a final observation may be in order. Namely, response is linked to the ability to arrive safely and in a way that promotes confidence. Even the most studied and totally justified programs can be offset by an officer's inability to properly respond. Such failures are often brought up by non-security personnel as a means of discrediting the total program. Here's an example:

Situational Case #2: The Improper Response

A security officer had to travel between two buildings to respond to a suspected burglary in progress. Since the incident was at night, the officer reasoned that no one would be walking around so she decided to take a shortcut between the two buildings, driving on the sidewalk with her headlights turned off. Both activities were in clear violation of established procedures. Unfortunately, she hit an employee who was working late and the accident prevented her from completing the burglary response.

The officer failed her mission in two respects: (1) She struck an innocent party, and (2) She failed to investigate the suspected burglary. The result was serious personal injury, and the loss of several expensive cameras, video recorders, and other miscellaneous electronic equipment.

Negative incidents involving a security officer's response will inevitably occur. The challenge is to be prepared when presenting them to your advocates. Typically those who are reluctant to support your programs are quick to use these examples as reasons for not giving you their support. The best strategy is to acknowledge the officer's mistake, thereby underscoring your experience and business acumen and setting the stage for introducing the final dynamic.

Dynamic #4: Incident Handling

Responding in a professional manner is only part of the reactive responsibility. The other half is measured in terms of how well the security employee handles an incident upon arrival using their training, maturity, and experience. How well the situation is handled is also a reflection of the established procedures (Dynamic #1), amount of available backup staff and equipment (Dynamic #2), and the timely response (Dynamic #3). Another way of viewing incident handling is as the end-result of each of the previous dynamics merging together.

When I was a rookie police officer, I remember asking my training officer what we should do if we ever responded to a situation that we didn't know how to handle. He shot back, "Fake it." He went on to explain that there would be times when situations arose that hadn't been covered in the academy. The nature of policing is that new twists or something unexpected always occurs. In many ways, the same can be said for asset protection. I'm not sure that "faking it" is the answer, though I must admit it works on occasion. The real measure, however, is the degree of satisfaction achieved. Even if the victim or complainant does not experience personal satisfaction at the time, the truer test is their satisfaction that the incident was handled in accordance with their expectations. Achieving this requires appropriate resources.

There are times, however, when in spite of the best planning, security officers will not handle the situation properly. Some are understood to be unforeseeable. Others involve how the officer reacts when confronted with an unusual situation.

I recall a time when I worked for a large bank and one of my officers mishandled a medical emergency. We received a report of a heart attack and all of our officers were trained in CPR. We set up staffing patterns to assure a response within five minutes and in this case the officer arrived in less than three minutes. Up to this point our procedures were in place, our staffing was adequate, our response time was excellent. The one thing we didn't expect was that he'd panic. He laid the person down, called for the paramedic unit, and never administered CPR. Sadly, the 37-year-old employee died before the paramedics arrived.

Our department suffered a significant loss of credibility. Some of our supporters tried to console us by saying there was nothing we could have done. But we felt we could, at least in case of similar situation in the future. We did a post-event analysis to find out exactly what went wrong and why the officer panicked. Several things were discovered and we set out a strategy to fix them. Afterwards, we conveyed the results of our analysis to senior management to assure them that the next event would be handled better.

Incident handling is more than just responding to and taking care of current events. Just as security administration requires an ongoing analysis to determine minimum staffing levels or appropriate preventive maintenance agreements, successful incident handling requires building on the lessons learned from previous situations.

What completes the actual loop is security's ability to assess the situation, note how it can be improved in the future, and offer appropriate recommendations. Take for example an investigator asked to handle an embezzlement incident. Case management systems typically close out an investigation once the perpetrator has been either identified or the case has been referred for prosecutorial action. Stopping there, however, falls short of completing the loop because there is no opportunity to review causes for the loss and recommend future preventive actions.

When closing a case, the investigator should be required to submit a recommendation on how this incident could be prevented in the future. Embezzlement, for example, could result from audit controls set too high or the lack of clearly defined procedures. A thorough case management system requires that the investigator begin the inquiry by citing the policy violation. Just as the public law enforcement officer is required to identify the elements of crime, so too, does the private investigator need to establish the basis for the inquiry. If an internal policy does not exist, it needs to be stated and an appropriate recommendation made to those responsible for setting such policies and procedures. Not all recommendations need be addressed by the policy makers. Sometimes circumstances and conditions exist that prohibit approval of the submitted recommendation; yet this is not for security to decide alone. Proactive planning requires feedback and recommendations serve as the responses. The process of establishing controls, using security to carry them out, responding accordingly and professionally—complete with remedial recommendations—creates the entire loop. Each dynamic builds on the preceding one; none is more important than another because of this interrelationship.

This then is the business case for seeking advocacy to promote support for security programs. It's a simple model, but a critical management tool. The looping concept can explain the complexity and less than apparent layers associated with asset protection, part of what I term Success Acquisition. Your success depends on supporters understanding the conceptual underpinning of asset protection who are willing to support your effort to acquire the resources necessary to accomplish your intended goals.

IDENTIFYING YOUR ADVOCATES

It's one thing to educate your advocates, it's another to choose the right ones. Who then should be your advocate? Unfortunately, there isn't a standard list to be found in the pages of some management text. Rather, advocates vary depending on programs, needs, and current events. There are, however, some that will remain more constant than others. Two in particular are your boss and your boss's boss.

To identify these two might seem somewhat simplistic, but many security managers complain that they are the last to know when a situation occurs requiring their attention. Many lament that they later discovered that either their boss or their supervisor's boss was fully aware of the situation and failed to inform them. This situation is quite common and more of an admission of their own failure than a flaw in the system.

Situational Case #3:
The Misguided Security Director

A noted security director in banking a few years ago enjoyed a worldwide reputation as a leader in his field. He sat on many commissions and served as a board member for several professional associations. His duties often required traveling to other countries.

He was often asked how he could afford to spend so much time on professional business and so little on his job as the bank's security director. His response was that he had a competent staff and the confidence of senior management. He would boast of how he was on a first name basis with his company's chairman and that his boss was one of his biggest supporters. One day, to the shock of many, the news spread that he had been fired.

Several stories were passed along as to why. Although many had some measure of truth, the real cause could be traced back to his lack of support. We learned later that his chairman barely knew him, and as for his boss, the degree of support he had always assumed to be there was lacking. In his continued absence, his assistant had judiciously stayed home developing the true relationships. His presence and availability put him in higher stead than the security director between both senior executives and middle managers. It wasn't surprising to those who knew the truth that the director's demise was inevitable.

THE ACCEPTANCE MODEL

While working on my doctorate at the University of Southern California, my research centered on the concept of organizational acceptance. Acceptance, as a concept related to advocacy, is important for our purposes here. To secure advocates, your ideas need to be accepted. My studies led me to conclude that there are four levels of acceptance or support (advocacy) present within most groups. Since then, I am always finding evidence that these same levels never change, whether in the public or private business sector.

Support can be found from a group of executives for a variety of reasons. Some are comfortable with their power base and see you as no threat. Others see that their success can be tied to yours. Still others will support you because they are truly concerned for the good of the overall organization. Whatever the motivator, within each organization there are those who will support you. Conversely, for the same reasons,

Figure 2.2:   Continuum of Acceptance

there are those who will oppose you at every turn. To them, you represent a threat and therefore need to be held at bay.

The four types of acceptance are always present. As a business manager you need to be aware of each and how they affect your success in seeking an appropriate level of advocacy. Figure 3 illustrates this acceptance continuum.

The highest form of acceptance is called the *advocate*, representing those who show a genuine and open willingness to sponsor you and your programs. Advocates rearrange their schedules to attend meetings on your behalf, confer with you on security strategies and techniques, and make personal interventions with key decision-makers. An example might include computer operations managers who value your services because their employees work late at night and use your escort program after-hours. Advocates may also include department heads whose programs are intertwined with yours. Payroll, for example, might use security's sign-in register or electronic access control system to track hourly employees for pay purposes. Advocates might be found in the facilities management group that uses your security console operators to authorize contractors in and out of the building.

Even line level personnel can be advocates. If enough employees are concerned about safety issues they might be able to collectively complain to their supervisors or personnel representative to senior management. More often than not, however, senior management's motivation to act on the line workers' recommendations will be based on emotion and not sound business reasoning, something that could cause problems later.

The second group is called *limited advocates*—people who appear to support you and do, until a conflict occurs between their needs and yours. Contemporaries who report to the same manager are often involved. Since most security departments are part of a larger division or group, at budget time there is inevitably competition for the same capital or operating dollars. As one asset manager once commented, "There's nothing like a budget process to determine who your friends really are." As jaded as this may sound, it contains a great deal of truth.

Limited advocates can also arise between competing entities. Facilities departments often offer services that are comparable with security. Responsibilities overlapping in systems design, life safety, and access control areas can create a threatening situation. Other divisions competing with security might include human resources' training or employment divisions. It is not uncommon for the HR manager to be an advocate of security until an issue involving training surfaces. The training division may view their role as providing all forms of instruction. Likewise, if security conducts new hire background investigations, HR may view this as interference in their area of expertise.

There are those limited advocates who harbor ill will from previous security administrations. If they feel threatened, their limited support may surface, when in reality there is no justification for them to feel that way. The challenge, therefore, is for the security manager to befriend these people, explain that a new direction is in place, and actively solicit the support of these "reluctant warriors."

The third group I term *bracketers*. These are organizational decision-makers who will only accept security within certain boundaries. They will "bracket" the asset protection manager and tightly define the limits of credibility. The head of Computer Operations, for example, may define your scope of responsibility strictly in terms of physical protection. Should you suggest that asset protection incorporate both physical and data security, the unit manager may challenge you, contending that data security is beyond your charter. He may want to restrict or bracket your scope within the confines of physical security only. This is not to suggest that all computer operations managers hold such a narrow definition for corporate security. Yet many do, therefore limiting the total effectiveness you might otherwise have within an organization.

Similarly, international managers may question corporate security's role in providing travel advice or other assistance. Patent attorneys can be very protective of intellectual property, and corporate lawyers may believe that interaction with prosecutors should be directed through them.

Some CEOs can fall victim to bracketing. They will limit a corporate security program to physical security only. Others will limit security's role to only investigations. On the other hand, the research conducted by Sam Martin, a security consultant in Dallas, Texas, suggests that most executives define security in ways entirely different from their own security directors.(3) This suggests that security managers may engage in their own form of bracketing or limit their own organizational accountability. Regardless of who is your organizational bracketer, identify them and develop strategies around them. Rarely will a bracketer expand their environment broadly enough to incorporate you as a complementary resource. They are threatened by you and don't understand your mission and will work hard to contain you. If they are influential in the capital or operating budget process, they are likely to scrutinize your requests as motivated by self-interest more than the organization's.

To this extent they are neither your friends, nor your enemies. Rather, they are an anomaly that needs to be addressed. Left unchecked they can influence other marginal advocates. Pushed too hard, they can reject you. Equally valuable, if pushed just right, they can broaden their perspective and become a strong supporter. Bracketers see the world in absolutes. Theirs is a world of organizational black and white. So long as you fit within the limits they define for themselves, you will be accepted and they will be your advocate. Should you step outside that predetermined role definition, they will reject you and feel comfortable not supporting you. After all, they reason, every one has their place and should therefore act accordingly.

The last category is *rejecters*, individuals who simply do not support you. Their reasons may be numerous; they cannot identify with your aims and are openly opposed to you and your programs. Fortunately, these types of people are few. It is critical that you discover who they are as soon as possible. To the surprise of many security directors, after years of working with certain managers, they discover that these managers never accepted the role of security in the first place.

I have found that rejecters are typically one of two kinds of managers. The first is someone who has had a very bad personal experience with either the police or the security department. These people are transferring their hostility to you and are so tied up with emotion that reasoning with them is nearly impossible. Their occasional support is fleeting or fickle at best and cannot be relied on even in the most mundane matters. The second type of rejecter is usually the macho type who believes security is for "wimps." They boast of times when they faced personal danger and did so without help. They defiantly challenge the need for a security program or scoff at most proposals. Here's an example of what I mean:

Situational Case #4: The Trapped Executives

An international retailer once called me for assistance getting two executives out of a foreign country's political crisis. Their executives were in the country when an attempted coup occurred. During the fight that ensued, these executives got trapped in the company's overseas office, which had been fired upon. After several telephone calls and some negotiating with experts on both sides, they were able to get out of the country safely.

As a result of this action, I was asked to develop an international travel plan, complete with an emergency evacuation plan. The program was never launched, however, because the director of international personnel was a former marine commander and openly stated that travel to developing countries included risks. He cited his days in Vietnam and suggested that if executives didn't want to face the possible consequences, they should resign. His assistant had a similar background and attitude.

A comparable situation played itself out with a company president who bragged about growing up as a gang member on the south side of Chicago. Thirty years later he would still recall times when he and his gang would fight it out on the streets. To him, organizational infighting was another form of street fighting, and his employees needed to learn how to fend for themselves.

Security, to him, was a waste of money and only an imposition forced on him by his legal staff to avoid potential lawsuits.

Each of these advocacy forms can be found in any organization. You may have said to yourself as you read each description that I was referring to so-and-so. They're all there in your organization. As noted above, the challenge is to identify each and build your strategy around them.

SECURITY'S THREE STYLES

Before closing this chapter, I'd like to draw your attention to another concept. Its purpose is to help you understand the type of department you have and how it can be leveraged to your full advantage. Basically, there are three different types of corporate security departments in today's business world:

   I. The Facilities-Oriented Department
  II. The Operations-Oriented Department
 III. The Advisory-Oriented Department

Actually, there is an emerging fourth type which incorporates those departments that have been set up as profit centers, but since it comprises so few, I have elected not to discuss it here. (This emerging style is discussed at the end of Chapter Five.)

The Facilities-Oriented Department

This orientation focuses largely on physical operations and is concerned primarily with guard operations and access control. There may or may not be a central monitoring station on the property. Nevertheless, some form of surveillance system detects intrusion after hours or into highly sensitive areas.

I refer to this style as "The Little Green Shack" approach. I think you know the type. A person approaches the guard at the gate and announces that they are here to see the security manager. The guard responds, "Oh yes, drive around back and you'll see the little green shack. That's where you find him." This was largely how security was defined for years and is still true today. For many companies security is seen essentially as night watchmen or gatekeepers. Even for many world headquarters operations, this approach can be found in main lobbies with security officers attired in policelike uniforms. I suspect this style still represents most of the security departments in the United States today. The director is really more of a guard supervisor and reports to the facility engineer. Duties are limited to entry control and officers are limited in career advancement and compensation. Turnover is high (over 100% annually) and security's role is clearly understood by the rest of the employee population.

The Operations-Oriented Department

Characterized by a large staff, the second style is what I call *operations-oriented*. The guard force is under the management of a protective services manager and may be either contract or proprietary. In either event they are charged with the same duties found in the first style. This system has several additional responsibilities. Reporting vertically to the security manager, this department will likely encompass an investigative unit, possibly a systems design group, console operations, a safety unit, an international group (if applicable), an executive protection unit, and a large administrative support staff.

The security manager is no less than a middle manager and often is a member of the senior (but not executive) staff. Compensation for the top manager could approach or exceed $100,000 and unit managers would be eligible for modest performance bonuses. The manager is instrumental in setting corporate policy and sits on several internal committees. The operating budget is likely to be at least $2,000,000. In recent years this style has expanded beyond a traditional security role, incorporating data security, compliance, risk management, environmental protection, and many totally unrelated support functions. In all, this type of department is considered a significant cost center that cuts across nearly every sector of the organization.

The Advisory-Oriented Department

The *advisory-oriented* approach, in contrast to the operationally oriented department, relies on a small staff, typically less than 10 employees including professional and clerical staff. This approach is commonly used in decentralized organizations where local management has direct responsibility for each support unit. Characterized by seasoned professionals managed by a director who is more business-oriented than technically security focused, this group of workers is viewed as internal advisors setting policy, engaging in strategic planning, and serving as a referral center for specialized needs. They are likely to conduct inspections, develop training programs, and serve as a liaison with external groups and agencies. As more corporations move toward strategic alliances with outside suppliers, this style is becoming more popular with executive management.

Having briefly described each, it is important to recognize that most security heads will define themselves as a blend between two or all three types. Security, like most support units, is a dynamic and evolving function. The important point is to decide which of the three most closely resembles your organization. Some may feel that the third style, Advisory-Oriented, is the upper echelon of security services. My experience suggests that such thinking is a trap. In reality, each style is as important as the other. Success is knowing what style your company wants, effectively managing that style, and knowing what is best for the organization.

As a consultant, I remember trying to move an operations-oriented department to an advisory style. My efforts were met with continual resistance from the security director—for a simple reason: He enjoyed being an operations manager and had no interest in the other style. For him, his identity hinged on managing many units. Unfortunately, that was not the direction his executive managers wanted to take. It was no surprise to learn later he was forced out.

The lesson is obvious. First, determine what the organization wants—not necessarily needs—and then ask if your personal management style fits. If so, there's a compatible match; no excuses or explanations are necessary. On the other hand, if either your personal style or the organization's expectations are out of sync, a change is in order. Something must give. Movement generally will be on the part of the security manager.

Knowing the organizational style is easy, accepting it may be another matter. Success is measured in terms of a person's level of comfort with their own identity. All too often I encounter asset protection managers who have a distorted sense of their own and their department's importance. When there is an appropriate alignment, success comes easily and everyone benefits. Misalignments can cause frustration, misunderstandings, increased liabilities, and most importantly, misallocation of valued resources.

CONCLUSION

Most security management texts do not begin with a call to seek out advocates. That's probably because most books are not designed to bring the asset protection manager into focus with the need for a strong business orientation.

In this chapter we explored the need to establish a group of advocates, those who can help you in becoming successful. We saw how managers need to define the essence of their corporate responsibilities in terms of four basic dynamics, establishing controls under an umbrella of customer service, administration of security resources, effective response, and professional management of incidents or requests for service. We examined the interrelationship of each and how they create a looping process designed to continuously refine strategies for protecting a company's assets.

Next we moved into a discussion of advocacy and examined four types of acceptance by those who influence certain levels of budgetary and managerial support. We analyzed the difference between true advocates and limited advocates. We assessed the impact that bracketers (those who narrowly define the scope of responsibility) have on job prospects for security managers. Finally, we looked at those that reject all that security stands for and how difficult organizational life can be without their support.

The chapter concludes with an examination of three basic styles of corporate security, facility-oriented, operations-oriented, and advisory-oriented. We described the characteristics commonly found in each, and noted that since it was an ideal construct, in reality most departments reflect a blend of two or all three. The chapter also ends with a warning that it is up to you to ensure that your management style matches the expectation the organization has for asset protection. Failing to recognize both will have an unfavorable outcome for any security manager. On the other hand, a symbiotic relationship can benefit you and the organization as a whole.

3

Developing a Successful Marketing Plan

INTRODUCTION

Security directors today are frequently asked to reduce their operating budgets or, at a minimum, justify their current level of expense, to facilitate the overall corporate mission of becoming "lean and mean." Many complain that they are already at their limit of effectiveness based on current resource levels. They ask: How can I market my department in a way that shows Security is more than an expense? How can I show senior management that my department truly brings added value to the business?

There are several ways. To begin with, let's clear up a major misunderstanding about Value-Added Contribution (VAC). The cynical view holds that it is a euphemism for cost cutting with the contention that it is a way for non-security managers to challenge the measurable value of asset protection. They argue that it is difficult to provide empirical evidence supporting the organizational value of asset protection, therefore it is easy to ask for a reduction in Security's operating budget.

Some ask: How can you measure prevention? As we saw in the second chapter, asset protection is more than prevention. At a minimum, it is a program designed to carry out senior management's desire to control their valued property and provide a safe and secure environment.

Actually, when properly understood, VAC can be one of your strongest management tools for assuring quality without necessarily taking a direct expense reduction hit. Adeptly used, VAC is a strategy that can transfer cost reduction to others, thereby lowering your operating expenses without adversely affecting your bottom-line. On the other hand, if you are still expected to make cost-cutting contributions, VAC can lessen the reduction or illustrate the associated risk and/or potential revenue loss associated with your operating expense reductions. Here are some examples:

Situational Case #5: The Mounted Patrol

The largest shopping center in a major Southwest market had a serious security problem in their parking lot. Police statistics indicated that auto thefts from their lot were the worst in the area. Physical assaults, indecent exposure, robberies, and auto burglaries were also so high that recent customer and merchant surveys showed that safety was the number one concern and a primary reason for a drop in sales at the mall. In response, the owners analyzed the feasibility of increasing lighting, redesigning the parking lot, installing security telephones, and adding more motorized security patrols. Against this backdrop was a decrease in sales. Management was looking for ways to reduce expense—security costs among them. Not only an interesting situation, but an excellent opportunity to demonstrate a case for Security's valued-added contribution.

After an initial analysis, the assessment team concluded that the solution was not any of the above. Rather than defining security in its traditional, singular role of crime prevention, the suggestion was made to tie Security's mission directly to the mall's marketing program. In so doing, the buying public would see that shopping at this center was both enjoyable and safe. To back this claim, however, something clearly had to be done about the crime rate—auto theft in particular. The solution was to introduce a mounted horse patrol. Why? For several reasons:

- An officer on mounted patrol can cover 20 times the area of an officer on foot and 6 times the area of an officer in a motorized vehicle.
- A mounted patrol program was compatible with a shopping mall in the Southwest.
- A mounted patrol could be positively and subtly integrated into print and television advertising. (4)
- A contest could be created, e.g., "Name Officer Bill's Horse" for families and small children.
- Officer Bill's horse could be used to pull Santa's sleigh at Christmas time.

The net result was a 67 percent reduction in auto theft within the first month of the program. All other crimes were reduced by 34 percent. Although the cost of providing security went up, the increase was significantly below the increase projected from added patrols, labor, equipment, and lighting. Post-implementation surveys showed that the program was widely applauded by the merchants and positively received by the buying public. The true acid test, of course, was whether sales increased. Result: Total mall sales increased 8 percent even after a major anchor tenant closed for unrelated reasons. In an environment that was seeking across-the-board cost reductions, with a little creativity, Security proved that it could bring significant added value to the center's overall profitability.

Situational Case #6: ATM Servicing

For those in banking, it is widely recognized that electronic banking divisions can be expensive, primarily due to the need to service and replenish the machines at all hours of the day, every day of the week. When an ATM goes down, there is a direct revenue loss because customers cannot make deposits. The profit margin for operating ATMs has always been a concern for the financial community. Generally, they view ATMs as an important customer service convenience, as opposed to a way to lower operating costs, as was originally envisioned. Many banks either use an outside service or rely on local branch management to respond to basic service needs after normal banking hours, including replenishing the machine when it is empty. Overtime is likely to be paid and the machine's downtime extended since someone has to respond from either home or a service center.

Some business-oriented security directors are seizing on this opportunity to integrate ATM servicing into their normal patrol services program thereby significantly reducing service costs and replenishment expense. Local branch management is grateful since they are no longer required to disrupt their off-hours to return to the branch. These directors report that customer service has increased and downtime has been dramatically lowered. Another benefit has been the opportunity to conduct added property checks without incremental costs since the officers had to be at the branch or ATM site anyway. For a large Western bank the net result was a savings of nearly $200,000 a year. A Midwestern institution saved over $100,000 and a Northeastern bank saved $65,000 a year. As with the previous situational case, VAC can be defined in terms of overall cost reductions, increased efficiency, and improved morale.

Situational Case #7: Quality Tenant Services

One of my clients is a major tenant in a 35-story high-rise occupying nearly 70 percent of the building. After suspecting a messenger service's employees of several petty thefts, they complained to the building owner's agent. Having had previous troubles with similar services, they asked if there was a way to keep these delivery people out and still send and receive materials. The owner's agent asked for assistance.

Aware that the security budget was fixed for the year, the director knew executive management would not be open to increasing security's expense in order to fill the void. After considering several options, she became convinced this was an excellent VAC opportunity for security. While it meant recommending an increase to security's cost, she was able to demonstrate a five-way win for everyone involved. Here is what she recommended:

- The property management company would send a letter to all messenger services informing them they had established a registry point in an area near the loading dock. A bicycle rack would be installed nearby, thus eliminating the need for them to park or chain their bikes in the front plaza. The letter would go on to inform them that all documents to be delivered would be left at this registry point, which would be staffed by a security officer. This would be the first win for the delivery services since their costs would go down—it meant one-stop deliveries—the time spent at this building would be minimal since all parcel deliveries would terminate at a convenient location.
- The second part of the plan would be to have security officers deliver and pick up parcels from all tenants. Using a radio-equipped roving force of two, tenants would be directed to call a number terminating at the delivery desk. Requests would be received by the officer and another one would be dispatched—a second win. Tenants would receive faster pickup service because the pickup person would already be in the building and only a few minutes away. They would also have their parcels picked up or delivered by a professionally attired, security-cleared individual.
- By having the security firm handle the internal deliveries, the third win would be for them. This meant that they would increase revenues resulting from increased staffing. They

could also expand their patrol services since two additional officers would be continuously traveling throughout the building. There would be the additional opportunity to introduce themselves to other tenants in a positive manner. Thus, if the tenants ever needed additional security service, they might be inclined to call the security provider instead of one of their competitors.

- The fourth win would be for the delivery company in particular. Since all outbound deliveries would be picked up by security and consolidated at the delivery desk, the property management company could competitively bid to have all outbound parcels handled by a single firm. The award recipient would enjoy one-stop pickup and could leverage the higher volumes to offer a lower price.
- By instituting the plan the property management would be the recipient of the fifth win, which actually consists of several wins. First, they could offer a valuable tenant service by making messenger services simple and much more professionally managed. They could negotiate lower delivery costs and either pass the savings along to the tenants or charge back the normal retail price, using the differential to offset the increased security expense. Thirdly, they could address the request of their largest tenant regarding their specific security concern. Finally, they could reduce the liability and unsightliness associated with outside messengers parking and locking the bicycles to posts, benches, and trees in the front plaza.

Each of these situational cases demonstrates that security divisions can be leveraged to bring added value. By integrating them into the problem resolution phase, a reverse approach can yield an actual increase in service while lowering total expenses and/or generating revenue for the company. We'll explore this idea of a reverse approach, or as I term it, "using the back door" and other creative strategies in Chapter Six. For now, the point is that asset protection managers should look to using VAC as another important management tool for demonstrating bottom-line contributions.

INTERNAL MARKETING—
THE UNDERDEVELOPED SKILL

Earlier I noted that security managers often feel frustrated about their inability to market their value effectively. Most have not been exposed to marketing concepts or are intimidated about promoting their programs. Many times I have listened to managers tell me that their programs' value should be self-evident and that they prefer a low-key approach. *Wrong!*

Even good guys need to let their internal customers know what services they can provide and why they are important to the customer. Name recognition is critical to the success of any business. Even if your company is not a household word, its success depends on establishing a name for itself within your industry. Marketing is the most critical aspect of running any organization. Marketing specialists such as Jay Abraham and Zig Ziggler underscore its importance by contending that it is the basis on which all success is built. Nearly every business theorist and practitioner would agree that marketing is the backbone of any business plan. I believe that the lack of internal marketing is what, more than anything else, has caused security directors to lose significant gains and even their jobs.

Below are 20 proven marketing techniques. Originally inspired by Jay Abraham and Paul Franklin (5), I have adopted several of their marketing strategies for assisting asset managers to become successful promoters within their own organization. When I first developed this set of internal marketing strategies, I asked Jim Wells, then director of security for John Hancock (Jim recently retired) to review it. I selected him because he has developed one of the most comprehensive internal marketing plans for his department. After he reviewed it, I asked for his reaction. He smiled and told me that he had already forwarded a copy to his staff and asked if they were employing three of the techniques I suggested. If not, he wanted to know why. Since then, it has become an integral part of my client work.

Though all 20 may not apply to your situation, most will. And of those you deem not applicable, I suggest you give them additional thought, for somewhere between the lines, there may be a hidden opportunity. Before beginning, allow me to suggest one guiding principle: Marketing begins with the understanding that it is selling and to sell successfully you must be in tune with your customer base. Even as a department manager, you need to develop a mindset that is always alert to an opportunity to promote your value, not necessarily in a flashy or slick way. Subtlety is acceptable, but your client must be fully aware that they are receiving value from your services, something easily done with a smile, a friendly tone, or simply asking "How can I help you?" Mary Kay teaches her sales force that one secret to success is to envision everyone carrying a large placard around their neck reading "I'm Important." This strong visualization can prompt each member of the security staff to respond accordingly, thus demonstrating the importance of each person and therefore the personal value security brings.

1. Go Where the Experts Are

Take the time to seek out marketing books at your corporate library, business school library, or even the local bookstore. Concentrate on those that focus on marketing strategies. You will be surprised how many points are directly applicable to your situation. This list of "20 sure-fire ways to market yourself" is perhaps a good example of what I mean. As I said above, its genesis comes from a manual on direct marketing by Jay Abraham. The book doesn't have to have the word "security" in the title to be relevant. Equally important, it doesn't even have to be about corporate cultures and internal politics to be on an approved reading list.

2. Walk Around and Observe

It's so simple and yet so few do it. An organization is, in many ways, a microcosm of our larger society, with a formal structure and an informal way of getting things done. A former boss once told me that success does not depend so much on what organizational box we occupy as on how well we manage along the lines that connect these boxes. In other words, our real success is based on an ability to get out into the organization and learn what our internal customers want or need.

When you see something, note it. This is particularly so for things that irritate you. Why does it upset you, and how would you change it? Once you have answered these questions, apply them to some of your own departmental procedures. In short, by looking at the world through your own eyes, ask how others view you. The converse is also true. If you see something that intrigues or pleases you, note it; there may be an application for your department.

3. Solicit Customer Feedback

Have you defined who your customers are? I'm not talking just about visitors, contractors, or your company's customers. While these are important, there are others. What about other departmental personnel? What about those within your own organization? Yes, that's right— even our own employees are also our customers. How do we interact with them? How do we treat them? Do we show favoritism toward one group over the other? If so, this is not necessarily bad. The secret is understanding why and asking if the same reasoning can be extended to your department. Directly ask your internal and external customers what they think of your operation. You might be surprised. Ask them what they want. You might be surprised again to hear what pushes their button. Asking doesn't necessarily mean you can deliver, but it may mean you have to develop some sort of educational program. Most people will accept, or at least tolerate, something they would otherwise not want if they understand the reasoning behind it.

> CAUTION: Be prepared to be challenged—and perhaps rightfully so. Here's an example: A client once asked why signing out of a building after-hours was necessary when she didn't sign-in when she arrived for work midday. She went on to say that the security officers didn't patrol the floors and thought it an inconvenience to

stop and sign out when departing. In truth, it was company policy (though not published) to use the register to track employees' leaving times for payroll purposes. When told why, she understood. Admittedly, it doesn't address why the company chose to keep this payroll practice a secret, but that is not a security matter.

4. Play the Role of Customer

Have someone call your department and request a service or product. Have the call critiqued. Next, have someone call and complain how they were treated and see how they are handled. Finally, arrange with another security director to call their department and see how well the competition treats their customers under similar circumstances. I tell my clients that there are two kinds of people in this world. In fact, this is true. There are only two kinds. There is you and there are customers. Everyone else is literally a customer: your stated customers, your fellow workers, your family members, even someone down the hall you hate. Given this, remember there is only one way to achieve success in marketing, the customer defines the relationship and that begins by analyzing how you treat them. In doing so, you learn how to treat the next one.

5. Listen to What Your Employees Are Saying

There's a biblical adage I often draw upon to illustrate one of the most overlooked resources available to managers interested in positively marketing their department's added value. Simply, "He came unto his own and his own heard him not." How many times has it happened to you? Another manager or your boss laments something going awry and you offer a good way to resolve it. Instead of listening, they ignore you and the situation either continues or gets worse. All along, you're saying to yourself, "if only they had listened." Are you guilty of the same thing? Your employees may be the very source to resolve some of your problems.

6. Encourage New Approaches

Abraham strongly suggests that success comes when salespeople, marketing staffs, or advertising people are given the freedom to suggest new ideas, different approaches, offers, and packages. The same holds true for an internal security department. Allow your staff to suggest ways not tried before. Free them from bureaucratic inhibitions. Do not placate or patronize them. There is a catch, however. Each member of the team must understand your basic philosophy, which assures not only continuity, but also focus and solidarity of direction.

7. Show You Care

Another often overlooked strategy is follow-up. Your customers want to know that you believe they are important, something that applies to past customers as well. For example, you may need to occasionally work with someone from Special Events, Research and Development, or another department not normally within the sphere of your responsibilities. A follow-up memo thanking them for the opportunity to be of assistance builds relationships. Such relationships are important for future encounters; yet, they are also helpful for building advocacy along a broad-based continuum when the need arises for new programs or defense of current operating levels.

8. Learn from Others Through Active Listening

Different from just listening to what others have to say, this tactic involves being tuned in to what captures your attention. You might receive a simple solicitation in the mail that really grabs you. Why? What is being said? How is it being presented? Similarly, you might see a commercial on television that holds your interest. Why? What technique is being used? What is the message? How does this differ from others?

Once you've tuned in, the next question is to ask if something similar can be applied to your situation. Here's an example. I recently received a copy of Gensler and Associates' annual report. The cover highlights the expression "redefining boundaries." As you skim the report other current themes are highlighted, including "designing for people, not publications," "commitment to our communities," "utilizing our strengths, believing in yours," and "empowered to evolve." So what does an annual report for an architectural firm have in common with a security department? If your task is to market security and illustrate added value to the organization's bottom line, this will require a demonstration of "designing systems and employing procedures for people, not for inclusion in a manual or set of regulations," "commitment to your customers internally and externally," "utilizing your strengths and believing in theirs," and "empowering your people and your customers to meet the ever-changing needs of your organization's asset protection needs."

9. Test, Test, Test

Both Abraham and Franklin point out, testing is the active ingredient for improvement. You want to test ideas and ways to present them with whomever the greatest interest or need lies. They illustrate that marketing is a constant activity playing to a moving parade, an excellent analogy for corporate managers to understand. We naturally tend to define our internal customers as though they are fixed. The people today, we assume, are the same ones tomorrow. For security departments, this is not necessarily true. Due to the nature of our business, those we deal with are continually changing. One day it might be facilities management, the next it might be human resources, and then it might be manufacturing or R&D. In short, the parade of corporate players is always changing. Although it is the same parade, different groups are continually marching by the grandstand. As they do, this is their chance to see and interact with you.

#10. Don't Always Focus on the Worst

It is human nature to want to improve. As such, we look for those things that we do not do as well as others and seek to change. An entire school of thought is built around the adage "if it isn't broke, don't fix it." While there is a great deal of truth in this, there is also a missed opportunity. Without necessarily "fixing it," we ought to seek out those things that we do well and build on them.

Promoting your overall program means knowing when to cut your losses and move on. Instead of examining only those things that have gone astray, a balance is often required. People like to be associated with winners. By focusing on those things that you do well, your department can build on these successes to promote others.

#11. Take the Soft Approach

Products and services should sell themselves. While it is necessary to promote them, sales inside a corporation typically need to be done using a soft approach. Using the professional approach requires use of the right words, tones, and attitudes. Written media should be simple and direct. Here's an example of subtle advertising that can be done even at the lowest level. Assuming your department offers an escort service for employees to their automobiles during off-hours, have the officer doing the escort inquire as to whether the employee(s) is aware of other services offered by your department. A safety brochure or other written piece can go a long way in delivering your service message without appearing as though you're being obtrusive.

Most of my clients have a great deal of difficulty with self-promotion. It is not something that comes naturally, but it is critical if you are going to be able to withstand the scrutiny of senior managers and/or cost analysts. They may not understand your value to the organization and are therefore quick to draw conclusions that are not in the best interests of the organization. Promotion is a fact of life and a primary obligation of any manager intent on meeting their corporate obligations to protect their clients' interests.

#12. Be Compelling Without Crying "The Sky Is Falling"

You have to market your services in a way that compels the listener, reader, and/or observer to believe that your value is more than just "nice to have." Your marketing must be stated in measurable business terms. It has to be based on facts that can be readily identified and understood. Reporting activity in security-related terms may make a great deal of sense to you, your staff, and other security professionals, but it tends to leave non-security personnel wondering about the significance of certain activities. Reporting on the number of open doors, unlocked gates, PCs stolen, auto burglaries, escorts requested, and even hours of executive protection offered does not justify your department's continued existence.

Levels of risk can be assigned that say the company can live with so many thefts or loss of personal services. To be effective, security needs to be postured in terms that show its value as a deterrent against huge losses resulting from negligence. It must show that without adequate safeguards, the organization's business interests are exposed. This can be defined in terms of those commodities that go to the core of the company's business. It's surprising how few of my clients understand the concept of "intellectual property." Yet, this is probably the most valued asset within the corporation. Intellectual property is more than trade secrets. It involves proprietary information, confidential records, valued processes, and customized equipment or software that give the company its competitive edge. The allocation of security resources needs to begin by showing what the asset is worth and how their programs are designed to protect it. Short of that, all other resource allocations can be negotiated away or lessened from current levels.

#13. Build Around the "One Great" Contribution

As with most things in life, there is always room to give a little. The successful marketing security executive understands what is absolutely essential and will fight for it. All else is negotiable. If protecting the company's intellectual property is the bottom line, then everything else is ranked on the priority scale at lesser importance. We have often heard our staff voice frustration over the loss of one program or another. They may lament the loss of equipment, deferment of prized programs, and cutbacks in staff. There are battles that may require certain losses, but the lasting measure of success is your ability to keep the core reason for your department's mission intact. Sports legions have been quoted as saying that "winning is everything." Actually, winning is important when it comes to the really important things. Many generals have lost battles because of the constant need to protect all fronts. Retrenchment can be positive. It allows an opportunity to regroup and reassess.

#14. Be Comprehensive

Sales are lost when not enough facts are available. Managers who pride brevity may be setting themselves up when it comes to marketing. People want facts, numbers, data. We are a society driven by data. We want to know values measured in quantitative terms as much as qualitative terms. We want to know that we're getting the most for our money. Corporate managers are no different in company life than they are in their personal lives. They want to see that there is a reason—or set of reasons—for supporting your program and resource allocation. Absent facts they question value.

Remember, the higher the price tag, the more likely they will want to know why. I used to tell my staff, and now my clients, "if you aren't prepared for the meeting, don't go." The same holds true for an internal marketing plan. If you can't articulate the many reasons why your programs should not be touched, or need to be expanded, then your chances of successfully selling are diminished significantly. Here's a simple idea to bear in mind. For companies, just as in the outside world we all live in, there is a scarcity of resources. Your job is to sell those who make the decisions to give you your fair share at a minimum.

#15. Keep a Good Plan Rolling

As noted above, successful marketing is understanding that we are continually playing to a moving parade. We may tire early of a certain plan; that doesn't necessarily mean our internal customers will, which is why we stress testing. I find it interesting that many of today's television commercials are reruns or adaptations from previous years.

Recently Nestle reintroduced their famous brown dogs singing the company's jingle that Nestle makes the V-E-R-Y BEST CHOCO-LATE. My fifteen-year-old daughter finds them a delight. These are the same puppets that entertained me when I was a teenager more than thirty years ago. Similarly, Oldsmobile has put a spin on its "this is not the same car your father drove" theme—clearly a throw back to several years ago.

#16. Their Agenda Is Your Agenda

One of the most overlooked opportunities in marketing your services is not determining what your customers' needs are. As security directors, we tend to believe that we are the experts and therefore should be responsible for setting "security's agenda." While this is largely true, equally important is the need to balance the equation with an understanding of what end-users need and expect. A great deal of latitude should be given to them. Here's a strategy I have found to be very effective:

Identify the key senior executives for each major business sector. (They are generally listed at the back of the company's annual report.) Arrange a 30-minute one-on-one meeting with each. For many this may be the first time they have meet with anyone from security; they will naturally be curious and concerned that there is a problem in their area. Assure the secretary that this is purely an introductory meeting and that you need their help. When you arrive, do so with a writing pad and pen. After a brief social introduction, tell them that you are putting together a business plan and want to know what service you can provide them. It's as simple as that. Tell them that your agenda will reflect their agenda, whenever possible.

This is also an excellent time to ask their candid opinion about the department in general. If they hold a negative opinion, you want to know that and the particulars. You'd be surprised by the number of "new corporate friends" you will develop by just that meeting, but it doesn't end there. Tell them you want to return in 90 days for another 30-minute meeting. At that time you want to update them on your progress and solicit any observations they may have—good, bad, or indifferent. Follow-up this second meeting with still another one, 90 days later. Just think of the feedback you'll receive, not to mention a sense of ownership that they will take on. This is critically important because ownership means advocacy—especially when it comes time to consider cost cutting.

#17. Look for Models Beyond Security

We can get so tied up in our own profession that we often overlook the obvious—the successes others are having. It's easy to say: "Well they're successful because they are so and so. They're not security. They're different from us." All of this may be true, but does this mean that there are not lessons to be learned? Here's a challenge: I have yet to find another corporate unit that couldn't teach me something about how to do my job as security director better. Even those who have failed have shown me what to avoid. The fact is simply this: Beyond the particulars of a department's specialty, organizationally there is little, if any, difference between operating units. This holds true even for security departments. The secret is to find another department that is particularly successful. Let's take properties management, or systems, or human resources, or food services, or any other department currently in your company's "organizational favor." You must ask what is it that they are doing right? What makes them a success? What can you do to emulate them? Even if you don't like the unit manager, move beyond the personal feelings and reassess the strategies they employ to be successful. There's an expression a pastor once said to me when I complained that his assistant gave poor homilies because he was such a bad public speaker. He said, "Don't listen to the medium, listen for the message." Great advice.

#18. Talk to the Marketing People

When we talk of marketing internally, we often assume that it is so unique that it requires special strategies. Internal marketing directly parallels many of the principles found in external marketing. Therefore, it is wise to seek those who engage in that business daily; e.g., your own marketing people. Explain that you're interested in "selling" your value-added service within the organization and ask what strategies or ideas they could suggest. You might be surprised at what emerges. Here's a quick example: The use of stanchions in elevator lobbies can send security messages about your escort service, travel advisory program, investigative capabilities, and training programs. Similarly, an internal newsletter or regular column in the corporate "rag sheet" can get your message out to the most people at minimal, or no, cost.

#19. Seek out Your Biggest Critic

When I first took over as director of security at a large bank there was an executive vice president for another department that had historically been very critical of security. I sought him out and asked what had turned him against the department. Displaying a macho attitude, he questioned its value. He told me that security was filled with wimps who spent more time scaring corporate travelers with stories of danger. He concluded that most security people were fairly inexperienced in international travel and didn't understand their end-users. I knew that anything I said would have fallen on deaf ears. When I left, I thought that he was a jerk.

A few weeks later I returned and said that I had a new program that didn't have anything to do with his area. I wanted his feedback. He asked why. I told him that if this program made sense to my worst critic, it might have a chance of succeeding. He said he would look it over. Later he called and said he liked it and wanted to know why I couldn't do something similar for his area. I told him I'd like to stop by and discuss how that could be accomplished. We met and after listening to him, although I still didn't like him, he gave me several good ideas. When I left the bank three years later, he called me and said that I would be missed.

#20. Define Your Specialty in Business Terms

Finally, your end product will only be successfully marketed if it is defined in terms that can be measured by your customer base. This means that each service and/or product needs to be postured in ways that have meaning for your customers. For example, solving cases, discovering open doors, or designing new access control programs really don't mean much to non-security people. They may think they understand the necessity for such programs and activity, but they may struggle with identifying the added value that such programs bring to them or to the overall business aims of the company.

Success lies in translating each of your programs and activities into terms that decision-makers can strongly relate to and accept. Though we'll have more to say about this in Chapter Five, let's briefly revisit each activity listed above and state them in business terms versus traditional security terms.

Solving Cases:

Traditional Security Approach—Reports findings based on loss, number of cases open versus closed, total recovery rate, number of responsible parties identified, and action taken.
Security Business Approach—Reports findings in terms of impact on bottom-line profitability, number of assets/sales required to offset loss, and "discovered" recovered earnings after a write-off.

Open Doors:

Traditional Security Approach—Reports on total number of open doors found over a certain period.
Security Business Approach—Demonstrates potential dollar impact on lost assets; particularly those associated with intellectual property (trade secrets, proprietary information, customer data, price listings, pending deals, etc.) directly related to number of open doors found.

Access Control:

Traditional Security Approach—Explains access control in terms of asset protection, control of people movement, audit trail.
Business Security Approach—Demonstrates access control as an inte-

gration with other business units to lower operating expense, limit exposure, and reduce insurance premiums, thus affecting total bottom-line performance.

A PRACTICAL GUIDE TO MARKETING

Earlier I mentioned that Jim Wells, former director of security at John Hancock, has developed a comprehensive marketing plan for promoting his department's services. With his permission, I'd like to share his approach since it serves as an excellent model for other applications.

The program is divided into five major parts:

- Development of the program's goal and objectives
- Identification of the targeted market
- Delineation of the marketing strategy and tactics
- Implementation of the program
- Development of a feedback loop for quality control.

Program Goal and Objectives: Wells suggests the following goal statement and corresponding objectives are achievable because they are specifically designed to be simple, straightforward, and easily understood by the entire security staff.

Goal: To develop a marketing plan that informs our clients of all our services, encourages them to use our services, and improves our image as a quality service provider.

Objectives:

- To ensure clients become aware and knowledgeable of services offered.
- To facilitate a favorable attitude by clients regarding our services.
- To encourage our clients to fully utilize our services.
- To increase client satisfaction and improve our image.

The targeted market is the security department's entire client base. This includes John Hancock employees, tenants, clients and customers, visitors, vendors, guests, and members of the public.

The marketing strategy and tactics consist of a multilevel approach using Hancock's publications, personal selling, and positive interactions between members of the department and the targeted market. Wells also integrates his fifth component, the feedback loop, into the overall strategy since it serves to gauge the effectiveness of his approach. Over 20 specific tactics were identified at the outset, including:

- Advertising services and programs through internal publications.
- Development and presentation of 30-minute security and safety seminars.
- Development of attractive promotional material for distribution.
- Development of a security services brochure.
- Development and internal distribution of quality client service bulletins for use by his staff.
- Establishment of an executive recognition program.
- Development of a new tenant briefing video.
- Development of a new employee briefing video.
- Development of a quality client service training program for security employees.
- Creation of a client resource center for security-related information.

Since the corporate office provides child care for its employees, corporate security instituted a special fingerprinting program and child safety program. By tailoring specific programs for specific client segments, security has been able to use them as advocates for other groups. When possible, testimonials are solicited and endorsements included in the written and video media.

The implementation and development of the quality control feedback loop are the driving forces that measure the success of the program and its continuous improvement. Client input is constantly sought. The management team takes an active role in assuring that security employees remain focused and don't overlook opportunities to sell the department. When an employee asks for an escort to their vehicle after-hours, for example, the security officer is encouraged to promote the department and ask the employee if they have any questions about corporate security or the services they offer. It's not unusual for the officer to hand the employee a security pamphlet at the end of the escort.

Surveys are passed out and feedback actively pursued, allowing management to assess the general and specific effectiveness of the program. Adjustments are made. Sometimes an entire approach is scrapped if it is not shown to be working as planned. Wells notes that success comes from a willingness to accept failure. "Not everything is going to work. And that's okay. At least we know what will and what will not be effective. We can be criticized for any number of things, but not for trying." More important, I believe, is his insight into overall business management. For the Hancock security staff, asset protection is their business and just like their own company finds it necessary to market their products and services, so too, must corporate security.

CONCLUSION

We began this chapter with a discussion demonstrating that security can be defined in real value-added terms. To be successful in the 1990s security directors need to redefine their approach to managing their programs. This requires a focus on business strategies, not a reliance on proving their worth as a security professional. As a party to this new business approach, they must also become comfortable with promoting their programs and themselves. Promotion breeds success. It's as simple as that.

Promotion does not have to be flashy or slick, it just has to be effective. To illustrate how, we examined 20 strategies that can be employed without expense or much fanfare. Hopefully you have found these 20 strategies helpful. Each is designed to assist you in better posturing yourself and your department within your organization. The underlying principles are based on the idea that success comes to those who want to define their role in terms of business management and not necessarily security administration. If only 20 percent of the ideas offered here produce results, you will be significantly ahead of others. Some, like those at John Hancock, have already discovered the necessity for marketing.

I have found that the underlying difficulty most security directors have in today's business world is an inability to translate their profession into measurable business language. They lack the skill set to define what they have to offer in the broader context of corporate survival. It is no wonder, then, that they tend to lose more than they gain when times are tough. Knowing how to market yourself leads to better positioning when it is needed. In a world that defines success based on "what can you do for me today" as opposed to past performance, only those who know how to respond accordingly will survive. All others will surely perish—unfortunately taking many good people with them.

4

Quality Assurance in Cost-Containment Times

INTRODUCTION

In the mid-to late seventies a new term began to catch on with writers and organizational theorists—turnaround strategies. Simply put, it meant exploring ways that could turn the company's fiscal direction around. Usually associated with firms in financial trouble, turnaround strategies typically entailed cost cutting, downsizing, or redefining the business to bring costs into balance with sales, thereby returning the organization to profitability. With the collapse of the junk bond market and financial institutions, increased foreign competition, and the increase in what has become known as 'corporate merger mania,' a lot of business people became familiar with the notion of turnarounds.

As the 1990s unfold, the term "turnaround" is not as prevalent as it was 10 to 15 years ago. However, many cost-control strategies remain. Though the end of the decade, the emphasis will continue to be on cost containment because those organizations that understood the dynamics of turning around their companies did so and are surviving today. Those who failed to do so are now corporate history.

While some companies continue to struggle, the lessons of business competition and profitability have captured the attention of even the healthiest firms. Staying competitive, and therefore profitable, requires cost containment across the entire business spectrum and at all levels of the company, including asset protection aspects. In the next chapter we will examine several of the latest quality-oriented trends. For now, however, we will explore a number of practical ways that a security manager can meet the challenge of delivering customer-oriented service in an era of shrinking funding.

COST REDUCTION REQUIRES CREATIVITY

The simplest way to reduce current costs is to take a line-item approach, which entails reducing selective budget line items by a certain percentage. As a first step this may be all that is required. Depending on the item, the quality of service may not be adversely affected. For most managers, however, this is not the case. Since security remains largely a people-intensive business, the most direct way to reduce costs is to attack those areas associated with personnel expense. What can you do then, especially if you are not a creative person by nature? Here are ten suggestions that have worked for others:

Strategy #1: Go to the Source

The line level—guards, console operators, analysts, and investigators—generally know their jobs well. Living with operational requirements every day, it doesn't take long for even the least committed employees to note ways where improvements can be made. How many times have we heard someone say, "I don't understand why they (that's you) have us do it this way. Anyone can see that by doing it that way we can do it better and cheaper!" Comments like this abound, even in the smallest organizations. Perhaps not all of their suggestions can be acted upon. Yet, by not drawing line personnel into your strategy for cost improvement, a valuable resource is being overlooked.

Strategy #2: Seek the Advice of Your Suppliers

Seek the advice of vendors, suppliers, and contractors. All too often we fail to see them as valued business partners. Later we will explore one of the latest trends in management, strategic alliances. This strategy links external resources to the management of internal processes. For our purposes here, these same resources can be drawn on to identify ways for improvement. Allow me to step outside security to illustrate my point.

Situational Case #8: Reducing Supplier Costs

When working with an industrial client on buyer-supplier relationships, I was asked to develop a survey instrument that could measure the client's effectiveness in procuring services and products from outside suppliers. As a part of this exercise, I interviewed the senior management of four vendors. When I asked them if my client's procurement requirements were increasing the supplier's production costs, each said yes. I then asked them if there were ways that they, as suppliers, could suggest to lower their clients' production costs without compromising the client's quality standards.

Collectively the focus group offered 26 alternatives. If implemented by my client, the suppliers stated a willingness to reduce their client charges 3 to 5 percent. This from a manufacturer that grosses more than $4.5 billion annually. Their procurement costs total into the billions. Even at 3 percent, this means significant cost savings. While it is not reasonable to expect comparable savings with security suppliers, the principle certainly holds true.

Strategy #3: Seek the Counsel of Other Unit Heads

Go to other department heads within the company. After all, they have the same mission to reduce costs. It is therefore conceivable that they have thought of ways that you have not identified. While the nature of corporate security may be unique to the company, the way that it is organized may not be. Facilities management, auditing, food services, corporate legal, and data processing divisions are all similarly structured. Each consists of different staffing levels entailing line personnel, professionals, and management. Each may vary in terms of the amount of capital goods and equipment they require, but each draw on the same back office support outside their specialty area. Consequently, they too face the same challenge when reducing costs.

Strategy #4: Go to the "Big Thinkers"

Larger organizations employ full-time strategic planners. Their job is to map out business plans that complement the company's long-term needs and goals. They are charged with viewing the company and the marketplace from a global perspective. To achieve the end result generally requires a creative mind that enables them to bridge the gap from the "what we ought to have" to the "what we have." In other words, by the very nature of their job, they may be a source of creative problem solving.

Similarly, the company's marketing department may also be a place where "big thinkers" reside. These are the people who generate profits for the firm. To do so requires an equally creative mindset. To stay competitive they need to constantly come up with new ways to sell the same product. They understand well the concept of the "moving parade," which simply means that the product doesn't necessarily have to change in order for it to sell. There is a constant flow of new buyers parading by the product. The challenge is to capture their attention. The same can be said for the security manager seeking ways to reduce expenses. For you, delivery of security services can remain essentially unchanged. Your parade is not a movement of people. Rather, it is a flow of ideas passing by. Below we will discuss over 10 such ideas. By drawing on the talents of those whose business it is to come up with creative solutions, there are probably 20 other ways that could be outlined.

Strategy #5: Seek the Written Word

Go to the written source—libraries, professional journals, and the latest management books. These sources contain the writings of the latest management thinkers. Although their comments may not be drawn from the security world, as we noted above, the parallel between security and other cost centers is close. The American Society for Industrial Security (ASIS) has been slow to effectively address the whole concept of cost management, but many professional associations routinely sponsor seminars, workshops, books and journal articles. The American Management Association, to name one.

Strategy #6: Seek the Advice of Consultants

Consultants should be viewed as one of the many management tools available to the asset protection manager. Be careful, however, not all consultants are creative. Seeking a referral from professional associations may not yield the desired result. While these groups can provide the names of several security consultants, they typically do not have a mechanism in place that differentiates between those that offer creative solutions and those who cannot. Be prepared to obtain a list of members and do some homework.

Even a cursory telephone interview will weed out those not capable of assisting you. When you find one, though, they can be extremely helpful. The really good ones can save you their fees by tenfold. Combining their talents with the collective experience gained through other clients, they can share their insights in a most cost-effective way.

Strategy #7: What Does Your Mentor Have to Say?

Go to your mentor, assuming you have one. This might be another security director, a college professor, an executive in another company, or even a relative. No matter who they are, they can probably provide that much needed slant alluding you. Just as the other professionals noted above can draw on their own experiences and innate talents, a person who has a vested interest in you might even be more helpful. After all, they want you to succeed. Part of their own psyche may be tied up in having you achieve your goals. They are, therefore, likely to spend enough time with you to explore alternatives or direct you to other sources.

Strategy #8: Conduct Informal Benchmarking

Another hallmark of nineties business management theory is benchmarking. We'll discuss this in detail later, however, this is essentially an exercise designed to survey how others are approaching similar endeavors. Benchmarking allows you the opportunity to discuss with others how they have found creative solutions to their own situations. They can also discuss with you the pluses and minuses of different alternatives since they may have already tried them.

Strategy #9: Attend Intelligently Chosen Seminars and Workshops

I use the phrase "intelligently chosen" deliberately. It is easy to justify attending a favorite annual conference or meeting. After all, colleagues will likely be there and generally they take place in nice locales that can double as a family vacation spot. In other circumstances this may be acceptable, for now however, the task is to identify cost-cutting alternatives. Attending a favorite meeting at the expense of depriving yourself or another staff member from alternate cost-saving strategies is both unwise and imprudent.

Note, however, that I suggest attending a meeting. Many times managers are quick to discourage or eliminate conference or workshop attendance altogether. This is shortsighted and can work against the goal of constructive cost containment. New ideas, products, and methodologies are continually emerging. Meetings and seminars are excellent venues for exposure to the most current ideas, especially those that work. Often strategies are discussed and analyzed at these gatherings long before they appear in print. The secret is in selecting the most appropriate one, which requires more than a review of the published itinerary. Often speakers cancel or the title alone sounds appealing and you then find that the speaker has missed the mark altogether. The best way to avoid this is to either call the speaker directly and discuss the intended format or ask around and determine if others have heard the speaker(s) before.

With respect to calling the speaker directly, don't hesitate to do so. I give an average of six workshops a year, pro bono. You will find most speakers to be approachable and willing to discuss their intended topic with you. The really good speakers will ask you if their remarks are on-target for your needs. If so, fine. If not, hopefully they will consider your needs and adjust their speech accordingly. After all, they've been asked to speak because their expertise is supposed to be of help to you.

Strategy #10. Begin Thinking Anew

This means asking questions like "Why do we do the things we do and why do we do them this way?" Or, "What would happen if we did what we do now in exactly the opposite way?" This type of unconventional thinking can lead to new and creative cost-cutting approaches. One of the best ways is to think about coming at the problem through the organizational back door. By that I mean thinking in ways 180 degrees different from how you would normally think. I have often found that by approaching the problem in exactly the opposite way, a more effective solution usually is in the offering. The best example for me came in creating different workforce constructs. When faced with a proprietary group of security personnel, I will immediately ask if there are more advantages to outsourcing. Conversely, when dealing with a third-party supplier, I will begin examining the benefits of a proprietary force.

Simply examining the values of using a proprietary force versus a contracted force can be equally limiting. Sometimes, the 180 approach requires asking more basic questions. In one case I asked what would happen if we eliminated or dramatically reduced the number of officers on each of the three work shifts. After our analysis, the client and I came to the conclusion that many duties and responsibilities could be shifted away from the security department on the day watch and transferred to the unit manager.

A Final Note On Creative Thinking

Before moving on, there is one final note I'd like to leave with you. Creative problem solving is not a burden to be borne by you alone. It is a shared process drawing on the collective input of many. In particular, you should engage the talents of your direct employees or an established security task force. Whether through a series of brainstorming sessions or some other methodology, these people should be brought into the process. After all, they will have to live with the consequences as much as you will.

Creativity, especially when it affects the professional reputation of those around you, can achieve a higher level of quality when the stakes are shared. Your staff, if they're truly professional, should rise to the occasion and contribute in meaningful ways. If not, for the more cynically minded reader, you may have just identified one possible resource that you can do without.

NINE WAYS TO REDUCE COST WITHOUT LOSS OF QUALITY

Regardless of how long you can stall and for whatever reason you use, if your company is like most others, the inevitable will occur. You will be charged with the seemingly impossible task of reducing operating expenses without reducing quality of service. How can the two coexist? Doesn't the former negate the latter? Traditional management theory may suggest yes, but in many ways, it is a myth. The truth is that you *can* deliver quality service at a lower cost. Let's examine 9 ways of doing it.

#1: Can You Create Partners?

Are you willing to take your scope of responsibility and share it with other departments? Partnerships do not have to equal a loss. The opposite can be true. Sharing responsibility with another department means dividing the workload and therefore resources. By shifting duties elsewhere you may actually increase levels of service, for two reasons. First, your partner may have additional resources and mechanisms in place that can better deliver the service to your corporate customers. Second, by redirecting nonessential duties away from your staff, you can dedicate quality time and effort to delivering primary services. Here's an example:

Many asset protection departments have responsibility for key control. The same can be said for other forms of access control, especially electronic card access with photo identification. Key issuance and control management can often be handled by your company's facility services department. This is not to suggest that security relinquish responsibility for setting standards, auditing compliance (although the audit department can do the same thing), and reviewing contractor performance (if your purchasing department does not perform this function). Similarly, issuance of photo identification badges and access cards generally falls under the responsibility of corporate security. By partnering with human resources, badges and access cards can be issued at the time of hire as a part of the employment process.

Here are two basic questions that need to be asked when considering partnering. Does it have a synergistic value? And, is it redundant? With respect to synergy, you might ask another question: Is there a department or business unit, due to their organization and scope, capable of doing what security is doing at a lower cost? Perhaps facilities or human resources both have the people and the mechanisms in place to deliver your service more efficiently. Here's another quick example: Can corporate training produce training tapes at a lower cost?

There's an interesting parallel outside of security that illustrates how two otherwise competitive interests have drawn together to benefit the other. For years the cable television networks saw AT&T and the

Baby Bells as deadly enemies. Conversely, the line carriers held an equally suspect view of the cable industry. As of late, they have begun to link their respective strengths.(6) Their motivation has been one of cost containment. Each realized that it would be prohibitively expensive to duplicate what the other had because the marketplace could not support both. Consequently, the telephone companies are now focusing on delivery while the cable industry is concentrating on programming. The same can be said for a corporate security department and another support department. Security should focus on program development while the latter addresses the issue of delivery.

To test for redundancy, ask yourself: Are you doing something that others are already doing? For example, many companies employ multiple console operations. Some are dedicated to facility engineering while others focus on security and/or life safety. With the advent of banking mergers, many of my financial clients are still using separate security consoles for each formerly independent bank. Even though banking laws may require the retention of separate corporate identities, there is no prohibition against joint administration of critical support units. Just as the parent bank can consolidate accounting systems and payment processing, so too can it consolidate alarm monitoring systems.

One large Northeastern financial institution, after a series of mergers with several smaller banks, found themselves with no less than five console operations and several independent contracts in two other states. In all there were more than 20 separate alarm monitoring centers handling less than 300 branch operations. After asking themselves if the subsidiaries were doing the same things as corporate headquarters, the solution was obvious—eliminate redundancy by developing a central station to handle each financial institution. In other words, partnering can occur right within the security department. Likewise, the issue of duplicated installation and maintenance services and inventories needs to be addressed.

You might also ask yourself if there are external partners available. I refer to this as the *consortium approach,* which entails joining forces with other organizations. Here's an example:

Situational Case #9: The Security Consortium

In Washington, D.C., five independent high-rise property owners entered into a common agreement with a third-party security services supplier. Even though each building was owned by a different builder or investment group, they found that lower costs with improved quality of service could be achieved by forming a security consortium—a partnership to share security services.

Prior to the alignment, two properties were viewed as small security accounts since less than eight full-time officers were required per site. Two others were considered moderate since they employed 15 to 18 officers each. The last was considered a large account since it employed nearly 40 officers. Through the consortium, the account now represents a weekly billing of more than thirty-two hundred hours, a large account by any contractor's definition.

By leveraging the relationship, even the smallest account now commands the same level of attention that would otherwise be reserved for a much larger revenue generator. Overall, the consortium obtained a lower contract cost based on volume. It also allowed for the creation of a contract manager position to be fully dedicated to the account at no extra direct expense, thus assuring closer attention to quality deliverables.

#2: Can You Assume A Higher Risk?

Are you willing to live with a higher level of risk? As times and requirements change, so too must your limits. Retailers may find that the cost of electronic article surveillance can be limited to higher priced merchandise than previously believed. Similarly, they may allow higher cash limits in their point-of-sale terminals. Bankers may want to raise the dollar limit of their teller stations and manufacturers may need to refocus security from production posts and concentrate more on distribution centers where higher priced commodities move in and out.

With the arrival of cost containment comes an opportunity to revisit basic assumptions regarding what it is corporate security is charged with protecting. Surveys of retailers suggest that the average shoplifting case involves less than $75 at full retail price, which translates to less than $50 at cost. (7) Is it cost-justified spend over $200 a day for security protection in order to possibly recover $50?

This is not to suggest that retailers stop providing security coverage in their outlets. It does raise the issue, however, of how much coverage is really needed. Put another way, is a cost four times greater than the potential loss essential? What limits can be placed on security without sacrificing the overall integrity of asset protection? Unfortunately, there is not a universal answer. Rather, it is an individual question that needs to reflect corporate culture, location, foreseeability of loss, potential liabilities, and a host of other factors. Nonetheless, when each factor is considered, the end-result should be a determination of whether the company can live with a higher risk level. If so, then security costs can be trimmed back without sacrificing quality, as defined by the new limits.

All too often senior management is willing to raise the level of risk to lower near-term expense. Should an incident occur above the previous level—even if it is below the new threshold—security is likely to be criticized. There will be those who lament the loss and blame security for failing or diminishing their level of service. You can anticipate that some will complain loudly that their workplace is no longer safe or their profit center results have suffered. These are unfair criticisms that cannot be left unchallenged. Any increase in the level of acceptable risk needs to be well documented and distributed to everyone prior to implementation. Without this, it won't be long before the security manager can anticipate hearing the cry of foul play. Risk-raising is a joint decision that translates into shared acceptance of the consequences and an understanding that asset protection is being redefined as the corporation goes forward.

#3: Can You Shift Services to Someone Else and Redefine Your Mission?

Are you bold enough to ask if some of the services you provide are essential or relevant? If you ask and discover that one or more is not, you may lose part of your charter or power base. The goal is not the size of your department, but rather the size of your contribution to bottom-line performance without loss of quality—a personally threatening situation; some might even suggest organizational suicide. If left to stand on its own, I might agree with that assessment. The secret to success is knowing how to replace these services with more meaningful contributions that are within the spirit of your charter at a more effective cost. The following two examples serve to illustrate what I mean.

In the first case, let's assume that your firm fingerprints all new hires and vendors, and your department is charged with this responsibility. You might elect to pass this responsibility to human resources as part of the initial hiring process. The chances are high that they can be trained to take acceptable fingerprints and easily integrate it into their routine. On the other hand, you may want to outsource this activity altogether or arrange with a local police agency to perform this task. Whatever the alternative, this is a responsibility that can be transferred from your department. In the second case, let us further assume that you are charged with handling external investigations involving customer defalcations. By shifting the responsibility to retail operations you may discover that they have a mechanism in place at their credit and collection division to handle much of your current case load.

Against the backdrop of these two services you might feel a significant loss in responsibility if one or both were transferred to other business units. Borne out of such loss an opportunity emerges, though you now have the opportunity to redirect your department's efforts in more significant areas. Perhaps your company is a multinational firm that has yet to focus on security matters at its foreign operations. Who is addressing the more substantive issue of protecting your company's intellectual property? I find that this is one area that most security managers totally overlook, yet intellectual property protection gets to the very core of a firm's profitability and ability to stay competitive. Intellectual property is more than trade secrets. It involves the organization's closely guarded processes, patents, equipment, customer lists, pricing strategy, and a plethora of other sensitive data. In short, by shifting lesser duties and responsibilities away from the department, opportunities can emerge for even greater contributions.

#4: Can You Eliminate Certain Services?

In his latest book, *Rethinking the Corporation, The Architecture of Change,* Robert Tomasko (8) underscores the need to blend the "big picture" perspective with a microperspective. He starts, however, with the macro view: There is no point fine-tuning something that really should be discarded—a valuable lesson for every manager, especially for security decision-makers. Over the last decade there has been a noticeable shift away from defining asset protection solely in terms of physical protection. As noted above, greater contributions can be achieved by focusing on intellectual property instead of exclusively physical assets.

The question that needs to be addressed is whether certain services or products can be eliminated. For example, many security departments provide guard services for unoccupied buildings. Their contention is that a fire watch is required or there is a policy that protection will be provided for any facility as long as the facility is still carried as an asset on the company's books. While this may have been true when the policy was first initiated, is it still relevant today? A large manufacturer discovered that it could reduce guard coverage by more than $1,000,000 a year by replacing the evening shift security force with intrusion alarms and eliminating guard coverage completely from unoccupied buildings with a low-cost alarm system. This system could be installed and dismantled after the property was sold off. The cost was less than $6,000 per system.

Before we eliminate anything, however, a word of caution. My father taught me a saying when I was young: "Never tear down a fence until you know why it was put up." I've never forgotten that advice and found it to be most helpful, especially since becoming a consultant. It is easy for a newcomer or outsider to look at something and scoff at something not obviously relevant. Many times a requirement can be discarded because it no longer holds its original value. Similarly, we are accustomed to hearing staff tell us, "Well, we do it this way because it's the way it has always been done." It's easy to laugh the response off as "typical," yet, there may well be a reason that remains valid today—it's just not so obvious.

Here's an interesting acid test: If you owned the company, would you spend the money you are currently spending on security? For example, say you want to build a house. The budget is limited. Where does a security system fit in the scheme of priorities? Is it as high as french doors? At first a security system may be high on the list, but as the architect's cost estimates begin to unfold for wood paneled doors and insulated glass, or the estimates for carpeting and kitchen amenities are more than originally planned, decisions have to be made. These are tough decisions that you and your spouse must deal with; something needs to give. How valuable is the alarm system now? Do you find yourself beginning to compromise on the type of system you originally required? Perhaps you might even consider just wiring the house now and installing the controller and alarms later. The point is simply that everything has its place on the priority list. The same holds true for your company. Given all the demands on a limited budget, is it possible that some of your programs and services can be set aside without sacrificing the overall integrity of protecting the company's assets and employees?

#5: Can You Redefine Your Workforce?

Chapter Seven examines the use of third party contractors in-depth. But there are other ways to meet financial cutbacks without resorting to this approach. One method is to redefine the configuration of your staff. The following case study illustrates one such approach.

Situational Case #10: Redefining Your Workforce

A few years ago, a major Northwest city was facing a financial crisis. It could hardly meet its current commitments, let alone increased costs. At the same time crime was escalating during nighttime in and around parks and the zoo. The unarmed security force demanded an increase in staff just to protect themselves. So they hired a consultant to assist them. He began exploring the possibility of replacing the proprietary force with a third party contractor. Much to his surprise, he discovered that the city force was competitively priced, and therefore, there was no economic gain to be achieved by outsourcing. He then called me.

After we discussed the situation, I suggested replacing the evening shift's full-time officers with part-time personnel. The net effect was doubling the staff during times when they were needed, but at a reduced total cost. Since part-time officers cost less than full-time officers, the city could put twice the number of officers on staff at a lower operating cost. Even if the city paid the part-time officers the same base rate of pay as it did to its full-time staff, the city would not have to pay the full benefit rate normally associated with full-time employees. Nor would they have to pay overtime. The idea worked. The city could now provide twice the number of officers to serve as backup and provide mutual assistance at a lower operating expense.

This case demonstrates that even when the costs are largely confined to one area, such as labor, there are alternatives. Here's another example. A large East Coast bank employed 12 investigators in their home office with 13 additional investigators assigned to one of two affiliate locations in neighboring states. In total, these 25 investigators represented a ratio of one investigator for every ten branches. After benchmarking with like financial institutions, it was discovered that the average ratio was closer to one investigator for every 19 branches. The East Coast bank had organized its investigator staff based on geography rather than function. In an effort to be responsive to local management they were incurring nearly twice the costs of their competitors.

#6: Can You Possibly be Planning for the "Great What If?"

As security professionals, it is natural to want to set up those procedures and commit those resources we believe are necessary to respond to almost any situation. Some loss prevention managers subscribe heavily to this approach, drawing on their experiences from the public sector, especially their days in the military. Unfortunately for them, most of today's corporate world does not define their ability to respond to emergencies in nearly the same manner. Practices instituted and resources committed should be enough to assure essential services are maintained.

Situational Case #11:
The Riot that Never Took Place

One retail security manager, motivated to prove his department's ability to respond, cost his company literally hundreds of thousands of dollars on two events alone. Despite receiving repeated advice from local officials that neither event warranted his preparations, he went ahead anyway. The first involved the election of the city's first black mayor. Since this was a major city, the security manager felt that if the black candidate lost, there would be rioting in the streets. Conversely he reasoned, if the candidate was elected there would be such jubilation that demonstrations would spill over into the streets and threaten some of his company's retail properties.

Local law enforcement officials and other security managers, using their own intelligence resources, assured him that neither scenario was likely to happen. Regardless, he hired extra off-duty police officers, guard dogs, rented an entire floor in one of the city's fashionable hotels to serve as a command center and rented two 40-foot-long trailers equipped with emergency generators in case power lines were cut. Total cost for the evening was more than $185,000.

Situational Case #12:
The Los Angeles Olympics

A few months later he was asked to coordinate with Los Angeles authorities to prepare for the Los Angeles Olympics. The retail chain was concerned that their West Coast distribution network could be disrupted by traffic congestion. After conferring with local officials and other security professionals, he was told that while no guarantees could be given, the probability of disruption was minimal. Instead of taking their advice, he rented an 18-wheel trailer truck and filled it with emergency rations capable of outfitting 50 security officers, complete with guns and ammunition. He secured a spot in the parking lot of one of his store's locations and set up a command center.

He also leased a helicopter and had it flown to the command center prior to the start of the Olympics. This, in spite of the fact that police officials told him that unauthorized aircraft would not be allowed in their "no fly zone," which is where the command center was located. He also leased a powerful radio and telecommunications system that was bigger than the Los Angeles County Sheriff's system. As history showed, there were no significant problems associated with terrorist activity or simple traffic congestion. Cost to the retailer in planning for the "Great What If": in excess of $250,000.

While these two examples are clearly extremes, they do underscore the need for security managers to reexamine their basic assumptions. Are staffing levels set higher than they need to be? Are access control systems or closed-circuit television systems more than necessary? Recently, I was part of an assessment team that examined a large corporation's use of CCTV. We found that in one parking facility for 800 cars there were plans to install 93 cameras. What was even more unfortunate was that every camera was going to be monitored by one officer working at a public lobby console. This officer was already attempting to view 28 cameras off a single monitor using sequential switching, and the plans called for each of the 93 cameras to share that same monitor!

Similar anecdotes abound. But perhaps one that rivals each of those conveyed above is an experience that happened to me when I took over the responsibility for a major bank.

Situational Case #13:
The Emergency Response Team

When I first arrived, I took a tour of the security guard room at the main office. I was accompanied by my manager who had just assumed responsibility for security. Our tour guide was the former acting security director, now deputy director. As we walked through the locker area, I observed four security officers sitting on a bench playing cards. I asked what they were doing since this was well after the start of the afternoon shift. The deputy director informed us that this was the emergency response unit. He went on to explain that the union contract called for a 4-officer unit to be on standby in case of a bank robbery during closing hours.

Under the contract each officer was paid a minimum of four hours at time and a half. Since the locker room was in the basement of the building and the banking floor was on the second floor, I asked how they responded. He said their only response route was to run up one flight of stairs and take the escalator from the main lobby to the second floor. Any casual observer would have concluded that none of them were physically fit to run up 10 steps, let alone a flight of stairs.

I asked when the last time the bank was robbed and was told that no actual robberies had occurred in the past ten years. Moreover, there had only been one attempt and that was over five years ago. At a cost of $17.37 per hour, per officer, times one and a half, that equaled an hourly rate of $104 for four officers. At a daily rate of $416, one year alone cost the bank $108,160. Needless to say the next contract was void of this arrangement.

Each of these situations illustrates that security managers can fall into the trap of overplanning. Many are borne out of a genuine concern for the safety and well-being of their organization. Other plans are the end result of a specific event or series of incidents. Yet, the tragedy is in a failure to routinely step back from the daily operation and question the value of such preparedness. Today's lean and mean times require a hard reassessment. In doing so, it is likely that you will find your area of overplanning and/or overresourcing.

#7: Can You Develop A Mutual Ownership for Security Among Business Unit Managers?

Another way of viewing the organization is to ask if procedural changes can replace capital and labor. Developing a sense of employee awareness is only half of the requirement for a successful quality driven program. The other half is to develop a strategy that assures their commitment. On a personal level, an individual may know the risk associated with leaving the front door of their home unlocked and going away for the evening. It is quite another matter when they take the precaution of actually locking the door upon leaving. The act of locking their door demonstrates an ownership of the responsibility for taking the proper security precautions. Similarly, in organizations employees must become more than just aware of the need for proper security procedures. Once they are, direct expenses associated with operating the security department can often be reduced without a loss in quality. The slack is taken up by those willing to assume a greater and more active role in their own protection. Another example:

Situational Case #14: Developing Mutual Ownerships

A large corporation recently set about the business of remodeling their world headquarters. The chairman was intent on reducing operating costs and it was determined that by restacking the building and taking advantage of state-of-the-art facility management systems, costs could be significantly lowered for heating, ventilation, lighting, and work flow. He also sent word out that he wanted the security budget reduced.

The resolution was to install card readers in each lobby and alarm the rear doors. Instead of requiring the security force to respond to each alarm activation during normal business hours, the decision was made to have the console operator notify the business unit manager that his or her rear door was in an alarm condition. By shifting the responsibility of responding to alarms to the local management team, the guard force could be reduced, thus lowering their budget as directed by the CEO.

As each floor was remodeled, the security director met with the resident managers and supervisors and explained that it was their responsibility to control their work area. This included responding to alarms. If the alarm was the result of a true emergency, they were instructed to notify the security console and an emergency response team would be summoned.

Each manager was told that the security officers were unarmed and had no special police powers. Further, the guard force was not trained in detainment techniques and was told that most alarms were false, generally originating because of someone sneaking into the stairwells for a cigarette, a maintenance person, or one of their own employees using the stairwells as a matter of convenience. Each manager understood that a record of received alarms would be kept and that if false alarms persisted, they would be cited in their annual audit and appropriate action taken at the time of their annual performance rating. Understanding the stakes, each manager knew the rules and was quick to pass along the new procedures to their respective employees. Needless to say the number of false alarms has been low over the past few years. The corporate security director also reports that there is clear evidence of a heightened awareness of employees and a willingness to challenge strangers observed in their work areas.

#8: Can You Find Significant Reductions in Non-Labor Areas?

Even though the single largest expense for most asset protection operations is labor, there are other areas offering potentially significant savings. Generally, the second largest area of expense is in the category of "occupancy," which is the charge allocated to security for occupying their space. It includes maintenance costs such as cleaning, utilities, and rent. By reducing the physical space the allocated cost should decrease correspondingly. Many times a department will continue to occupy space long after they have downsized to considerably less space. The same holds true for departments that outsource the security guard force but allow the facilities division to carry the locker room or other guard space on security's books.

I have frequently found that corporate security is charged with main lobby occupancy charges because they staff a console there. Since facilities is anxious to allocate expenses back to any department but their own, they will quietly charge off the entire expense of maintaining a large lobby to the unsuspecting security department. Many times the central lobby space exceeds the entire square footage allotment provided to security. At one large manufacturer, I found that facilities had allocated the cost of an entire employee parking lot against security's budget because they were the only department to have three reserved spaces for their vehicles.

There are other opportunities that may be hidden as well. Telecommunications may not cancel line charges or equipment lease costs every time an instrument is deleted. One security manager discovered overcharges by her telecommunications group in excess of $16,000 annually because they had failed to terminate line service with the local carrier, opting instead to pass along the charges to security because it was more administratively expedient. For the sake of convenience, security was expected to pay. If telecommunications determines that it is not in their best interest to set up a cost management system tied to deletions and add-ons, then they ought to be willing to absorb the cost via a similar charge-back.

Is this all funny money? Yes and no. Here's why: You are an independent department manager. You are responsible for your total budget. By scaling back direct and indirect costs, actual savings can be achieved. Auditing, human resources, facilities, telecommunications, payroll and other support units all have allocations. If you downsize, why shouldn't your allocated expense be reduced accordingly? For many corporate asset protection programs this could mean a savings of as much as 20 percent or more without loss of deliverable quality service.

#9: Can You Identify Hidden Opportunities?

Qualitative cost reductions can take on other forms, many transparent. Earlier we discussed the concept of creativity. This is an area that requires some creative processing. For example, in negotiating a service contract here are a couple of reduction strategies that can yield some surprising results.

First, consider monthly prepayment. In one contract, I asked the supplier to identify his "cost to carry." By this I meant his costs associated with making his payroll commitments between the time he paid his salaries and the time his client actually processed his invoice. On a net 30-day basis, he told me his bank charged him 6 percent. This was the interest he paid each month in order to draw off the needed funds to meet his payroll requirements before depositing his accounts receivables from his client. By encouraging his client to prepay monthly, he could forego his bank's interest charges and meet his payroll. In turn, he was willing to lower his billing rate correspondingly because this was an accompanying fee calculated into his original rate charged to the customer. Since this was a million-dollar account, the savings were substantial.

Similarly, he was asked to lower his rate because his client was a well-recognized firm in the area. By obtaining this account, certain marketing advantages flowed back to his company. This being so, why shouldn't the client receive some compensatory consideration based on the marketability of their name? Again, the supplier was willing to lower his rate because he knew well that having this client as one of his customers would likely increase overall sales. The same strategy can be said for requiring a "most-preferred customer status." This simply means that you, as client, are assured that throughout the term of the contract, the supplier will pass along all billing rate reductions if he should sign an agreement with another similar client for less than he is charging you. For a number of my clients this has meant that they have not had an increase in their billing rate for three years. This is because over the course of a year, the supplier has signed contracts at a lower rate, thus passing the savings on to them. These lower rates have more than offset the incremental increases resulting each year from inflation or other escalators.

For companies that employ external alarm servicing and/or monitoring services, similar strategies are available. Of particular note are monitoring fees. Banks typically suffer the most, especially with their automated teller machines. Usually they are charged for four contact points, e.g., tampering, duress, robbery, and trouble. In reality the alarm company only monitors two points, trouble and all others. For their purposes, the first three all require the same level of response and they're treated simultaneously. They will terminate the four alarms at a data gathering panel and route only two actual points back to their center. The unsuspecting customer is charged for four points, or double the cost. It's worth checking out.

CONCLUSION

In this chapter we examined two sets of 9 strategies for dealing with cost reductions without sacrificing loss in quality service. The first set delineated 9 ways to find creative solutions for reducing operating expense. The second set identified 9 ways to achieve such results. In the next chapter we shift our attention to several strategies currently being pursued by many companies. As a part of cost containment, we will examine how they can help you measure your effectiveness as a contributing business partner.

5

Today's Strategies— Management Fads or Management Tools?

INTRODUCTION

As a consultant I travel a great deal, and over the past couple of years many of my clients have been located in Boston. Each time I go there I try to stay at the Le Meridien Hotel, because of the way I'm treated there. It is one of the few hotels where I have stayed that consistently provides high-quality customer service. On one trip I had lunch with the general manager and I told him that I was very impressed with the hotel's level of service.

I explained further that I observed the staff in action with other guests, and found the same high level of quality service being extended to them as well. This level of service extended throughout the entire staff, from the bellman to the front desk staff, to the concierges and housekeeping. The same could be said for the food service personnel and the security staff. In my discussion with the manager, I commented that it must take a considerable amount of time and money for programs to continuously assure such a high level of service.

I was surprised to hear the manager tell me that while he was extremely proud of his staff, he spent very little time and money on quality improvement programs. He said that from the time the hotel opened, the issue of quality service became an intricate part of the hotel's culture. Dedication to providing topnotch service is a characteristic that job applicants at the hotel must demonstrate.

Building on this intrinsic concern for customer satisfaction, the hotel, in its initial orientation and training programs, emphasizes to new employees that their job is to provide high-quality customer service. From there it becomes part of the employee culture and is continually reinforced by both management and peer pressure from other workers. As the manager observed, "Anything less is just not tolerated, not by myself, my other managers, and perhaps most importantly, by the other employees. It's as simple as that." In short, providing continuous quality service need not be an undue burden if it is properly managed.

In this chapter we're going to explore several quality improvement programs. We will look at both their advantages and disadvantages. Stressed throughout this chapter is the concept of customer satisfaction. As security managers, achieving customer satisfaction is intricately tied to the overall success of the asset protection program. Whether the customer base is other employees and end users within the organization, or those external to the organization, their satisfaction is directly tied to the security department's ability to continuously show that they care and are genuinely interested in improving their department's quality of service.

CONTINUOUS QUALITY IMPROVEMENT PROGRAMS

The concept of continuous quality improvement became popular in the late 1970s and early 1980s. Born out of a need to maintain a competitive edge and/or regain market share, executives began looking for programs and strategies that could deliver goods and services in the most cost-effective manner. Continuous quality improvement programs appear to have had a positive effect on U.S. productivity.

In September 1993, the *Wall Street Journal* carried a front page story comparing U.S. productivity output against Germany, France, Italy, Canada, and Japan. (9) They noted that the hourly output for U.S. workers had risen 4.6 percent and had a better showing than eight of ten other countries surveyed. They found Germany had risen 0.6 percent, while France rose 2.9 percent, Italy 3.7 percent, and Canada 4.2 percent. Japan's productivity levels, by comparison, had fallen 6.2 percent.

The article discussed associated labor costs. The *Journal* noted that while the United States had increased its level of productivity, its associated labor costs had fallen on a per unit of output cost by 1.5 percent. This decrease was in sharp contrast to the comparative base that showed Japan had increased its labor costs by 18.3 percent, followed by Germany at 12 percent, the Netherlands at 11.3 percent, and 7.2 percent in France.

What these statistics show is that the United States, on whole, has reestablished itself as a leader in productivity while simultaneously reducing labor expense. This achievement, however, has not been without its own associated costs. Within one day of the *Journal* article, the *San Francisco Chronicle and Examiner* reported the results of a survey conducted by Proudfoot Change Management, a Winter Park, Florida-based consulting firm who commissioned the Gallup organization to survey 400 executives from large manufacturing and service companies. The focus of the study was to assess how these executives were perceiving change within their own organizations. (10)

The study found that 79 percent believe change is taking place either rapidly or extremely rapidly. Sixty-one percent of the executives said that the pace of change at their companies was expected to accelerate, and yet nearly 60 percent admitted that there were no mechanisms in place at their organizations to manage this type of change. According to the survey, the fastest changing areas are cost pressures, information technology, government regulations, customer demand, quality programs, quality in advancement of workers, and automation. The message here is that in order to sustain higher levels of productivity and customer satisfaction, change, as a dynamic within a company, needs to be better managed. This being so, there is an obvious role for agents of change to institute formerly established quality improvement programs.

All of this change has had an impact on corporate security. As John Fay notes, "Corporate security is the child of change and the product of its environment. It was born out of a need and grew up learning how to cope and survive. It is what it is and does what it does because of the dictates of external and internal forces. Carried with this condition is the inherent danger that change can become so demanding that corporate security may be unable to cope, and therefore not survive, at least not in the way it presently operates." (11)

He continues, noting that for the corporate security manager, the mandate is to achieve the same or higher level of results, except to go about it differently. The organization's top leadership wants the asset manager to embrace bold new concepts, yet wants an assurance that there will be no diminishment in asset protection. As Fay observes, "Whether the corporate security manager likes it or not, he or she is caught up in a process of learning, adapting, and above all, accepting the proposition that the change which has begun will continue well into the foreseeable future, and that corporate security must be a constructive part of the process. This is a hefty challenge for an asset protection manager. If they lack a basic business management orientation and a working knowledge, what is meant by the term continuous quality improvement?"(12)

In a separate article for *Security Technology and Design*, Fay outlines a six-step strategy (13) that can help security decision-makers adapt to their changing environment and focus their programs on value-added contributions for their organization:

Step 1—Improve On Quality and Cost.

Fay says, "The successful security operations are those which strive to be the best in their class in all the main performance activities." This best-in-class concept is discussed in greater detail below. For our purposes here, however, it is important to note that quality can only be found where there is an emphasis on implementing those practices that represent the security industry's best efforts.

STEP 2—Forge Close Links to Customers.

As noted earlier, customer satisfaction is the root purpose of the professional security service. To stay focused on this fundamental building block, it's incumbent on security managers to understand the customer's needs, or as Fay would put it, "This is less like making friends through public relations and more like getting into 'the mind' of the customer, so as to increase the manager's ability to respond rapidly and appropriately." (14) This notion ties back to our earlier discussion on internal marketing strategies, where I suggested it is the security administrator's responsibility to think like the customer to best understand their needs.

STEP 3—Establish Close Relationships with Suppliers.

As we shall see in Chapter Seven, outsourcing is a significant management tool available to security administrators, particularly those faced with a challenge of downsizing or reorganization. The asset protection manager needs to maintain a hands-on relationship with suppliers. The courts have consistently held that asset protection for a firm is a duty that cannot be delegated away to a third party and therefore requires continuous management of suppliers. Moreover, the idea is to select a few capable suppliers and work closely with them to achieve the desired level of cost containment without sacrificing quality performance.

STEP 4—Make Effective Use of Technology.

This is consistent with one of the basic themes of this book. Effective management requires balancing operating procedures, staffing assignments, and use of appropriate technologies. The operative word here is *balance*. In today's high-technology world, it's easy to become seduced into believing that efficiencies are achieved through application of the latest device or system.

Such an entrapment can lead to overspending and a misapplication for the end-user's requirements. For example, a data processing manager was interested in providing a higher level of security for his tape library. The room itself was equivalent to a large walk-in closet and only three staff people had authorized access. Instead of changing the locks and using nonduplicating keys, the security manager proposed the installation of an electronic access control system, complete with a card reader and controller. What should have been a couple of hundred dollars expenditure, soon became several thousand and was ultimately rejected by the user as too expensive. Even worse, the security manager's credibility was brought into question.

STEP 5—Operate with Minimum Layers of Management Hierarchy.

By flattening the organization there is more reliance on higher trained and more competent staffing. The net effect should be an improvement in quality if the residual staff is given the appropriate resourcing and support. Such support can, and often should be, a blend of both external and internal resources. As Fay notes, "Execution of the security strategy in a flat, lean organization will, in most cases, rely upon a small, yet well-rounded staff of the highest quality, working in partnership with suppliers who bring to the arrangement a broad array of technical competencies."(15)

STEP 6—Continuously Improve the Security Staff.

Continuous quality improvement programs are a direct reflection of the evolving quality of those delivering such service. Just as the general manager at the Meridien Hotel noted, employees need continual support and incentives to be assured that their contribution is appreciated. Improvement of the security staff may require a considerable learning curve and coaching, formal classroom instruction, and special training as it relates to on-the-job requirements. Fay concludes that the desired

CUSTOMER

	ANGRY/UPSET CUSTOMER	INDIFFERENT CUSTOMER	PROBLEM-SOLVER CUSTOMER
ANGRY/UPSET SEC OFFICER	LOW OUTCOME	LOW OUTCOME	MODERATE OUTCOME
INDIFFERENT SEC OFFICER	LOW OUTCOME	LOW OUTCOME	MODERATE OUTCOME
PROBLEM-SOLVER SEC OFFICER	MODERATE OUTCOME	MODERATE OUTCOME	HIGH OUTCOME

SECURITY OFFICER

Figure 5.1: The Customer Service Matrix

outcome of successful staff development is technical competency, quality output, teamwork and a flexibility that permits the acceptance of daunting challenges.

THE CUSTOMER SERVICE MATRIX

The business of security is to protect assets. To be successful, it must be done within a customer service context. As with any other service-oriented business, security draws on its ability to serve by maintaining a focus on customer satisfaction. The whole movement of quality improvement is based on the premise that output—products or services—are valued only to the extent that they are customer-driven. In this context, the balance of this book emphasizes customer satisfaction heavily. It is the cornerstone determining your ultimate success as a business manager specializing in asset protection.

Several years ago I participated in a seminar on customer service styles. I was given the matrix presented below in Figure 4. The source for this matrix was not provided, and while the author is unknown, I have found it to be an extremely worthwhile tool to illustrate the potential outcomes between a customer and service provider. It has a direct application for the security professional because it underscores the need for security personnel to always maintain the position of the independent problem solver. Since then I have adopted it for use by security personnel. The matrix shows that there are only three outcomes possible: low, moderate and high. It's surprising that there is only a one in nine chance of the service outcome being high. There is a four in nine chance that any outcome will be moderately successful, and an equal four in nine chance that it will be low. Since the potential for a high outcome is so low, the matrix deserves a closer analysis.

You may think that something is wrong. After all, you might reason, most of the customer service encounters you have had would not be considered low. This is probably true. Where then does the discrepancy arise? I believe it is found in the moderate outcome categories. When one of the two parties maintains the problem-solver mode, the outcome will likely be moderate. If the problem-solver is the customer, the security officer cannot legitimately take credit for the success; the security officer is the reason for the outcome not achieving its full potential. Since the outcome is moderate, there is little likelihood the security manager will receive a complaint. Yet, the encounter itself was not highly successful.

Conversely, if the officer maintains a problem-solving attitude, there is a high probability that the encounter will not drop below a moderate outcome. Here the officer is a contributing factor. Even though the outcome is only moderate, both the officer and you can take pride knowing that the outcome was driven by security. While techniques can be developed to move the customer into a similar problem-solving mode, the outcome for this particular encounter would be rated successful. Let's look at what happens when the outcome is not so successful.

If the customer comes into a situation angry or upset, and the security officer is equally angry, the service quality is, predictably, going to be low. The reasons why each party is upset may be worlds apart; yet, if they are both in the same mindset, the results could be disastrous. A third party's intervention will be required and credibility will be lost to both the individual and the department. There is really a no-win situation. At best, damage control might win the customer back at some point in the future. The interaction can be characterized by either covert or overt conflict, leading to reduced esteem by both parties. Put another way, anger begets anger.

When the customer comes to the situation angry and confronts a security person who is passive, complacent, or indifferent, the service quality will again be low. In this case the customer may either bully the security person into meeting the customer's demands, or the passive security officer may resist the customer's influence. The latter case will only inflame the situation and lead to a greater level of customer frustration.

On the other hand, if an aggressive customer confronts a problem-solving–oriented security person, there's a high probability that the service quality will at least have a moderately successful outcome. By maintaining a pleasant but neutral position, the security officer stands a better chance of getting the customer focused on problem resolution, and will avoid inflammatory words or actions, which would only serve to aggravate the situation.

Similarly, if the customer is indifferent and approaches an angry or upset security officer, the service quality outcome will be low since the customer may become overwhelmed and confused. Although the customer may succumb to the power tactics of the security officer, there's a feeling of low satisfaction with the outcome.

If both parties involved are indifferent, little action is likely to result since the relationship will never get beyond superficial or preliminary issues.

> On the lighter side, a security manager once told a group about a time when he observed his officers in action on the midnight shift. He arrived at the property unannounced and positioned himself to watch his nighttime security officer working the main lobby post.
>
> From his vantage point it looked as though the officer was reading a book. When the security director heard the elevators open and watched as an employee went over to the desk to sign out, he observed that this employee was walking very slowly and was noticeably exhausted from having worked so late.

> The security director then told of how he watched as the employee approached the lobby console. The security officer never looked up. As the employee was signing out, the director saw that the employee's head began to nod, and within a matter of seconds, the pen fell from his hand onto the ground.
>
> At first the security director was alarmed that the employee had taken ill. On second glance, it became clear that the employee had only fallen asleep. As he approached the console, he confirmed his worse suspicions—the security officer was also sound asleep!

This is probably an extreme example of what can happen when two indifferent-passive people encounter each other late at night. But it illustrates the potential outcome.

When a passive customer is approached by a problem-solving–oriented security officer, the service received is likely to be moderate judging by the customer's passivity level. In this situation the security officer is obliged to question the customer as much as possible to determine his or her needs and intent. The security officer must be patient when giving and receiving information because a tenacious attitude may be perceived by the customer as hostile, aggressive behavior.

If the customer has a problem-solving orientation but the security officer is angry or upset, the service quality is likely to be moderate, but through no contribution of the security officer, however. The customer devotes time and energy trying to get the officer focused on the job at hand so his service needs are met. If this strategy fails, the customer may ignore the security officer's behavior, request a third party (a supervisor), or go elsewhere.

If the customer retains a problem-solving orientation, but encounters an indifferent-passive security officer, the customer may not get adequate information upon which to base decisions. In many instances the security officer's behavior may provoke the customer into a different mode altogether; e.g., hostile-aggressive or passive-dependent.

Finally, as the matrix demonstrates, a high customer service quality outcome can only be achieved when both the customer and the security person are simultaneously displaying problem-solving attitudes. The interaction is characterized by a mutually respectful "let's get on with business" approach. Information and facts are brought to bear, with both parties eliciting required data and responding accurately to legitimate questions.

As the matrix illustrates, security employees need to be aware that they are the controlling variable in determining the outcome of a customer service interaction. Any abrogation of this responsibility places the customer at a distinct disadvantage. Unless the client is willing to take up the slack by maintaining a problem-solving attitude, the outcome will undoubtedly remain low. If properly presented, the customer service matrix can serve as a powerful management tool for building quality improvement programs.

TOTAL QUALITY MANAGEMENT (TQM)

By the early 1980s, quality circles and quality teams started being replaced by an entire process designed to improve quality in measurable terms. Originally designed to improve and speed up the product manufacturing and delivery process, TQM programs (and experts) began sprouting up by the dozens. Soon TQM processes made their way into service organizations as well. Today there are literally thousands of organizations engaging in some form of total quality management processing. TQM, as it is commonly known, is not without its critics. Many believe that as a process, it is so internally directed that it forces entire support units away from the focus of providing quality service in an effort to meet the rigors of internal demands. Alternatively, there are many who believe TQM in the workplace is long overdue, believing it to be a critical management tool for redefining how businesses can effectively meet their overall objectives.

Among those who criticize TQM, noted consultant, W. Edwards Deming, author of *The New Economics for Management* and *Out of the Crisis*, says that TQM is nothing more than a buzz word and carries no meaning for him. Conversely, Robert Galvin, chairman of the executive committee of a board of directors and former CEO of Motorola, believes that TQM programs are successful, and that more emphasis should be placed on them. This view is shared by Lewis Platt, chief executive officer at Hewlett-Packard. He notes that with TQM programs, HP has saved more than $800 million in warranty costs during the past ten years, not including the tens of millions of dollars that the company saved through process improvements in manufacturing, marketing, and field support.

Noted author Tom Peters believes that TQM has failed for three reasons. First, like the manager at the Meridien Hotel, Peters contends that TQM, if done right, is a way of life and not a program. Second, for TQM to be successful, front line employees must be given both the resources and the authority to fix customer problems immediately. He argues that most managers are reluctant to empower employees with this authority. Finally, Peters notes that many quality programs are simply not customer-focused, but instead are internal programs run by technocrats.

Rosabeth Moss Canter, Harvard Business School professor and author of eleven books, takes a more moderate stance, saying that TQM is here to stay. She notes that the International Standards Organization is setting de facto world standards with its ISO-9000 criteria, and the Baldrige Award (discussed below) in the United States makes quality processes and outcomes an essential feature of business—even though they ought not be regarded as the primary feature of business success.

Perhaps the sharpest critic of TQM is Oren Harari, a University of San Francisco professor and a consultant with Tom Peters' group. In 1993, the American Management Association's publication, *Management Review*, ran an article entitled, "Ten Reasons Why TQM Doesn't Work," written by Harari, which sparked a series of letters to the editor over the next several months from both supporters of Harari and proponents of the TQM process. (16)

Since quality improvement programs have captured corporate management's attention and are now being implemented in literally thousands of companies across America, it is appropriate to review some of Harari's criticisms. My purpose here is to put the process of continuous quality improvement into focus by suggesting that if left unchecked, as Harari suggests, it will not only become another in the series of passing management fads, but also can be damaging to the organization's goal of providing customer service at a higher level.

Harari's comments have direct application for asset protection managers because we, like other business unit heads, can easily fall into the trap of following what is currently in vogue and unwittingly set ourselves up for failure.

Ten Reasons Why TQM Doesn't Work

Harari's first observation is that TQM focuses people's attention on internal processes rather on external results. As we shall see below in our discussion of the Malcolm Baldrige process, quality improvement techniques require the establishment of a structure and application of a series of mechanisms to monitor the progress made within the structure. It is Harari's contention that it is easy to become too internally focused, overemphasize internal performance measures, and lose sight of the larger picture, which is to achieve a process aimed at meeting the customer's requirements.

His second criticism is that TQM focuses on minimum standards. It is his concern that quality management processes "seduces many people into believing that minimum standards define quality." He challenges its advocates by saying that "quality means offering your customers products and services and personal experiences with your company that they will find easy, useful, intriguing, and even fun."

This is particularly relevant for security managers who, in an attempt to quantify customer service activities, establish quotas for security officers, and preestablished response times. Assigning a certain number of doors to be checked, work areas to be walked through, or emergency response within a prescribed period of time, are valuable measures provided they are kept in balance. The manager should not lose sight of the fact that it is not the number of tasks accomplished in a given shift, or the time it took to respond from Point A to Point B, as much as it is the quality of the activity that takes place during routine patrols and the level of service provided once the officer arrives on scene.

Harari's third point is that TQM develops its own cumbersome bureaucracy. In the life cycle of any organization this is not an uncommon trap. Most organizations start off in a strong entrepreneurial mode, and as they grow, more controls are required to assure continuity and consistency of approach, which leads to the establishment of bureaucracies. One need only look to such corporate examples as Apple Computer, Microsoft, IBM, and Xerox. For the security director, establishing a TQM process is only as valuable as the ability to accomplish the end goal—a high level of customer satisfaction. If in so doing, security officers find themselves excessively bound by rules and expectations regarding performance criteria, then the end result could be in serious jeopardy.

The fourth point is that TQM delegates quality to quality czars and experts, rather than to real people. Harari's experience is that large organizations seeking to implement an across the board quality program, find it necessary to establish an entire department, or designate someone with ultimate accountability for quality improvement. Similarly, within an asset protection program, it is understandable that the manager would select an individual to spearhead this effort. Doing so is certainly reasonable, provided the individual works diligently to maintain a connection with the rest of the security staff and is not waylaid by theories or other organizations' success stories that have little or no relevancy to their particular situation.

Harari's fifth point is that TQM does not demand radical organizational reform. If the process does not force flatter structures and an ability to delegate critical decision-making to line level personnel, then the firm will not meet its goals. The same is true for a department within a company, such as security, that wants to set up a quality management process. As Harari notes, "The problem is that while TQM gives these issues lip service, it rarely confronts them head on. Too often, for TQM, tough, painful, structural changes play second fiddle to the more visible carnival of motivational balloons and wall posters, innumerable classes with big binders and slick presentations with fancy graphics." (17) Harari's point is simply that if quality improvement is limited to management hype with little substance to back it, the program will ultimately be a failure, and will actually have cost the organization a great deal of expense in terms of both money and time.

The sixth criticism is that TQM does not demand changes in management compensation. To be effective TQM must be an incentive-based program. Security personnel need to know that they have an investment in delivering quality as an end result of their efforts. For the past fifty years, organizational theorists have consistently shown that successful programs will more often hit their mark when an economic incentive is tied to the efforts of those responsible for the program. This is not to say that compensation is the only motivator. Far from it. But the undeniable fact remains that when people are economically motivated, they do a better job.

Harari's seventh point is that TQM does not demand entirely new relationships with outside partners. As we shall discuss in Chapters 6 and 7, establishing relationships with outside vendors is not inherently flawed with respect to total quality management processes. If not properly managed, however, the actions of your suppliers can have a dramatically adverse impact on your total quality program. TQM, to be successful, requires full participation and commitment from everyone, both internal and external to the organization. As Harari warns, if these new relationships are based on soft, squishy concepts like trust, honesty, inclusion, mutual support, and candid, nonlegalistic expectations of both parties, there is no management stick to keep external relationships in check.

When all is said and done, the truth is that suppliers need to believe that the security department wants to establish a two-way street that assures them reasonable profit margins. They also want to know that there's an opportunity to continue the relationship beyond a time frame defined in months. A true quality management program looks for long-term partners and a willingness to commit to them by drawing on their ideas, resources, and expertise.

Harari's eighth criticism is that TQM appeals to faddism, egotism, and quick fixism. Today there are hundreds of companies offering seminars on the latest TQM success stories and processes. The challenge for security managers is to decipher which companies have programs and/or techniques that are truly substantively based. Unfortunately, even in the world of total quality management, some talk a better game than their abilities demonstrate.

The ninth criticism is that TQM drains entrepreneurship and innovation from the corporate culture. As Harari says, "Bluntly speaking, TQM programs attempt to standardize and routinize internal processes with a carefully developed set of measurements and methodology."(18) As we shall see below, quality improvement programs do represent an organizational paradox. On the one hand, by empowering line personnel and encouraging innovative thoughts, a certain level of quality can be achieved. For the asset protection manager, there must be a mechanism in place showing that innovative approaches and line-level decision-making contributes to bottom-line performance. What this means is that the adopted TQM process needs to force people to focus on the goals of the program without an overly burdensome infrastructure.

Harari's last comment is that TQM has no place for love. His point here is that while TQM attempts to make quality happen via an analytically detached, sterile mechanical path, it often misses emotion and soul. My experience is that any program developed by management, lacking a similar human dimension, can be equally criticized. If the security manager develops a "by the book" quality program that doesn't reflect the human spirit and needs of the staff, then the program will fail to reach its full potential. On the other hand, if the spirit of customer satisfaction is driven through the department and supported by everyone, as a people-oriented process, then it can sidestep this trap.

As noted, Harari's article sparked a feverish debate on both sides of the continuous quality improvement issue. Defending TQM was Donald P. Jackson, vice president of corporate quality for the Durametalic Corporation, in Kalamazoo, Michigan. Individually refuting each of Harari's ten points, Jackson notes that TQM must focus on internal processes if external results are going to occur. He challenges Harari's contention that TQM focuses on minimum standards, saying that the essence of TQM is on developing processes that force managers to seek continuous improvement above previously established standards.

In contrast to Harari's sixth contention that TQM does not demand changes in management compensation, Jackson notes that compensation changes from "pay for performance" to "pay for knowledge." Bonus payments based on profitability and profit sharing with all employees are parts of the TQM process. He dismisses Harari's TQM faddism comment as a negativism that is so absurd that it does not deserve a response. Finally, responding to the contention that TQM has no place for love, Jackson notes, "I feel sure that Dr. Harari has never seen a quality awards presentation. He would have a different opinion of how "real" people are affected by recognition for their commitment to the TQM process." (19)

These comments, coupled with those of Galvin at Motorola, Platt of Hewlett-Packard, and Professor Cantor, indicate that total quality management is controversial. I believe that like any other management tool, quality improvement programs can be successful if they're properly understood by management and properly applied. When misunderstandings and abuse set in, it's only logical to conclude that they will not only miss their mark, but also discredit the values they're intended to achieve.

One final word on quality improvement programs. The Forum Corporation of Boston, Massachusetts has created an acronym called P.R.O.G.R.E.S.S. (20) to help their clients develop CQI programs:

- Pick the issue
- Research the current situation
- Obtain root cause(s)
- Generate possible improvements
- Run a pilot
- Examine the results
- Set up transfer
- Seek further improvements

These eight steps are self-explanatory. Forum suggests that quality begins by picking a specific issue and then researching the current situation. As part of this research, the security manager needs to identify strengths and weaknesses and whether the issue is still relevant, given the overall climate of the organization. Obtaining the root cause(s) challenges the manager to identify fundamental reasons, situations, and factors that define the current state of affairs. By generating possible improvements, Forum means articulating those strategies that have a realistic chance of demonstrating improvement.

Before investing considerable time and money, they suggest that a pilot program be initiated to test the validity of the assumed improvements and their impact on the root causes. Once the pilot test is complete, it's important to examine the results, or conduct a thorough analysis of the effort to determine its applicability as a whole. By setting up the transfer, Forum means those improvement steps that have been pilot tested can now be transferred to the broader context in dealing with improving/resolving the current issue. Quality service demands continuous improvement, therefore, it's important to continuously evaluate the new program, making refinements as necessary.

THE BALDRIGE PROCESS

In 1987 the U.S. Department of Commerce began recognizing American companies committed to customer satisfaction. Limiting award eligibility only to for-profit organizations, the winning companies are honored with The Malcolm Baldrige Award, named for former Commerce Secretary Malcolm Baldrige. Covering three broad categories: manufacturing, service, and small businesses, the award is given yearly to a handful of companies by the National Institute of Standards and Technology (an arm of the Commerce Department) under the direction of a board of examiners. In 1992 this board consisted of 250 quality experts, including 9 judges, 50 senior examiners and 191 examiners.

Use of the Baldrige Process is not limited to just those seeking the award. As a TQM process, business units and companies are encouraged to subscribe to its methodology to provide higher quality service. Because of its rigorous standards and past success, it deserves a special discussion here. If properly applied, the Baldrige Process tests your program's ability to maximize overall productivity and effectiveness while continually improving customer value.

Applying the Baldrige TQM Process

Richard M. Hodgetts, a professor of strategic management at Florida International University notes that the Baldrige Process centers on ten core values:(21)

1. *Customer Driven Quality*—Identifiable strategies that contribute to customer satisfaction.

    The first strategy for a security program should be to define a mission. For a company with international operations it might be to provide assistance to XYZ's global business unit network by developing and delivering asset protection programs designed to promote a safe environment for their clients, assets, and business operations through customer-driven quality services and state-of-the-art technological support. Building on this mission statement, the security department can now articulate any number of identifiable strategies, including:

    - A customer service feedback survey administered semi-annually,
    - A security council consisting of selected business-unit heads and employees from the general workforce that helps develop relevant customer-driven services,
    - Specific contract language for suppliers requiring customer satisfaction performance criteria, and
    - A series of one-on-one meetings with corporate executives to measure their satisfaction with the overall security program.

2. *Leadership*—An active commitment from management (e.g., the security director) to create programs and introduce systems designed to achieve excellence.

    This second core value recognizes that success is a top-down driven process. Subordinate staff cannot assume sole responsibility for quality improvement. Achieving customer satisfaction requires commitment from the top. This commitment is best displayed by the director setting forth specific quality improvement programs such as:

    - Quarterly performance reviews with merit increases based on measurable criteria,
    - Redefining job descriptions to reflect an emphasis on providing customer service, and

- Publishing the results of specific programs to senior management, end-users, and staff in quality-oriented terms. (Note: to do so requires that programs be initially designed with quality-oriented criteria.)

3. *Continuous Improvement*—A demonstrated commitment to ongoing improvement by taking steps to improve productivity and provide enhanced value through service offerings.

This may require a continuous review of current staffing patterns. As opposed to establishing a fixed schedule, a more fluid pattern might be instituted using a flex-force or external suppliers. Other ongoing improvement steps might include:

- A review of maintenance records on equipment and establishment of criteria for replacement based on preset thresholds,
- Establishing an automated case management system to track investigative workload and clearance rates, and
- A required postevent analysis on all major incidents to determine causes and offer realistic changes.

4. *Full Participation*—The process must incorporate a system of incentives and recognition that encourage all employees to participate.

The security director may need to establish specific incentives for the staff, including third party contracted officers. This latter group can be appropriately addressed via the contract. Opportunities would include:

- Training programs, career development programs, and opportunities to attend professional meetings,
- Awards that are meaningful to the staff (more than a certificate or uniform ribbon). Theater tickets, for example, or dinner for two at a nice restaurant—including babysitting money—or a weekend getaway, etc. (we'll have more to say about this later), and

- Opportunities to make presentations before senior managers.

5. *Rapid Response*—Institution of strategies that illustrate a faster response to requests for service.

   Recalling our discussion of the asset protection looping model, this might include:

   - Establishing response time criteria such as 85 percent of the time, security will respond to an emergency within five minutes,
   - Setting criteria for console operators on the maximum number of telephone rings before answering—this may vary from shift to shift or day to day,
   - Contractually obligating the alarm company to provide notice of an alarm within a set time frame or police dispatch, and
   - Establishing minimum times from receipt of an escort request to an employee's vehicle until the officer actually arrives to provide the escort.

6. *Design, Quality and Prevention*—There must be a clear demonstration that there is a program for building quality into the service and product offerings.

   For the staff this may involve:

   - Developing a standards manual for state-of-the art technologies,
   - Updating post orders,
   - Interfacing with facilities management on new designs,
   - Working with the auditing department on controls,
   - Becoming an integrated support function for due diligence activity on potential mergers and acquisitions, and
   - Working with human resources to develop a drug testing program for new hires and establishing background investigation criteria for new hires.

7. *Long-Range Outlook*—The department's strategies, plans, and resource allocations should reflect forward-thinking and a long-term commitment to customers.

This is one of the more challenging continuous quality improvement measures for the security manager. Due to the dynamic nature of security and the potential for changing customer bases, it is difficult to develop a strategic plan that extends more than three years. Yet, by making certain assumptions, a long-range outlook might involve:

- A plan for evaluating the merits of one type of workforce over another,
- A shift in level and type of services offered, such as a move from physical asset protection to intellectual property protection,
- A transference of physical property protection duties to facilities management, and
- Integration of other departments into security, such as safety and risk management, to achieve greater synergies at lower costs.

8. *Management by Fact*—Security must use facts to illustrate its progress toward quality goals.

It would be incumbent on the security manager to direct the analyst, investigator, and head of the guard force to submit regularly scheduled progress reports. These reports should identify the project name, it's purpose, defined objectives, a detailed time and action plan, the individual(s) responsible for each action and the progress to date. The report should also illustrate definitive results, for example:

Status Report for March 15

Project Name: Office Escort Program
Project Purpose: Increase customer satisfaction by providing an escort for all guests from the main lobby to the office of the individual being visited.

Project Objectives:

a. Develop Office Escort Program by January 15 for all Managers and professionals staying after close of business, e.g., after 5:00PM Monday through Friday and all day on weekends.
b. Communicate program and its purpose and value by January 31 to all managers and professionals by conducting one-on-one meetings, creating and distributing brochures, publicizing the program in company newsletter, and notifying personal contacts at the lobby post as they leave.
c. Establish staffing schedule by February 10, identify appropriate personnel for escort responsibilities and train them accordingly.
d. Institute program by March 11 and begin bimonthly customer feedback program to measure effectiveness and make necessary adjustments.

Time and Action Plan: Objectives 1 through 4: (Delineate the necessary steps to accomplish this objective, identifying completion dates and naming person(s) accountable.)
Results to date:

- The program was instituted on February 20, eight days ahead of schedule.
- Five officers received training and were assigned according to the established schedule.
- Estimated costs for the program remain on target for the year.
- First bimonthly feedback survey completed. End-user satisfaction rated 4.35 on a 5.0 scale. External customer satisfaction rated 4.75 on a 5.0 scale.

Two noteworthy comments made by end-user:

- Officers should wait with guest until received by manager/professional. From a security perspective, this makes sense. This will, however, prolong response time and could therefore lower our overall effectiveness. Suggestion requires further review.
- Officers should not ask guest the nature of the visit. Some managers/guests may feel that this is an invasion of privacy or an indication that "big brother" is watching. Comments very good, adjustment made immediately.

This example tracks the project from the beginning through its implementation and into the ongoing operation. Each status report can be written as an addendum to the first, thereby creating a complete history and assuring that earlier comments and suggestions are addressed.

9. *Partnership Development*—The security manager needs to develop and maintain partnerships with external and internal sources.

The word partnership here means those with an ability to assist and does not mean to connote any legal relationship. As we shall see in Chapter Seven, security managers may elect to develop such a legal tie through strategic alliances or joint ventures. These external relationships may involve for-profit third parties such as security companies. They may also involve alliances with police departments, public agencies, other security departments, professional associations, and educational institutions. Internal partnerships would involve any business unit that could either support or benefit from a direct relationship with the security unit.

10. *Public Responsibility*—The security manager has a responsibility to know that security personnel are trained and ready to respond to an emergency that might affect the community at large.

The security department might offer crime prevention and safety awareness programs. Some departments provide free fingerprinting for the children of local residents as part of child abduction deterrence efforts. Others have developed mutual-aid pacts with local fire departments and police agencies for emergency response while others sponsor law enforcement appreciation dinners.

The Baldrige Categories

As noted, even if your company isn't pursuing the Baldrige Award, you can still implement the Baldrige Process. Security departments at these companies have successfully implemented the TQM process:

- Solectron Corporation
- Federal Express
- AMP Incorporated
- John Hancock
- AT&T
- Motorola
- Kodak
- Mobil Oil

Mark Graham Brown, author of *Baldrige Award-Winning Quality*, (22) notes that the process focuses on seven major categories:

1. Senior Executive Leadership

The leadership category entails a demonstration of senior executives' personal involvement in creating and sustaining customer focus with clear and visible quality values. How are quality values integrated into the company's management system and reflected in a way that demonstrates public responsibility?

To achieve success and hold the support of executive managers, the security department will need to make a definitive demonstration of leadership. Since 1984, Mobil Oil's corporate security department has hosted an annual training conference for their security managers. Each year, executive level managers, including the president and CEO, address the group. They outline their expectations and provide reactions to implemented programs. This is commitment.

At AMP Incorporated quarterly status reports are sent from security to the director of general services. The reports are then forwarded to the vice president for general services and technical operations for review and comment. Unedited, these same reports are then submitted directly to the chairman of the board of directors. As Paul Workinger, Vice President for General Services and Technical Operations notes, "We may be a big company, but through these reports I get to know who my business unit managers are and they get to know me. It's a great vehicle for getting things done in a way that assures we are focused on quality customer satisfaction." Another demonstration of executive commitment.

2. Information and Analysis

This category covers scope, validity, analysis, management, and use of data and information to drive quality excellence and improve competitive performance. Examined here is the adequacy of the data, information, and analysis system to support improvement of the department's customer focus, services, products (if applicable) and internal operations.

This category can give security managers fits if they are detailed or statistically oriented. The process is critical, however, because it measures progress or the lack of it. Development of criteria and a means of measuring it is required. For me, it is one of the key indicators that separates a business manager from a security professional. Data and information analysis requires rational business-oriented decision-making.

The security manager cannot build a program based on the "great what if." Many do and are not even aware of it. They will submit budgets and program requests based on the belief that a certain level of resource allocation is required to assure that the company is ready for an unexpected event, an approach likened to the "Chicken Little syndrome." They exclaim that without certain funding or commitment, the sky might fall. Lacking any substantive analysis and business reasoning, they "feel" it is necessary and cite another catastrophic event that occurred elsewhere as proof.

Quality depends on quantitative measures—it is not a pure art. Quality is the end-product of analyses and deliberations. To assure that focus is maintained requires definition, collection and analysis of customer-related data, and formulation into action plans and programs. Prompt solutions must be found to customer-related problems; relationships determined between the security department's services and products; and quality performance and key customer indicators shown, such as satisfaction, continued requests for service, and retention of advocates and supporters.

Essential financial and market data are also required. Cost-benefit analyses need to be completed and comparisons made with others who engage "best-in-class" practices to meet customer satisfaction requirements. Cycle times need review to assure that they are as short as possible. These activities will guarantee that the asset protection program remains directed and that activities and processes are designed to enhance overall corporate profitability.

3. Strategic Quality Planning

This category involves the planning process and how key quality factors are integrated into the company's total business plan. The department's short- and longer-term programs need to reflect how quality and performance requirements are deployed to each unit within Security.

Protection managers need to develop strategic plans for the near and intermediate terms. I recommend that plans be limited to no more than three years. Anything beyond that remains academic. Variables change rapidly in today's overall dynamic environment—senior executives change, mergers occur, economic recessions and a host of other noncontrollable factors enter in, making it nearly impossible to plan effectively. Although a three-year window is considerably less than what other business cultures subscribe (the Japanese typically make 10-year plans), it is a significantly more long-range view than the 90- to 120-day window most American businesses use.

Conversely, short-term planning generally encompasses 12 to 18 months. Whatever the company size, moving a program from the conceptual stage to full implementation often requires months. This is largely because organizations operate in quarterly cycles. Budgets, performance measures, compensation reviews, and go/no-go decisions are generally made quarterly. Advocates for the Baldrige Process and other TQM programs criticize this type of thinking. Today's reality, however, is that American business is driven by the fiscal quarter. Unless the entire company commits to changing this approach, the security director will be further ahead adapting to the general norm.

Variables to consider when engaging in quality-oriented strategic planning include a summary of key requirements and indicators deployed to work units and suppliers, resources committed for capital improvements, equipment, training, and staff allocations, and implementation of new or revised operating practices. Longer-term quality-oriented goals and objectives need to be addressed, along with projections on how these programs will compare with other similar departments.

4. Human Resource Development and Management

This category reflects how asset protection departments develop and realize the full potential of their proprietary or contract workforce. Programs must assure an ongoing commitment to personal, professional, and organizational growth.

For most security directors, sending a subordinate to a conference is difficult—particularly true in an environment that emphasizes the lean and mean approach. Senior executives are quick to limit or eliminate altogether professional seminars, education reimbursements, and annual conferences. To them, many of these meetings are boondoggles or perks. Admittedly, there is some truth here, especially annual conferences supported by large professional associations.

Conversely, large associations do offer specialized workshops that are valuable, particularly for subordinates. These workshops are specifically tailored to topics that can enhance their technical skills. They also orient them to new technologies, methodologies, and/or review current issues relevant to them. The net effect is a more informed staff wanting to do their job in more efficient ways. Security managers intent on providing quality service need to stress the importance of these experiences to senior executives and fight hard to retain them.

Human resources development includes creating incentive programs and promotional opportunities. The former may entail traditional recognition programs such as certificates and letters of achievement, but there are several nontraditional ways of encouraging quality service.

Situational Case #15: The Bank Guard

A bank guard observed an elderly man enter the main lobby of a large retail bank. The gentleman appeared to be unsure of himself and sat down in a nearby chair. Concerned about the man's health, the guard moved closer to watch him more carefully. After a while the guard approached the man and offered assistance. The gentleman looked up when he heard the guard addressing him and said that he was physically OK but needed some financial help.

The guard directed the man to a nearby teller but the gentleman rejected the offer and said he wasn't certain if he should deposit his money in this bank. He went on to say that he knew that the bank had recently had financial problems and he wasn't sure his money would be safe. He also told the guard that he had just come from his own bank and was upset with the way they had treated him.

The guard sat down and explained how she had all her money in the bank and how comfortable she felt with how things were going now. She assured him that as both an employee and longstanding customer, she would encourage the gentleman to deposit his money with her bank. She suggested that she introduce him to a new accounts manager. Impressed by the guard's treatment, he agreed. After he left, the guard noticed that the account manager went to his supervisor and began what was a rather intense conversation. Several minutes later the banking managers approached the guard and asked her to meet with them. She went with them to the bank president's office.

They told her that because of her care and concern, the elderly gentleman deposited a settlement check from his attorney for more than $600,000. Moreover, he authorized them to transfer his assets from the competing bank—total value: $3.5 million. Obviously the guard had no idea of the account's total value. She smiled and said that she was glad she could help and left. Stunned, the managers, felt that her effort could not go unrecognized. Knowing she had a brother several thousand miles away that she wanted to visit, they arranged for her to take time off to visit him at the bank's expense.

This gave the security director an idea. He developed an incentive plan for his staff depending on the level of quality service they performed. The incentives varied from dinners and theater tickets to gift certificates at local stores. Customer satisfaction surveys showed a dramatic increase within a year.

Employee development involves their participation as well. A quality program emerges when the employee is given the opportunity to contribute, otherwise popularly known as *empowerment*. It requires management to let go of some of its authority and let employees make critical decisions. Through delegation, staff members make decisions and take action to satisfy customers' concern. The Ritz Carlton Hotel corporation allows employees, including housekeeping personnel, to make decisions costing up to $2,000 to resolve customer problems.

With this responsibility, employees must demonstrate their willingness to provide quality service. It is therefore incumbent on management to develop practices and specific mechanisms to promote and monitor employee contributions, individually and in groups. Today's employee wants to be treated with dignity, respect, and fairness. They understand that the company can't assure them of lifelong job security. By being treated honorably, more often than not, they will treat others—notably their customers— with the same degree of respect.

5. Management of Process Quality

The management of process quality category refers to systematic processes the security department uses to pursue ever-higher quality performance. This entails key elements of process management, improvement, and assessment.

In the next chapter we will discuss several axioms for success. I relate one in particular: "Don't tell me what I know, show me what I don't." Implied here is the notion that to sustain quality requires a concerted effort to continually push for newer and higher levels. To do this requires a break from the arena of familiarity and a willingness to venture into new territories. In doing so, quality improvement can be assured. Although some programs tried may fail, others will have far more success than anticipated, thereby pushing quality to an even higher level.

The notion of process quality is especially adaptable to the security design work associated with new technologies and facility improvements. Working in the early stages with facilities management or real estate development departments, security requirements can be coordinated and integrated into all phases of the design, construction, and final review process. The same can be said for the process related to new products or services. With the introduction of ISO 9000 standards for international production requirements and TQM strategies such as the Baldrige approach, process quality is an accepted practice that needs to be integrated into the normal course of business.

Continuous improvement begins with the identification of the basis underlying any practice or service offering. The asset protection manager must challenge basic assumptions and test their relevancy in today's organization. Process quality also involves establishing a mechanism for dealing with out-of-control occurrences and corrective actions to minimize their recurrence. For example, a fire broke out in the warehouse of a large corporation. The firm's records were nearly lost when the suppression system flooded the top floors and the excess weight caused the floors to cave in. Since fire safety was the responsibility of corporate security, they were hard-pressed to explain why bearing load ratios were not addressed when the sprinkler system was installed. The cause was traced to engineering oversight. Regardless of the blame, a plan to correct the situation was required. Process quality demands that when unpleasant situations arise, they are dealt with just as expediently as when positive situations occur.

Process quality management extends to suppliers. With more and more outsourcing occurring, this is critical. Performance criteria need to be spelled out in detail and quality checks installed. The security manager needs to develop a mechanism to continuously monitor suppliers to assure quality measures are followed. This includes strategies and actions to improve supplier delivery time for security devices, responsiveness for service providers, and ongoing development programs. As Brown notes, these might include partnerships, training, incentives, recognition, and supplier selection.

6. Quality and Operational Results

This category focuses on quality levels and improvement trends in operational performance, including those of suppliers. As part of this, performance levels should be compared with similar security departments. The security decision-maker needs to develop specific programs aimed at identifying trends as early as possible and test them for their relevancy within the company. Such trend analysis needs to be made against a backdrop of the factors that predict customer satisfaction and quality in customer use. Being a beta site (first of its kind, or testing ground) for a new product may not be in the security department's best interests. In highly entrepreneurial environments, being a leading-edge user may work well because it is expected, and therefore, there is a higher tolerance level. The converse can be true as well. In a more conservative setting, being just behind the edge, but part of the power curve, is likely to be far more successful. Simply stated, it is a matter of the security director intimately knowing the organizational climate and tolerance for new approaches.

7. Customer Focus and Satisfaction

The customer focus and satisfaction category incorporates the security department's relationships with its entire customer base —internal and external—and its knowledge of customer requirements. It also involves the methods to determine customer satisfaction, current trends, and levels of satisfaction.

The Baldrige Award judges emphasize this last category. Of the total 1,000 points used in the 1992 examination, 300 were allocated to customer satisfaction. After all, it is the heart of any quality-driven process. Each program within the security department should carry a clearly and easily identifiable tone of customer service. Each project should underscore a strategy aimed at fulfilling basic customer needs, capturing opportunities to enhance relationships, and a means to communicate customers' proper expectations regarding security's services and products.

This category also forces the asset protection manager and subordinate staff to identify and develop standards that define reliability, continuity, responsiveness, and effectiveness in meeting customer requirements and requests. As part of this process, there should be a description of how these standards are deployed to other corporate support units and how overall performance is monitored and improved as the need arises. This means that surveys, questionnaires, reports, and other data must be readily available and routinely used by security personnel and others.

Control Processing
as a Management Tool

Winners of the award typically determine implementation and control steps at the time they develop their total quality plan. The controls are pegged to key results that can be charted and measured. Each company has its own vernacular and way of tracking. For example, AMP Incorporated uses Highly Leveraged Achievements (HLA); Westinghouse's Commercial Nuclear Fuel Division, a 1988 Baldrige winner, uses Plus Points; Federal Express has Service Quality Indicators (SQI); and AT&T has modified Deming's Plan-Do-Check-Act (PDCA) model for their control purposes, calling theirs Plan-Do-Measure-Improve (PDMI). Each has their own unique characteristics but share a common link by using a specific methodology to maintain focus on providing quality service.

A critical management tool for providing customer-oriented service is the use of charts, graphs, and other statistically based measures. Their use displays an ongoing commitment to the quality goal by evaluating performance, identifying both successes and problems. A variety of process measures are available, including flow charts, matrices, bar graphs (from simple ones to more sophisticated ones like Pareto charts), and diagrams. Hodgetts provides a brief review of these and several others such as scatter diagrams, frequency histograms, and control charts.

One of my favorites is the *fishbone diagram*—a cause-and-effect decision-making tool that forces the manager or analyst to take a particular issue and break it down into specific components. From here an examination can be made concerning what factors are affecting other factors and why. If the asset protection manager is concerned about an unacceptable response time to emergencies, for example, the following abbreviated fishbone diagram can offer some interesting insights. It shows that response time is directly related to four primary factors: equipment and the general employee population as well as the security officers and associated training.

Within each of these four primary factors there are several subfactors, all of which when combined, provide a vector-type analysis to

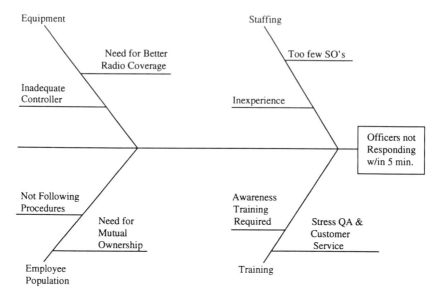

Figure 5.2: Fishbone Diagram for Response Time Analysis
(Abbreviated for Illustration Purpose Only)

pinpoint why the desired response is not being met. By isolating each factor, specific programs and strategies can be developed.

Cycle Time

A term popular in today's corporate parlance is *cycle time*. Drawn from the manufacturing sector, the phrase has come to mean the time from the inception of an idea or process through to its completion. Cycle time is now used in both the production and service sectors of American business. Operating and support units within companies are commonly asking questions regarding cycle time issues. The hypotheses associated with cycle times are based on the premise that if cycle time is reduced, higher quality goods and services will result. Another perceived value is that shorter cycle times allow companies to respond more quickly to their customers' needs and desires. Today, it is commonly accepted that the company that is first to the marketplace will gain a significant foothold ahead of the competition.

These basic business principles have a direct application for security administration. Reduced cycle time, if properly managed, should yield a process of identifying those factors that limit quality service and therefore need to be corrected. This analysis often leads to an opportunity to redefine or re-engineer the security delivery process. This re-engineering, as we shall discuss below, should lead to lower operating costs from fewer steps and more direct action by individuals across the entire organizational continuum. If successfully followed, cycle time improvement should mean less need for future cycle time analysis, thus shortening the cycle even more.

BENCHMARKING

Today one of the fastest growing management activities is benchmarking. In some circles this is known as comparative analysis. Regardless of its name, the concept is not new. Companies have been comparing themselves against their competition for decades. What is new, however, is the formality and openness in which it is conducted. Benchmarking usually dictates one company identifying others whom they believe deserve emulation. These latter companies are known for their "best-in-class" practices, meaning that they are recognized as conducting their business in the best possible way.

Best-in-class practices usually result in providing a higher level of customer service. Those who follow them therefore have significantly higher customer satisfaction ratings. Defining what constitutes best-in-class is not easy; there are no standards upon which to judge such practices within the corporate security sphere. Lacking established codes and widely accepted norms, the security administrator needs to rely on a variety of indicators or resources.

The following two case studies show how best-in-class practitioners can be identified and emulated.

Case Study #1

One strategy is to identify best-in-class practitioners by looking for a composite blend from a variety of sources. In one recent benchmarking assignment, for example, a matrix was developed to identify those recognized as best-in-class by pinpointing specific interest areas and then seeking input from industry-accepted resources: universities, professional journal and newsletter editors, independent consultants, professional associations, other widely respected security directors, and forensic litigators. Each of these resources was asked to identify three security departments they believed engaged in world-class practices for each area specified below:

- international security
- executive protection
- protective services, and
- investigations.

If one or more companies were consistently named by resources for that particular category, the assumption was made that these companies were at least above average in performance. The procedure above was followed by a security department participating in their company's pursuit of the Malcolm Baldrige Award. The methodology was reviewed by the examiners and given high marks, so much so, that several other operating units adopted the same procedure.

Once top companies were identified, each was contacted and told that they had been identified as a department broadly recognized as following best-in-class practices. They were then prescreened and asked for their cooperation in the benchmarking exercise. Those who agreed were sent a copy of the questionnaire below and asked to answer the questions in a subsequent telephone interview.

BENCHMARKING QUESTIONNAIRE

COMPANY NAME: _____

INTERVIEWEE'S NAME: _____

INTERVIEWEE'S TITLE: _____

1. Describe your organizational structure and reporting relationship (i.e., facilities-oriented, operations-oriented, advisory-oriented.)

   Structure: _____

   Reporting Relationship: _____

2. Assign the percent of your resources dedicated to:

   Physical assets: _____

   Investigations: _____

   Intellectual property: _____

   Data security: _____

   Other: _____

   Please list by function: _____

   _____

   _____

3. Identify the total number of proprietary staff by:

   Managers: _____

   Supervisors: _____

   Professionals: _____

   Specialists: _____

   Clerical: _____

   Contract: _____

4. What is the size of your 1993 operational budget?

5. What is the size of your 1993 capital budget?
   What is (are) the major funding project for 1993?

   _____

   _____

6. What are the critical factors, major programs and/or attributes about your organization that contributed to your company receiving the Malcolm Baldrige Award?

7. What aspects of your program would you say make you world-class?

8. Do you have an established international security program that reports directly to you? If so, briefly describe its extent, focus, etc. If not, does this fall to some other business unit's responsibility? (Delineate on Addendum, Question #1)

9. Do you have a special unit that is responsible for establishing security standards and/or design of systems and devices?

   Standards: Yes___ No___ Sys/Dev Design: Yes___ No___

10. How would you describe your organization's reputation within the company? If highly positive, what accounts for this? (Delineate on Addendum, Question #2)

11. What new programs are you currently working on which will demonstrate your value added to the company?

12. Briefly describe your executive protection program. (Delineate on Addendum, Question #3)

13. What are your largest challenges?

14. Anything else that you can add that differentiates your organization from your counterparts? Or, another security department we should look at? (Delineate on Addendum, Question #4)

ADDENDUM:

1 International security program (Question 8):

   _____
   _____

2. Internal acceptance program (Question 10):

   _____
   _____

3. Executive protection program (Question 12):

   _____
   _____

4. Other comments or security organizations (Question 14):

   _____
   _____

Once the second telephone interviews were completed, the security manager then listed those companies that warranted a site visit. After obtaining their agreement to host a half-day visit, each company was reviewed in-depth by the security manager or a department staff member. During these visits more detailed information was gathered by on-site observation, documentation reviews, and selected interviews.

After the site visits were completed, the data gathered was detailed and the most salient points identified. This exercise provided a wealth of information gathered from a variety of sources. By the time the benchmarking exercise was completed, the security director had a comprehensive understanding of how others approach similar responsibilities, and knew the pitfalls to avoid and the more successful strategies to implement.

Case Study #2:

A Midwest-based property management company wanted to outsource their security operations for 13 properties in their portfolio. Since they limited their contracts to a specific geographic radius, they were comfortable approaching other facility management companies outside their marketplace for benchmarking purposes. To identify companies subscribing to best-in-class practices, they also approached several professional associations and solicited their input. Among those contacted were the Building Owners and Management Association (BOMA) and the Industrial Development Research Council (IDRC). They also sent representatives to national conferences on security and facilities management. The aim was to gather participants' opinions on those firms known for their world-class approach to property protection. They took an additional step—the corporate legal office searched for premises liability cases wherein the facility management company was a named party. Those most frequently found were rejected. Because of these independent efforts, they identified 10 companies outside their market to benchmark.

As with the first case study, they contacted each firm to solicit their cooperation. Six companies were willing to participate, provided they had access to the information when completed. An agreement was reached and the following questionnaire was sent to them:

Questions Specifically for Outsourcing

1. What were the factors that lead you to outsourcing this function; e.g., economic, risk transference, expertise, lack of internal resourcing, etc.?
2. Specifically, what security functions are outsourced?
3. Do you use a single supplier or several?
4. Who do you use?
5. What criteria did you use to select your supplier?
6. Who else did you consider?
7. Who in your organization oversees the contract?
8. Please explain how the contract is administered; e.g., does a single source request all services? Do selected managers have direct access, etc.?
9. We're considering allowing each of our site managers to establish their own account relationship with the selected vendor. This means that the vendor could have as many as 13 or more reporting relationships. Is this feasible?
10. What have you experienced as some of the more significant advantages to outsourcing this function?
11. Conversely, what are some of the more significant traps, obstacles, disadvantages?
12. Is your vendor using union labor? If so, what are the contractual safeguards regarding right to strike? If not, has this presented problems in the past?
13. Does your vendor supply all materials and equipment? If not, typically what do you provide; e.g., radio communications, office space and supplies, vehicles, etc.?
14. How do you manage on-hand inventory?
15. What provisions have you instituted to measure your vendor's capability to respond to and appropriately handle emergencies/disasters?
16. Does your vendor routinely participate in your staff meetings, planning sessions, etc.?

Of the companies receiving the questionnaire, all but one completed and returned it by the requested due date. Once all the data was collected, a report was generated and an edited copy was sent to each participant. Follow-up telephone conversations were conducted with three of the firms and they agreed to a day-long site visit by a representative of the facility management company. During these visits a review of the security company was made and a series of discussions was held with different managers of the host company. Here the facility management company learned how the security firm was selected and the lessons learned to date by the host.

These two case studies demonstrate that benchmarking can be applied in different ways. The common thread is the identification of those who engage in highly regarded practices and the use of their experience to help you decide what is most appropriate for your application. Benchmarking, like any other management tool, has its limitations. Timothy Ogilvie, an experienced consultant specializing in benchmarking for Price Waterhouse, warns that comparative analyses can be shocking. Those who use the process may find a significant gap between how they do things and how those identified as best-in-class approach the same issue. This discovery can be emotionally upsetting if the benchmarking results are not put into a proper context. He observes: "The problem with simplistic portrayals of benchmark gaps, however, is that they do not provide an adequate basis for deciding among alternatives."(23)

Without a reference point to distinguish between you and the world-class performer, Ogilvie notes, you can get "lost in space." Using this graphic metaphor, he suggests that the way through the confusion is to engage in "decision science." The decision-maker, he says, in this case the asset protection manager, needs to ask six basic questions that can serve as a guide through the space:

1. Is This a Space That You Should Care About?

It's commonly understood that no two organizations are alike. Even between the most competitive companies, there are differences. As a result, these disparities need to be reflected in the comparative analysis. This is even more important if the benchmarking is with a company outside your industry sector. After all, it is likely that a more apropos comparison in security programs needs to be drawn from a variety of sectors. Given the nature of internal investigations, for example, a best-in-class program may be found in the financial services arena. If you are in manufacturing, you may find it necessary to cross over to the banking environment to make your comparisons. With this likelihood, it becomes critical not to draw any false conclusions regarding one's own organization compared to the benchmark.

2. Are These Points in the Same Plane?

This question is a derivative of the first. Ogilvie cautions that unless adjustments are made, leaving comparability issues open can lead, at best, to credibility problems when setting performance goals based on the benchmark. At worst, it can result in erroneous decisions.

3. What Are the Time Dimensions in this Space?

Benchmarking must be understood within the context of a defined window. Comparisons drawn from performance data that is relatively new will not be as valuable as data gathered over a longer stretch; Ogilvie suggests a three-period trend. Just as crime comparisons require a period of time dating back from an event to establish a pattern, the same can be said for program performance. Here's a general rule: The newer the program, the more likely its validity will be challenged.

4. What Are the Boundaries of this Space?

This refers to the limit of theoretical performance. If the measure is response time, in an ideal world the limit may be an ability to respond 100 percent of the time within a preestablished period. Similarly, if the measure is number of cases closed versus number of cases opened, or value of recoveries to number of cases opened, the ratio might be one to one or a value recovered over an established threshold for every case assigned.

Such measures need to be adjusted to reflect realistic targets. Ogilvie calls this the historical evolution of the process and suggests that it is the most crucial boundary. If the process is fairly developed, the improvement level may be reaching its optimal state. Conversely, if the process is fairly new, there may be a great deal of room for improvement left.

5. What Is the Customer Dimension?

Benchmarking needs to identify how customers react. While an improvement level may be appreciated by the security staff, it may fall short of appreciation by the customer. During peak arrival times, the decision may be made to staff the front lobby console with two officers to expedite inquiries and requests. While this may increase efficiency, it may be viewed as overstaffing. Especially if the company is downsizing.

6. How Do Movements Along One Dimension Affect Related Measurements?

Benchmarking efforts need to identify the vectors that exert influence on an issue, a responsibility, or a service. These vectors may come from within or outside the organization. Nevertheless, a vector is any force—person, place or thing—that influences an outcome. They need to be identified to ensure that a like comparison can be made.

These six simple questions make the difference in defining what constitutes a meaningful exercise. They also differentiate between those with experience and those who talk a good game, but fumble about knowing what they are doing. Two organizations that can help you are the International Benchmarking Clearinghouse, a service of the American Productivity & Quality Center, Houston, Texas, and the American Society for Quality Control (ASQC). Both were principal drivers in the development of the Baldrige award and have established protocols and codes of conduct. They can assist you by working with prospective benchmarkers to properly prepare for on-site visits, release of information, questionnaire formulation, and defining confidential property limits.

RE-ENGINEERING

Another TQM concept introduced in the late 1970s was *re-engineering*. Two noted management consultants, James Champy of CSC Index, and Michael Hammer of Hammer & Company, have collaborated on and published *Re-engineering The Corporation: A Manifesto For Business Revolution*. (24) In their book they hail re-engineering as a new beginning and a reversal of the industrial revolution. For them and other advocates of re-engineering, the challenge is to start over and redefine the way in which a manager goes about conducting business. As they note, "Re-engineering isn't another idea imported from Japan. It isn't another quick fix that American managers can apply to their organizations. Business re-engineering isn't about fixing anything." (25)

Continuing, they emphasize, "It means forgetting how work was done in the age of the mass market and deciding how it can best be done now. Old job titles and old organizational arrangements—departments, divisions, groups, and so on—cease to matter. What matters is how we want to organize work, given the demands of today's markets and the power of today's technologies." (26) For Champy and Hammer, re-engineering is the fundamental rethinking and radical redesign of business processes to achieve dramatic improvements in critical contemporary performance measures such as quality, cost, service, and speed. In short, their definition focuses on the words *fundamental, radical, dramatic,* and *processes.*

By fundamental, they mean to challenge managers and decision-makers who ask the most basic questions about their operation. Why do people do what they do? And why do they do it the way they do?

Radical for them means identifying root causes and addressing them head on. Since re-engineering is about the business of reinventing, dealing with ways to improve, enhance, or modify the current method of operation are unacceptable strategies. This is an easy organizational trap to fall into—most people find it easier to simply modify what they know best (improve, enhance, or modify). It is a difficult challenge to accept the responsibility of delivering the same type of service in an entirely different way. Lacking proper guidance, it is easy to get mired down quickly.

By dramatic, the authors mean making changes that require quantum leaps in performance; making marginal or incremental improvements misses the mark and is not true reinvention. As they note, re-engineering should only be brought in when the need exists for heavy blasting. One quick example may help to illustrate the point. As we shall see in our Chapter Seven, sometimes it's necessary to replace an entire staff with another work force. In a traditional environment, particularly a unionized one, such a change would be viewed as a dramatic way to go about securing the assets of a corporation.

Finally, the word *process* is meant to be a collection of activities that takes on one or more kinds of input, and creates an outcome that is of value to the customer. Champy and Hammer note that this is the most difficult aspect of re-engineering confronted by corporate managers. Processing is the collection of activities that result in the organization's ability to deliver services or products to the customers. As the authors observe, "The individual tasks within this process are important, but none of them matter one wit to the customer if the overall process doesn't work, that is, if the process doesn't deliver the goods." (27) This means that as an asset protection manager, your processing (e.g., collecting the necessary data associated with your operations, investigations, and training) needs to be sharply defined, tuned to a specific focus (customer/end-user), managed smartly, and continually monitored.

Re-engineering, though intended to reduce long-term operating and capital expense, may cost you up-front in terms of both money and people. As Tom Davenport, author of *Process Innovation: Re-engineering Work Through Information Technology*, points out, "Thinking out of the box means spending out of the box. There are times when that's necessary, but to say it's typical is just not realistic." (28) By this he means that achieving re-engineering may mean dismantling what is in place, and spending extra to rebuild a new structure.

An example is the security program at Kodak. They elected to retain their proprietary operation but wanted to lower expenses. To do so required an initial cost increase of both energy and money. The energy cost increase came from eliminating a number of security officers (fewer people covering more territory and handling more activities). The money cost increase came with the purchase and installation of systems and devices. On whole, however, the net effect has been a significant reduction in total operating expense, and therefore a contribution to the company's general bottom-line performance.

Bob Tomasco cautions managers not to get too carried away with concepts and ethereal thinking. In an interview with George Harrar of *Enterprise Magazine* in January 1994, Tomasco notes, "The fallacy shows up in some of the re-engineering hype about starting from a blank sheet of paper. I think that that's a great concept—go up to the mountain, have a retreat, and plan; the reality is, we pay people who run companies to play with the cards they're dealt. You have to start with where you are, not where you want to be. The really creative executives are the ones who can use re-engineering to build on what they have, to move the company along, and not get caught in some fancy world thinking what it would be like to start all over again."(29)

As we saw in Chapter Two, asset management is a looping process, beginning with controls, passing through the administration and management of these controls, responding to events and properly managing them, concluding with recommendations for preventive strategies. This basic four-part structure needs to remain constant if security directors are going to be true to their ultimate mission of delivering quality customer service. Re-engineering suggests that there may be new ways of administering and managing as well as responding and handling, but the fundamental activities need to be held constant. In short, re-engineering is about process management, not about redefining asset control.

Situational Case #16: Re-engineering Security

To illustrate the methodology associated with business process re-engineering, let's take a brief look at a large Northeastern company. To begin with, they defined re-engineering as an integrated process to realign and change the operations of their business with a goal of achieving a significant increase in the value it delivers. Their reasons for re-engineering were to "energize the organization around the needs of its customers." For them re-engineering meant following a five-step process: goal-setting, defining, re-engineering, designing anew, and implementation.

By goal-setting they meant developing a new mission statement for corporate security. This meant first identifying where the organization was now and where it wanted to be tomorrow. To help do this they created a vision statement. They then identified those forces (some re-engineering specialists refer to them as *drivers* or *vectors*) that affected their mission: internal and external customers, the corporation's business plan, and the physical aspects of the complex. Next, the security director established a conceptual plan and sought commitment from executive management. Finally, the vision statement was distributed to all unit heads.

The second activity, defining, involved developing the actual workflows within each security unit. This meant breaking each component of their department into designated work flow patterns, beginning with protective services (guard operations and console monitoring), to investigations (internal and external threats to the organization). Data was collected and analyzed. The expertise and knowledge of selected security officers, investigators, and staff analysts were assessed. To assure a comprehensive review, opportunities were given for the staff to exchange ideas and perceptions as well as review and sign off on final work flow charts and diagrams.

The third step, re-engineering, involved identifying principles and best-in-class practices, in an effort to streamline the organization and its associated processes. Areas ripe for re-engineering were identified and feedback, interview, and documentation methodologies were defined.

The fourth stage of activity, known as the "design anew" segment, involved refinement of newly identified operating practices gathered from the internal interviews and benchmarking process. In this phase, it was important for security management to field test new work flows and their impact on the staff and customer service.

The final phase, implementation, was designed as an ongoing process for both management and operating staff. It meant putting the re-engineered process into effect, assessing its effectiveness, making adjustments, and enhancing as required. This chain of events repeats until either the particular process is abandoned or it reaches such a level that it requires radical redesign; which in essence means starting over.

The Shamrock Organization

This five-phase methodology shows how a particular company went about re-engineering many of their business units, including security. Others have taken a more radical approach. Following the precepts outlined by Charles Handy in *The Age of Unreason,* (30) there are those who have adopted his *Shamrock organization.* This construct sets aside traditional hierarchical organizational structures and recreates an organization as a three-leafed shamrock. The first leaf represents a small core of professionals, managers, and skilled technicians. Their skill sets have been identified as being absolutely critical to the organization. This small group is apt to interact in a more collegial manner in a traditional boss-subordinate relationship. The organization is flat and information flows freely between the participants. Considerably larger than the first, the second leaf consists of third-party suppliers who have been chosen for their expertise and ability to provide quality service. Such contractors may often employ former members of the organization. The third leaf consists of part-time and temporary workers who are employed as needed. Commonly known as a flexible work force, these are employees who require minimal support and draw a greater identity from their profession than from the company. This is not to say, however, that they lack loyalty and commitment to the company when on the payroll.

The Shamrock organizational structure reflects the direction that many of America's largest companies are currently pursuing. Workforce downsizing is virtually inevitable. Since labor costs represent a significant part of any department's operating budget, downsizing's appeal is obvious to those who want to pursue the lean-and-mean approach. We'll have a great deal more to say about downsizing and outsourcing to third party suppliers later. Outsourcing is not an excuse to abrogate business unit responsibilities, however. While the function may be operationally performed by temporary workers, management of that function still remains a primary responsibility of the department head.

As John Fay points out, there are security problems associated with the Shamrock organization, and therefore, it's incumbent on the security decision-maker to build into the department's mission a mechanism for monitoring controls and protecting assets when placed in the hands of non-company employees. Remembering that the asset protection manager's primary responsibility is to satisfy all customers, internal and external, the challenge escalates with the introduction of employees who are not directly under a unit supervisor's control. For Fay, organizations considering the Shamrock approach need to be concerned, among other things, about how sensitive information is shared and made available to outside parties. "Business information," he notes, "including the most sensitive process by an organization, is valuable to the extent that it's put to work. Although the corporate security manager's instinct is to keep sensitive information under lock and key, the reality is that sensitive information is widely scattered and in flux at any given time for the simple reason it is in use or in movement." (31)

Given the dynamic flow of such information and it's value for maintaining both competitive market position and profitability, the security manager by default is required to re-engineer the deliverability of his service. Guards, cameras, and access control devices may be totally inappropriate when information can be removed from the organization electronically or in other ways totally outside the bounds of physical protection methods. Fay also cautions that with respect to the second tier of the Shamrock organization, corporate security needs to be part of the process when sensitive materials are made available to contractors, especially when they work for competitors. As corporations experiment with the degree to which they can outsource, this becomes even more important.

Continental Illinois Bank, for example, has pushed the outsourcing envelope to limits well beyond what other companies of comparable size have done. Their operations center is run almost exclusively by third party suppliers. A property management company subcontracts security for the facility to an independent contractor, who in turn is charged with monitoring the movement of the facility's assets and people, who are employees of still another independent data processing company. In order for the data processing contractor to maintain its low cost, it subcontracts temporary workers to any number of flex force providers. In this example, you have contractors employing contractors to watch other contractors, who may be employing still another level of contractors. Assuring that each contracted level ardently prescribes to and follows quality hiring standards and related performance criteria, is *critical* to the success of the company's total profitability. This critical factor demands an integrated approach between selected business heads and the corporate security director.

With respect to the third part of the Shamrock work force, Fay notes, "There are few reasons to believe that part-timers and temporaries who replaced regular employees, are of the same caliber." He says that in this group one should anticipate a higher level of drug-related accidents and incidents, pilferage, vandalism, confrontational behavior, and occasional acts of violence. "The vendors of flexible labor are focused on providing orders, not on conducting pre-employment background checks. Without screening, the professional core will likely be working next to people with pasts checkered by crime."(32)

I take exception to Fay's observation. Often, people working for temporary agencies are drawn from sectors of society that have the lowest crime rates (homemakers, senior citizens, recent high school graduates) and therefore do not necessarily have checkered pasts. To categorize temporary and part-time employees as former criminals would require definitive empirical proof. Nonetheless, by implication, I believe that Fay would agree that despite an individual's background, the onus is still on the organization to require background investigations and hiring criteria comparable to those required for full-time workers. Moreover, the same high-quality performance expectations should be imposed on flex-force employers just as they are on the core corporate group and approved third-party suppliers.

Misguided Re-engineering Models

As asset protection managers intent on developing quality driven programs, it's easy to be misled by would-be theorists who have developed their own quality models. Such models are sometimes based on esoteric principles in a spirit of trying to better position security management as a viable entity within the company. While their intentions may be admirable, the end product can be dangerous and yield the opposite effect.

One example would be the Value-Added Model developed by Stephen Gale, Keith Duncan, Rudolph Yaksick, and John Tofflemire in December 1990, which included research supported by the American Society for Industrial Security Foundation. (33) The researchers attempt to present a management model for security directors' consideration, based largely on economic principles designed to assist government policy setters and executive managers of large corporations. Nevertheless, it is the foundation on which the writers attempt to build a profit-center oriented model for security administrators.

They miss the mark from the very outset by pegging their value-driven model to the basic principle of maximizing shareholder value. "The share price represents the capital market's assessment of the expected future earnings of a firm, given available information. Thus, the value of equity (shareholders' claims) is the risk adjusted, capitalized value of the firm's expected earnings stream. Thus, use of value maximization implies that security directors will seek to maximize the size of the firm's future earning stream and/or minimize its level of risk." (34)

Fundamentally, there is nothing wrong with this statement if it's properly understood to mean that any program that the asset protection manager develops must reflect an eye toward the organization's bottom-line performance. Developing programs that cost too much or fail to adequately protect critical assets clearly could affect profitability and therefore shareholder value. It must be stressed, however, that to affect shareholder equity, the loss would have to be incredibly high and in all likelihood involve an entire tier of management decision-making outside the control of most security directors.

Gale and his associates continue to obfuscate the issue by saying,

> "At this point it is appropriate to address two related questions. First, is the financial concept of share value maximization compatible with the economic concept of profit maximization? The answer here is yes, since value maximization is the multi-period, risk-adjusted analog of single period profit maximization. In other words, maximizing the capitalized value of future economic profits is tantamount to maximizing share value.
>
> The second question is: Is value maximization too narrow of a corporate objective since it concentrates on the interest of existing shareholders to the neglect of other (conflicting) interests (e.g., bond/debit holders and creditors)? Doherty (1985:20) argues to the contrary. He observes that the value maximization objective allows for the risk costs imposed on other corporate claimholders who have contracts with the firm.
>
> Furthermore, by impounding the risk cost of various claimholders in a single claim—the value of equity—the value maximizing objective provides a resolution of these conflicting claims."(35)

Perhaps such verbiage may be relevant for chief financial officers and business strategists, but it has little relevancy for the average security director of a large corporation. Such a foundation is so esoteric that it fails to establish credibility for the serious-minded security administrator. It is their conclusion that security in large, for-profit corporations, should be viewed as a specialized application of financial management. Asset protection administrators should focus on the sources and uses of funds for security investment decision-making if shareholder wealth is to be maximized. "Security management may thus be defined as those management activities associated with making and implementing security investment decisions undertaken by firms in anticipation of or following contingent losses, as well as the selection of related means of financing such investments."(36)

Unfortunately, even among the largest Fortune 100 security operating budgets, their total value contributes or detracts very little from the ultimate shareholder value of the corporation. Costs, of course, should still be controlled and programs still designed to enhance the corporation's ability to protect their assets. Attempting to tie asset protection to a financial management model as a means of redefining security as a profit center, however, misses the mark.

Revenue Generation

Despite these critical comments, Gale and his colleagues do offer us the opportunity to analyze the contribution (or possible distraction) of re-engineering corporate security programs in a way significantly different from past approaches. For them, security achieves its fullest potential when it contributes to the profitability of a corporation by generating revenues. I'm not convinced that this premise is necessarily valid. While it is true that there are opportunities for security directors to generate revenue from products and services, unless there is a mechanism in place to differentiate revenue-generating activity from basic asset protection, the security director would be wise to focus on controlling assets in a cost center environment.

Revenue generation, if properly managed, can enhance the total value of the security department. It can also compete with daily operations by dispersing fragmented resources and misaligned priorities, however. Security managers who are successful in generating revenue to offset their operating expenses typically are those who either (a) have standalone units whose sole purpose it is to offer for sale certain products and services; or (b) deliberately limit what is for sale so as not to distract the staff from meeting its primary mission of providing a safe and secure environment.

Generating revenues as an offset to operating expenses can be fun and rewarding if the proper controls and mechanisms are put into place. Revenue programs require a business mindset that can properly define the value of the product or service, pricing it to be competitive in the open marketplace. Some security directors are finding that their organizations are forcing them to competitively bid their services to internal customers against the open market. Since the emphasis today is on value-added contributions, let's take a brief look at some potential revenue generators.

To begin with, some security executives are finding markets for their internal training programs. A few years ago one large West Coast bank developed a robbery prevention training program for its tellers. The security director had the program designed generically to allow them to sell the film through the American Bankers Association for distribution to other retail banks. Other organizations have turned lemons into lemonade by developing disaster recovery and business resumption programs borne out of real-life experiences and selling them to other corporations. Still others sponsor seminars to explain how they were victimized by either a large fire, bombing, or natural disaster, and what lessons they learned so others wouldn't suffer similar catastrophes.

For another organization, the cost of fingerprinting the company's employees and contractors was offset by developing a fingerprint program as a service that could be sold to other companies. Specifically, a specialist was trained in the proper method of taking fingerprints. The department was then given the opportunity to sell that service to competitors who did not have such a sophisticated program but nonetheless required the service. Other examples of revenue generation include offering concierge services, valet parking, investigative services, and a host of safety products ranging from brochures and posters to evacuation and crowd control programs.

Explaining Your Business In Their Business Terms

As we have previously seen, success is based on your ability to communicate the value that you bring to an organization, in a way understood by decision-makers at the highest level. This communication simply means that the security manager must develop an ability to speak their language. That is to say, an ability to restate the business of security in a way that convinces senior management that you not only understand the business you purport to protect, but also do so in a way that complements their overall business aims. A couple of examples will help to illustrate the point.

Situational Case #17: Three Examples of Security-Business Communication

The director of a large retail operation began an internal investigation on an alleged kickback scheme involving a buyer and an outside supplier. The buyer had come forward and informed security that one of his suppliers offered to pay him $28,000 in kickbacks, based on a $2.8 million buy order. As the investigation unfolded, the buyer was outfitted with a listening device provided by the local police department to tape the conversations between the supplier and himself. In addition to recording these conversations, the buyer was instructed to accept the first $1,500 payment.

Shortly after that, the supplier became nervous and told the security manager that he no longer wanted to participate which, in essence, brought the investigation to a close. Given the small amount of money paid to the buyer, the local prosecutor and police task force assigned to the case lost interest. The security manager, however, wasn't satisfied. He directed that the accounts payable department withhold $75,000 due to the supplier, and further instructed them that when contacted by the supplier, to direct him to the security director. (As the security director later explained to his corporate counsel, he came up with the $75,000 based on the triple damages formula provided in federal racketeering statutes.)

When the supplier contacted the company for their late payment, he was forwarded to security. He was informed that the $75,000 would be released when he was willing to cooperate and identify other buyers he had offered similar kickbacks. The supplier refused and told the security director that the retailer could keep the $75,000, saying that he was going to retire and sell his business.

When the security director filled in the CEO, he became outraged and exclaimed, "All we got was a lousy $75,000? I wanted bodies to hang from the flagpole so everyone could see I don't tolerate such behavior!" The quick-thinking security director shot back that, while he understood the CEO's disappointment, the CEO should also recognize that this $75,000, when measured against the corporation's profit margin of 1 percent, represented one-third of the annual sales of one of their largest stores. Caught by surprise, the CEO thought a moment, smiled, and replied, "Well, I guess that's a job well done." In other words, the CEO recognized that he was talking to a retailer and not necessarily just a security director.

Similarly, a former bank client was struggling with the decision whether to outsource the security department. Concerned about the impact it would have on the other employees, the company president was reluctant to go forward, saying that he needed a compelling reason to present to his board of directors. He was told that the annual savings was equivalent to an increase in his asset base of more than $500 million, without the added burden of associated administrative expense tied to such an increase in assets. Like the retail CEO, he smiled too and realized that he had not only found his compelling reason, but also was talking to another banker, as opposed to a security director.

Still another example: The security department for a large utility wanted to introduce a drug awareness and testing program. After completing their research and benchmarking against other utility companies, the security director statistically showed that drug testing for new hires was directly related to a decrease in employee theft. This decrease in theft was used as an offset to the cost of implementing the program and restated for senior management in terms of new revenue to be received by bringing more than 270 new units on line.

Each of these examples helps to illustrate the point that the success of a security program is directly related to the security director's ability to define asset protection as contributing to the overall business plan of the company.

CONCLUSION

In this chapter we have seen the necessity for posturing the security program under the umbrella of customer service. Equally important, while recognizing that the primary mission is to control assets and provide a safe and secure environment, the goal of an asset protection program needs to be reflected in a value-added contribution to the organization. In doing so, customers, whether they are internal or external, need to believe that the security department is there for their benefit.

We examined in detail the concept of value-added contributions by analyzing many of today's continuous quality improvement programs. Among them has been an analysis of total quality management programs, with a specific focus on the Baldrige process. We also examined the notion of re-engineering as a way of redefining security's contribution as an integrated member of the business management team. We analyzed the value that benchmarking, sometimes known as comparative analysis, can bring to the asset protection manager. And we saw that benchmarking can identify those who engage in "best-of-class" practices and how such practices can be applied to the security administrator's benefit.

In this chapter we also cautioned against falling into the trap of believing that every value-added model necessarily contributes to an effective business approach. On the other hand, we explored the potential associated with developing revenue-generating programs as an offset to managing operating expenses. Finally, we underscored the need to present security's contribution in terms that could be understood by those in the ultimate decision-making position.

6

Strategies for Success

INTRODUCTION

A sense of humor is the mark of a good manager. A friend of mine is a very successful radio executive. For years he has worn a Mickey Mouse watch for a simple reason. It continuously reminds him that business cannot always be so serious as to let the lighter aspects of life slip by. It's his way of keeping things in perspective.

As I said in the Introduction, this is my "fun" chapter. Despite the fun, however, there is a sobering message. Just as we have seen that the success of a security program is tied to organizational theory strategies, it is also contingent on several practical tactics. I have found over time that successful managers routinely follow certain valuable axioms. Each can lead the administrator through the organizational maze— sometimes more aptly characterized as the corporate minefield. Some are humorous, some are not. Yet, they all are intended to help.

Today the business sections of book stores and libraries are full of new approaches to management. In the previous chapter we examined several of them. Despite all these new theories, there were two books that emerged in the 1970s that continue to have as much relevancy today as when they were first published. Smart business managers often look to the past for advice. In doing so, the works of Richard Buskirk and Roger Golde need to be revisited.

Buskirk's *Handbook of Management Techniques* is designed as a quick guide through a plethora of strategies that can affect the success or failure of managers trying to make their way through the morass of organizational life. I have read it dozens of times and still learn something new each time. It's definitely worth inclusion in any manager's permanent reference library. For the astute manager, it is a wonderfully humanistic and slightly Machiavellian approach to organizational survival. He offers over 120 management techniques, ranging from operating tactics to negotiation and persuasive tactics. One of my favorites for security managers is one of his timing tactics.

> *Let the Situation Worsen:* "Occasionally the best one can do is to let a bad situation get worse, for if he acts too soon he will be criticized as taking unwarranted action. There are some dangers in using this tactic, for some situations may worsen to the point where a manager cannot straighten out the mess, thereby causing losses. It takes great forbearance to let a situation worsen to a point where action can be taken."(37)

Asset managers are generally conditioned to react at the first sign of a problem. We take great pride in fixing wrongs sooner than later. Yet, in doing so, we often discover that more would have been gained in letting the situation come to that point just below full boil. Buskirk's advice is based largely on a style that encourages managed risk. Since success requires a degree of risk-taking, his insights have a lot of merit. The axioms discussed below are not necessarily out of *Management Techniques*. I guess that Buskirk would endorse them, however, since they are guidelines aimed at helping the manager find an approach to constructively position the security department within the greater organizational context.

Golde's book, *Muddling Through: The Art of Properly Unbusinesslike Management*, is a light read with practical overtones. His chapter titles immediately give the reader a hint of what is to follow: Discretion: Do It My Way or Your Own; Dealing with Experts: The Art of Managing from Ignorance; and The Fuzzy Side of Management: An Introduction. Each chapter focuses on specific strategies that are as equally hard-hitting as Buskirk's. Here are two quick examples:

> "Just as your boss's ultimate weapon is his capacity to fire you, so your ultimate weapon is the ability to leave the job (which, when you think about it, is actually a way to fire your boss). But the ultimate weapon has no power unless you are willing to use it. It is difficult to bluff your willingness to leave; your true state of mind will show through. The key to how willing you are to leave is simply your knowledge of other job offers or your confidence that you can find them if need be."(38)

This type of advice is not for the faint of heart, especially in a climate of downsizing. Being overly tied to job security, however, can put you at a distinct disadvantage when it comes to taking unpopular stands. A successful boss-subordinate relationship needs to be based on the implied understanding that both of you know the value of the other. Such an implication includes knowing that your services are of value to others.

According to Golde,

> "By not facing up to the basic fuzzy, vague character of objectives, the standard approach to delegation can create unrealistic expectations and harmful attitudes. The boss tends to feel uncomfortable, admitting he is not really clear about exactly what is wanted. So he may try to sound clear and precise, even to the extent of making spurious statements about the situation. What is worse, after these apparently logical statements have been repeated long enough, the boss actually begins to believe in them himself. As a consequence, he resents spending more time later on to further define the objective, because a clear objective should not need continual explanation or modification."(39)

How many times have you experienced this? How many times have you been guilty of this? Both Buskirk and Golde represent the type of management challenges that are confronted in the real world of organizational life. Despite their 20-year-old counsel, what they offer remains extremely relevant today.

As promised, below are my twenty axioms for success. Alone they cannot guarantee the desired result. Without them, however, your chance of reaching your full potential within the organization is far less likely to occur.

AXIOM #1.
Sometimes the Boss Is a Jerk.

At first glance this may strike the reader as somewhat crass. But it underscores a perspective grounded in understanding who we are and our effect on a subordinate staff. Most readers of this book are either a boss or have a desire to become one. It is important to realize that success begins with an understanding that all subordinates will, at one time or another, see you as a jerk. For most, this perception may not be long-lived. Conversely, for others, it may be a lifelong perspective. The point is this: As a boss, you need to recognize that on occasion others in the organization will not understand why you do what you do. From their perspective, you may be a person who does not know or appreciate their needs. They may become mad at you or perceive you as insensitive to them. Nonetheless, you will not always be liked.

This is important to understand at the beginning since it frames how you should approach your job. Knowing that you could be a jerk at times can serve as a natural check on your way of managing. Sometimes it may be necessary for someone to tell you how you're acting. If your style is one that does not allow this, neither you nor your department can probably reach full potential.

Situational Case #18: The Promoted Manager

An up-and-coming manager had recently received a promotion. He was responsible for the national organization involving security of the company's distribution network. The initial challenges were somewhat overwhelming due to the company's size and the number of problems he inherited. Although the promotion included retention of his other duties, he shifted most of his attention to the new aspects of the job, leaving the rest of his staff to carry on by themselves. Though not his intent, he failed to give many of his managers clear direction on how to handle aspects of their job. When they came to him for guidance, he was short with them.

As time went on, the staff saw him becoming more of a jerk with each passing day. Finally, one of the unit managers confronted him. When he first approached the boss, the unit manager was very nervous, fearing that the boss might overreact and fire him. After explaining how the rest of the staff felt and that they were perceiving him as a jerk, the boss sat silent for a moment and took in what he heard. A few moments later he pushed back from his desk and laughed, acknowledging the truth. Having become so absorbed with his new duties and their accompanying problems, the boss lost sight of how he was acting out his own frustrations and anxieties. He called for a staff meeting and apologized for his behavior.

This situation underscores several other factors for success. To begin with, this young manager had enough self-confidence and patience to hear what was being said. It also underscores the corollary: *Insecure managers are an organization's worst enemy.* Successful managers respect their subordinates as people. They see themselves for who they are and understand the importance of an open and participatory climate.

AXIOM #2.
Don't Tell Me What I Know,
Show Me What I Don't.

Security directors are often criticized for defining their contribution to the company's performance along a narrowly defined framework. By limiting themselves to only what they know well, they restrict opportunities for greater contributions. Although it's natural for a manager to build programs around their specialty area, today's security administrator needs to stretch into uncharted waters to achieve success.

Managing the familiar can lead to mediocrity. Complacency creeps into the organization. Defining asset protection in traditional terms should become second nature to the manager after a couple of years. The end result is a program that may not be keeping pace with the rest of the organization. Earlier we discussed the need to define contributions in terms that can be appreciated by other managers. We noted, for example, the need to equate a new capital program in terms of retail company sales, or the equivalent increase in bank assets. To do this the security manager must step away from classical definitions and seek new perspectives.

This willingness to take risks is also necessary for a number of aspects within the asset protection program. To demonstrate your value-added contribution requires an understanding of each business unit so that a comprehensive response can be developed. Many security directors, for example, define their limits of responsibility in terms of physical protection. For many companies, however, the highest valued asset may be their intellectual properties: processes, confidential lists, and/or pricing strategies. One bank president told me about his dissatisfaction with his security director. He said that the director was fixated on robberies, going on to explain that while he, too, was concerned about robberies, the greater threat was losses from fraudulent loans and wire transfers. The security director later confided that he didn't fully understand the nuances of the latter and therefore built his program around what he did understand: bank robberies.

There is a corollary to this axiom: *Results are what count, effort means very little by comparison.* This may sound somewhat harsh. In today's corporate world, however, it holds a great deal of truth. Quality requires a tangible result. Effectiveness, and therefore competitiveness, leaves little room for a good effort that fails to yield meaningful results. A security program that fails to deliver can cost more in terms of loss than it does to operate.

AXIOM #3.
Without Controversy
There Can Be No Success.

Any manager is naturally inclined to minimize controversy. The belief is that greater efficiency can be achieved when the organizational components are in harmony. This is not always true. Disagreement can allow new ideas and approaches to surface. Unchecked conflict or prolonged controversy is negative. However, if properly managed, the asset protection manager can leverage such conflict to the advantage of the department. This is particularly true when new programs are being considered.

As companies redefine their business approach, it is essential for security to be part of the business plan. Unfortunately, this is rarely understood by unit managers—especially if it means added expense or unplanned changes. Security directors must be able to finesse departmental requirements through without alienating senior management. Misunderstandings may still surface or changes introduced over the objection of others. This is acceptable provided the differences stay on a professional level and do not become personal. Properly handled, these differences of opinion can create positive controversy. Handled improperly, however, they may lead to long-lasting hard feelings.

Situational Case #19: The IA Controversy

A security manager was hired by a large financial institution and assigned to the bank's general services division. Before his appointment, security had always reported to the internal auditor (IA). As a department, security had historically been responsible for all fraud investigations. Since the auditor supported the change in reporting relationships, it was assumed by the general services manager that the security director would retain responsibility for fraud investigations and he stressed this to the new security manager.

Shortly after the security manager came onboard a serious internal fraud was discovered. The security executive directed his staff to begin an investigation. Not long into the inquiry it was discovered that internal auditing was also investigating the matter. The security director called the IA. The internal auditor informed the director that auditing was still responsible for all internal fraud investigations. The IA reasoned that just because he transferred the reporting relationship, he did not necessarily transfer all of the department's functions. He had elected to retain fraud investigations.

Unfortunately the auditor failed to tell this to anyone. The security director took exception and escalated the matter. The auditor did likewise, which meant getting his boss involved, who happened to be the bank's chief executive officer. Not put off, the security director asked for a meeting between the CEO, auditor, his boss, and himself. At the meeting, the security director told the group that he would not have taken the job had fraud investigations not been a part of his total duties. He suggested that they accept his resignation since he was over-qualified and volunteered to help them find a lesser-qualified person.

Not wanting to lose the security director, the CEO decided to leave fraud investigation responsibilities with the security director and informed the auditor that he would now head the bank's newly created credit review program. Even though the auditor was not completely satisfied with the end result, he gladly accepted the new responsibility.

AXIOM #4.
In Any Organization There Are Always Two Spheres; Politics and Competency.

This is a particularly important concept for security decision-makers to understand. Asset protection managers tend to place a high value on an individual's competency. Credibility is based on a person's technical proficiency. This means a thorough understanding of protective service strategies, investigative techniques, and/or systems design. In each situation there are prescribed ways of demonstrating one's capabilities. By following the rules, one gains respect and admiration. Clearly, competency plays a significant role in being accepted as a security expert.

On the other hand, organizational life consists of an equally important dynamic, commonly referred to as "corporate politics." Over the years, the concept has come to have a negative connotation. Yet, it is a real, and significant, factor in all companies. Politics is the ability to influence final decisions. It requires a skill set entirely apart from the technical aspects of the job. Within this sphere controversy can thrive. When abused, the conflict can have negative results. When adroitly handled, it can be a very effective management tool.

Politicking a new program through the organization requires the manager to assess the controversial aspects of the entire program and develop strategies that position everyone as a winner. No one person usually gets everything they want. The successful security manager/ organizational politician knows how to influence the right decision-makers. They know when to raise an issue and when to withdraw. The successful asset protection manager accepts the reality of political strategists.

Often I will hear security directors talk about how they hate the "game of corporate politics." Unfortunately for them, such a position assures their programs will never achieve their full potential. Typically, these same directors will say, "I don't believe that I should have to sell my ideas. If they are sound and we do our job right, the programs will sell themselves." Upon hearing this, one cynical corporate president replied: "And there is a real Easter Bunny, too."

As we saw in Chapter Three, success is more than just doing the right thing. Good ideas have to be sold. People have to be educated. Until they accept ownership, however, little can be accomplished. In an environment based on limited resources, good ideas and programs require a certain degree of politicking, and with politics, there comes conflict. It is often said that government politicians lack technical competency. Why then are they in positions of power? Often it is for reasons totally unrelated to the technical aspects of the job. The same can be said for those charged with heading divisions within a corporation.

Politics represents more than a way of corporate life. It represents the persona of one in a position of power over another. In other words, a leader will choose to be surrounded by trusted people who can represent the leader when he or she is absent. If an individual is highly competent but not in synch with the manager, there is little chance of joining the inner circle. This can be very frustrating—most people are told from childhood that hard work and competency are rewarded.

AXIOM #5.
Despite All the Evidence, There Are Those Who Continue to Believe That All Is Well, or This, Too, Shall Pass.

Though humorous, the axiom carries a very serious message. As companies reorganize, security managers are routinely being asked to hold or reduce expenses to the previous year's levels. Despite daily media reports about mass layoffs and stories from managers about downsizing, there are staff members who refuse to accept this reality. When the employee is in a position of authority, this is particularly troubling. Recently, one security director was faced with mounting opposition from two of his trusted assistants. Both were company veterans who refused to believe that they needed to cut operational spending. Even though they participated in the budget process, when it came to holding costs down, they refused to do so—opting instead to spend as though there was no directive to curtail unnecessary expenses. When asked why, both informed the security administrator that they had been through tough times in the past and that this was only an aberration. Even though the company had filed for Chapter 13 protection under bankruptcy proceedings, these managers still were not in tune with the reality of the situation.

Perhaps a fitting corollary would be: *Despite all the evidence to the contrary, there are those who believe that there are adults somewhere who know what they are doing.*

Again, a humorous look at an all-too-frequent reflection of reality. As children, we naturally assumed our parents knew what they were doing. Believing otherwise would have been rather disconcerting. It's easy to assume the same about those above us in the corporate world. We want to believe that senior executives got to where they are based on demonstrated abilities. As we saw earlier, people somctimes ascend to high-level positions for reasons other than technical know-how.

AXIOM #6.
Organizations, Like Water,
Seek Their Own Level.

Organizations mirror the personalities of those who run them. If a security manager is content to maintain the status quo (which is not necessarily bad), the security department will reflect this approach. Similarly, if the department head does not want to be assertive and seek new areas of responsibility, the department will not seek them out on its own.

Conversely, assertive managers will likely seek new duties and not settle down until they have achieved their goal. Some managers may find that this requires leaving the organization or redefining their goal. Regardless, the organization will follow suit. In short, dynamic leaders are usually supported by dynamic departments. Similarly, complacent leadership promotes a mediocre staff and programs.

AXIOM #7.
Organizations Begin to Die the Day
the Sense of Urgency Begins to Fade.

It may take some time, but when a department loses that "can do" spark, it isn't long afterwards that they become something significantly less than their former self. This should be evident to both those within and outside the company. Today, we all are frustrated with the amount of time it takes to process most things and receive timely service. Whether in our personal lives or on the job, unexplained delays, apparent inattention, or just plain old slow service leaves an impression that departments don't subscribe to high professional standards. This is one particularly important reason for lobby officers and console operators to responsibly answer the telephone after-hours.

Another area to watch is providing timely turnaround for the issuance of access control cards. New employees are quick to judge the merits of a security department if they have to wait several days to receive cards. Until then, they may feel hassled when they have to sign-in or get someone's approval before being allowed into their work area. New employees want to impress their new boss with on-time arrivals. Delays from slow security service only serve to alienate both the new employee and their boss.

AXIOM #8.
Security Ought Not Be That Department Where an Individual Goes to Get the Answer No.

I'm not sure why it is, but I frequently find asset protection managers are quick to say no to new ideas. Perhaps it is linked to our backgrounds in maintaining control. Venturing into uncharted areas is a naturally scary proposition. It is therefore easy to discourage new ideas, especially if there is a potential for loss or injury. Yet, in today's highly competitive world, companies need to explore new directions. Therefore, it is incumbent on security to embrace new approaches. The challenge is to look for ways to protect the company's assets, employees, and customers within the context of these new definitions. The successful security program should always stand ready to embrace new challenges.

This doesn't mean throwing caution to the wind. As the person charged with protecting the assets, there is an obligation to voice concerns so that they are adequately addressed. Even here, these concerns should be stated in a way that is positive and contributes to the overall success of the project. Each year many of my clients are corporate executives who need assistance in finding a more cooperative security director. The commonly heard complaint is that the asset protection manager is more of an obstructionist than a valued resource. That is a profound message for our profession.

AXIOM #9.
Radical Ideas Blossom When Line & Staff Merge.

There is a natural tendency to separate staff and line functions. Yet, often suggestions regarding the best approach to greater efficiency can emerge from the rank and file. My experience is that most line members want to perform professionally. Since they have to work each day with the existing conditions, they know best what pragmatically works and what does not. Staff members are sometimes disadvantaged. Although they know the technical aspects of a certain job function, they may not be fully aware of its operational nuances simply because a long time has passed since they last performed the job.

Line level personnel know the reality of the operating environment. What they lack may be the business reasons for doing things one way versus another. That is why staff-level input is critical when there is dissidence between staff and line workers. Line workers believe that "they" (e.g., corporate staff) don't understand them and talk of the "ivory tower" syndrome—a concept predicated on the notion that some bosses are out-of-touch with the real world. The staff, conversely, believes that line workers are antimanagement and looking for ways to counter management's aims. Yet, studies show that a merger of staff and line perspectives not only diminishes a significant amount of infighting, but actually builds better teamwork and better products and/or services. The very essence of re-engineering is built on the belief that when both teams merge better ideas surface.

Situational Case #20: Merging Staff and Line Ideas

A health-care provider wanted to improve its security program. The regional security manager understood the need for balancing technology with staffing, but lacking the technical resources to develop a full business plan, he employed an established security engineering firm, Gibbs & Associates, of Fremont, California. The owner, David Gibbs, recommended a two-pronged approach: an end-user needs assessment study coupled with his own company's review of staffing and technology needs. The regional manager agreed.

When the consulting staff began their review, it became apparent that there was a significant difference of opinion between some of the management staff's ideas and the line workers' ideas. After reporting the differences to the regional manager, Gibbs recommended that his company serve as the catalyst for merging the best of both levels. The result was a natural blend of the benefits of both perspectives. For Gibbs and his staff it was business as usual. For the client it was quite a different story. At the local hospital level, security management was pleased to discover that their recommended technology needs could be integrated into the overall business requirements of the hospital administrator. At the line level, the officers were equally pleased to see that their ideas were being reflected in the final design of the security plan. The regional manager was equally pleased because Gibbs had found a balance between the line workers and management staff without disrupting either.

For Gibbs, there was a four-way win. His staff designed the project integrating the real world needs of the line workers (Win #1). They also reflected the business requirements of the management staff (Win #2). Since the regional manager was pleased (Win #3), this in turn led to additional work for Gibbs & Associates (Win #4). Clearly, not all line-staff mergers require an outside consultant. There is an important point to be made, however. When staff and line personnel clash, the use of a neutral third party tuned to their respective needs may be required. Here, Gibbs & Associates merged the two and formed a strategy not only amenable to both, but also far more efficient, thus yielding significant cost savings.

There is an interesting corollary to this axiom. Namely, *Success is achieved only when the new and old teams can blend together; this is one of the greatest myths.* As company mergers continue to flourish, turnaround specialists enter organizations, and consolidations unfold, it is often said that it will be beneficial for both teams to work together. This is corporate bunk. Pure and simple. It is not only a myth, but a dangerous one at that. The new team has been given the charter to meet the new goal and objectives. This will require a *single* mindset.

There is no room for two teams that might be at philosophical odds with one another. Members of the previous team need to merge with members of the new team. This is not to suggest that the "old team" members shouldn't voice their opinions. They have valuable insights and bring a strong sense of continuity to any given issue. When all is said and done, however, the two teams need to be working toward the same goal with the same plan. Organizational theorists who advocate retention of both team perspectives really offer a strategy for unnecessary and unhealthy conflict. If a member of the previous team cannot accept the ways of the new team, they should leave. It's as simple as that. The ultimate success depends on everyone coming together for a single purpose.

AXIOM #10.
Document!! Document!! Document!!

In today's litigious world and overregulated society, it is important to document most decision-making activities. But many protection managers are reluctant to fill out the necessary paperwork. Personnel actions cannot be made without the required documentation; especially if the manager is looking to fire the individual. Capital expenditures require written business justification, and requests for added staff and equipment need to be supported by written facts, service requests, or documented maintenance costs. Despite this requirement, most security managers do not do a good job at preparing the necessary papers.

The corollary is equally simple: *Document both the good and the bad.* Even if you intend to ultimately seek the firing of an individual, there is the need to document the good things the person accomplishes. Some courts have awarded wrongful termination suits to the employee because the only documentation available was negative. Rightly or wrongly, juries are hard-pressed to believe that employees only commit bad acts. Balance is required.

AXIOM #11.
Success Comes to Those Who Orchestrate It.

A security executive once told about when she knew she was a success: "When I could finally take a moment away and not have to think about my next move." She knew well that achieving success is hard work. It requires a long-term vision coupled with a plan of attack. While there is undoubtedly some truth to the adage "being in the right place at the right time," some organizational theorists would argue that even this is the result of a planned effort. Nevertheless, success is an end product that can be measured. To achieve it requires a thought process that takes controllable variables into account. Some would argue that winning the lottery is an example of luck. Still others would contend that even lottery winners need an orchestrated plan. At a minimum it requires some selection criteria for picking the winning numbers.

Corollary: *If you are going to wait to be discovered, you better pack your lunch. You will have a long wait.*

A famous rock star was once asked how he was discovered. "It was easy," he answered. "I just spent six years singing every night, in any city and for any gig that someone would have me. During the day I practiced and wrote songs. At night I played, and somewhere in between, I'd occasionally treat myself to a meal and a little sleep. After that it was all downhill." Similarly, organizational success is earned.

AXIOM #12.
An Organization's Greatest Cardinal Sin Is to Allow the Norm "We've Always Done It This Way" to Exist.

We are all victims of the dreaded saying, "We've always done it that way." It's a common phenomenon. The critical factor is that we recognize it when we hear it. Equally important, we must continuously ask why procedures and practices are followed, staffing assignments made, and systems and devices used. If the answer is, "We've always done it this way," that should be reason enough to explore the matter further.

I'm not suggesting that established ways of doing things should be discarded. (Remember my father's advice about tearing down fences without knowing why they were built?) More than once, this sage advice has prevented me from making decisions that only appeared to be correct on the surface. Established practices serve their purpose provided the conditions for which they were developed are still relevant. Frequently post orders are outdated, but they're still followed because no one has thought to update them.

Failing to challenge the "why for" of a security practice causes both embarrassment and loss of credibility. Here's a quick example: Why do most organizations require employees to sign-out after-hours when they are not required to sign-in upon arrival during normal business hours? There are some valid reasons for this practice, but does your staff know them? Or, do they offer explanations that are no longer valid? If your circumstances are such that you really don't gain true value from a sign-out procedure, you should be willing to drop the practice.

I recall leaving a building one evening with a client, a senior executive. As we left, he asked the security officer why employees sign-out. The officer said it was one means security uses to know who is still in the building. When asked how they know that, since employees leaving hadn't signed-in, the officer got flustered. As we left, the executive said he had not intended to embarrass the officer. Rather, he had always been curious. He went on to tell me that a proposal for a new access control system was on his desk awaiting approval. Until then he had planned to approve it. Now, however, he had more questions and intended to have a long discussion with the security director. I suspect it was a long meeting.

AXIOM #13.
Nature Didn't Give the Buck
Its Antlers Just for Looks.

Use the resources you have been given. There is nothing wrong with self-promotion. Earlier we saw how one major company's security department actively embraced a formal program of internal marketing. Other tools include access to certain senior managers, use of compliance and regulatory requirements, employee concerns, benchmarking against similar institutions or departments, and legal rulings.

These tools, like any other resource, can be abused. That's where your professional ethics comes into play. Without drawing on your assets, the wolf pack will take advantage. Just as the buck has learned to effectively fend off attackers by lowering his head and using his antlers, security directors need to use the tools provided to similarly fight. It is unfortunate to have to describe corporate life as sometimes being a battlefield, but the reality of working in an organization with scarce resources and competitive personalities makes it true sometimes.

Just because security "wears the badge and carries the gun," there is no guarantee that it won't have its enemies. The successful security director recognizes that aside from the professional service his department offers, his department is also a part of the organizational structure. To this end, battles will have to be fought. Many asset protection managers look with disdain on "corporate politics" and choose to stay out of the way. Sadly, many of them fall victim to these same politics. Assuming the mantle of leadership requires a willingness to fight. To do otherwise is a disservice to those below you.

As a corollary, it might be helpful to remember that *today's Mr. Big is, at best, tomorrow's fading memory.* By this I mean that mid-level managers shouldn't be intimidated by senior level managers. Many security managers have confided that they are intimidated by their company president, CEO, or another executive. They fear power or are uncomfortable interacting with people in such positions. This intimidation works against them and lessens their effectiveness, particularly in cases where an executive must be told that certain things he or she wants done cannot be honored.

Situational Case #21: The Retiring Executive

A former corporate executive in charge of 22,000 employees announced his retirement after working for the company for more than four decades. One up-and-coming manager told the executive how much he would be missed. The executive responded that he didn't believe this would necessarily be so. He said that there is a short life cycle to remembering former executives, which goes something like this:

- At the retirement party everyone talks about how he will be missed.
- Over the next several weeks many employees will ask one another if they have heard from him and will wonder how he is doing.

- In a few months his replacement will have arrived and everyone will challenge the new incumbent with phrases such as: "Well, when so and so was here, we did it this way. If it worked for him, why won't it work for you?"
- Within six months the new boss will have asserted himself and the former executive will be blamed by his former trusted friends and colleagues for everything that is wrong.
- By the end of the first year an occasional voice will be heard asking if anyone has heard from the retired executive lately. Nearly everyone will answer no.
- After eighteen months, reports and memos will surface with the executive's name at the bottom. The employee will smile and remember the time when the executive was around.
- Somewhere in the middle of the third year, a new employee and an experienced employee will be talking. The executive's name will surface and the new employee will ask who he is. The answer will be, "Oh, just some guy who used to work here."
- By the end of the third year, a new employee will find a directive signed by the former executive and scoff, "Hey, this can't be relevant. Look, it's got some guy's name on it that no one even knows!" With that, it will be tossed aside and discarded.

A somewhat sad lifeline. Unfortunately, it's more often true than not. Even today's Mr. Big will one day be not so big. It helps to remember this when feeling a little intimidated by executives.

AXIOM #14.
Women Need to Be Better Prepared If They Are Going to Survive, Let Alone Make It to the Top.

The bibliography contains several recently published works dealing with the issue of women in corporate leadership roles. As a profession, security is still largely dominated by men. Finding a female security executive is still unusual. Yet, lacking any definitive study, my experience suggests that proportionately there are more women managers on the contract side of the security field than at proprietary operations.

Because there are so few, finding appropriate role models is difficult. This is especially true for newly appointed managers. Recently, a large East Coast financial services organization promoted a woman to security director. When asked if I could direct her to other counterparts, I could offer the names of only two women directors in the banking community responsible for a like program. One was located in the Midwest and the other on the West Coast. Given the geographic spread, developing a working dialogue becomes difficult. Something needs to be done, though.

The primary issue is women's ability to be taken seriously by other corporate executives, most of whom are men. Though few will admit it, many male executives have trouble taking direction from a female security director. In time I believe this attitude will change. Until then, women generally will need to look outside the profession to seek the necessary advice and guidance.

In an attempt to counterbalance this sometimes explicit, but most often implicit, discrimination, some male security managers have attempted to take on the role of mentor. Unfortunately, in doing so they have assumed strong paternalistic roles, just the opposite of what is required. To be successful, women need to better understand how the male psyche works in order to understand the competition and established mores. Only then can they work around them to achieve the desired outcome. This is not to suggest some sort of diabolical, evil-driven plan. Instead, just as any manager needs to first understand the corporate landscape, female asset protection managers need to understand men's initial resistance to their leadership. It's another sad commentary on our times, but all too often I have seen senior managers not take women seriously, simply because of their sex.

AXIOM #15.
There Are Some Events That
Are Simply Out of Your Control.

A controlling-type personality in security can easily get frustrated in the security field. For several years I've been a registered Stuart

Atkins LIFO trainer. This is a program that instructs people on the four basic life/personality styles commonly found among the population. Atkins' studies show that in dealing with issues, each of us tends to adopt one predominant behavioral style, or a combination of two. Essentially these styles are the Controller, the Adaptor, the Supporter, and the Analyzer. Other behaviorists have developed similar models. In my seminars and workshops, I have found a preponderance of controlling personalities among security personnel. This shouldn't be surprising since it is a profession that requires people to take charge and control the situation. As we discovered in the second chapter, the very nature of asset protection begins with the development of controls.

The point is that we are a profession of control-oriented managers. When events occur that are outside of our control, we get frustrated, angry, believe ourselves to be failures, and try to capture control of the events. Often all in vain. Mergers and reorganizations take place, valued allies leave, priorities shift, and natural disasters happen. These and literally dozens of other events continually unfold and cause us to reexamine established plans.

At a recent national meeting, a security manager told me that he intended to resign and move his family to another state in an effort to improve his quality of life. Three days later his company announced that they were being acquired by a larger firm. Shortly after that he called me and said he was very frustrated because his plans were upset. He felt helpless and out of control; his situation is not uncommon. Many security administrators voice similar frustrations over decisions made at higher levels. This can lead to deep-seated resentment, unhealthy cynicism, and even outright contempt for others. It is little wonder that these employees are eventually asked to leave. The answer, it seems, is to expect control over only those events you can truly influence and build in enough flexibility to adjust to circumstances and events as warranted.

AXIOM #16.
Ask a Manager Where He Wants His Organization to Be in 10 Years. If His Answer Is Not Significantly Different

from How It Is Now, You Know You're Talking to a Maintenance Manager.

There are fundamentally two types of managers—maintenance providers and creative builders. Neither one is better than the other. Both serve a role. The difficulty comes when one or the other is misassigned. Longstanding departments with established programs generally do better with a maintenance manager. A creative mind still needs to be somewhere in the organization to challenge the status quo and offer new insights. Conversely, a company wanting to develop a new program or redefine an existing one needs to employ a creative thinker. This individual can see the big picture and is open to alternate approaches. Yet, like his counterpart, the creative manager also needs a maintenance manager nearby. This individual can assure that the creative effort becomes a working reality.

A side corollary is *How do you kill a creative manager? Put him under an insecure maintenance manager.* Creativity can be very threatening to an insecure manager. The maintenance-driven individual may not see the value of the creative person. They are quick to say, "If it isn't broke, why fix it?" Sometimes this is true. Sometimes it can be a camouflage for much needed change.

How do you know if you're one or the other? Here's a simple test I use. Ask yourself, if you were given only two career choices, which one would you select: The pit boss at the Indianapolis 500 on race day? Or a member of the race car design team? The first suggests a maintenance manager because it sees the necessity for keeping the car in peak performance throughout the race. The other requires a creative thinker; someone willing to test new ideas and build the bigger, faster, safer racer.

AXIOM #17.
There's a Lot to Be Said for Survivalists.

In a book like this, it's easy to incorrectly conclude that being a survivalist is somehow equivalent to being a second-class citizen. Let me be clear: this is not true. Survivalists offer continuity and a balanced perspective. What makes a security organization work is a blend of approaches. Survivalists have an innate skill at detecting the corporate potholes; especially hidden ones. They also have the knack of getting themselves and others out of trouble when necessary.

The survivalist often serves as a mentor to new employees or upstart executives. They know the personalities of those who currently sit along executive row. Often the survivalist can remember when the executive was a budding superstar. He or she may also know about a few skeletons in the closet or other embarrassing trigger points and can guide the security manager into safer, calmer corporate waters.

AXIOM #18.
Organizations Are Like Waves. Some Crash, Some Just Fade; Yet One Thing Is for Sure, All Waves Crest and End.

For years I've been intrigued by the wave theory of organizations. I've seen it unfold again and again. The theory contends that every organization has its own wave. Just as a natural wave begins far out at sea and builds to a crest as it nears shore, the same can be said of an organization. After the crest, it has only two options. It can gently fall or, in more troubled waters, crash. Regardless, it falls. If the wave is really far out, it may build, crest and fall several times over. The same can be said of security departments. Some will fall for any number of reasons, only to build momentum and eventually crest and fall again.

For the astute security manager, the skill is to assess where your organizational wave is and prepare accordingly. Some enter the wave at its peak only to have it suddenly fall. Others see that the wave is just beginning and enjoy a long ride before facing the crest. Still others may see the crest coming and look forward to riding the wave in much like a surfer enjoys catching "The Big One."

If you know where to look, there are signs that can tell you where your wave is. Comments from your boss, the amount of respect shown by others, events that lead to your hiring or promotion, are to name but a few. As a former turnaround manager for three large companies, I found that working for a troubled corporate giant proved to be an excellent time to catch the wave at its beginning and ride it for several years. These companies are looking for help. They have problems and need solutions. Consequently, they are more apt to allow you to develop programs, seek alternatives, and work autonomously. In time, however, the crisis will pass and they will develop new priorities. When this begins to happen, the wave is about to crest. Knowing this, you can exercise one of several options. Leave and move on to another stormy sea, ride out the wave and enjoy the fruits of your efforts, or seek new opportunities within the company by assuming more or different duties. Regardless, the wave you're currently on will end. It's a matter of physics.

AXIOM #19.
The Best Way to Enter a Building Is Not Necessarily Through the Front Door.

We naturally try to solve problems using established methods. And why not? They worked in the past. The difficulty is not all problems can be solved through conventional means. Asking a security manager to increase service while reducing his operating budget is a significant challenge. Typically, increased service means increased expense. Similarly, investigating internal fraud usually requires a trained investigator. What happens when you don't have one? Or, what if an executive receives a threat but doesn't want security coverage? You know the executive is at risk but you don't want to risk upsetting him or his family.

These problems are common in our profession. Under normal conditions there are answers to resolve each of them. But when the resources are not available, or if there is a reluctance to follow prescribed procedures, what can you do?

I use a methodology I call the "180 degree approach." This involves studying the problem and asking what the conventional answer would entail. I then look at the problem from the opposite perspective (it's like walking into the building from the rear loading dock). In this way, the answer may arrive from a completely opposite strategy from the more conventional approach. But, if it works, it works. Especially if it costs less and is accomplished in less time.

The best example is in working with workforce assessments. If quality improvement is required, training is usually the first remedy, followed by setting performance standards. Next, incentives, penalties, or a combination of both should be used. Sometimes the answer may be through attrition. Another alternative is to replace the entire staff. In today's parlance that is called *outsourcing;* we will explore it in more detail later. For now, however, it serves to illustrate that quality improvement can be achieved by entirely replacing the workforce. As drastic as this may sound, it is often less painful, more effective, and less costly in terms of both time and money. Conversely, the same can be said for replacing an external provider with an internal operation.

I have found the following corollary to be particularly apropos: *There's nothing like a crisis to allow small minds to rise to the occasion and think small.* Desperate times call for radical ideas. Generally this means thinking in much broader terms and setting aside conventional approaches. In a natural disaster, for example, quick decision-making is critical. Resources need to be immediately identified and procured. In some cases financial commitments need to be made outside the normal procedures. Once, following a tornado, a security director requisitioned needed supplies from a nearby supplier. Going directly to the vendor, he bypassed the usual purchasing requirements. Still being confronted by many difficulties, he soon received an angry call from a purchasing agent who accused him of not obtaining a purchase order first and threatened to cancel the order. In another case, an asset protection manager was asked to submit ideas on how his department could cut costs in light of his company's deep financial troubles. He offered two recommendations: encourage his investigators to use low octane gasoline in company vehicles and discontinue the flower service.

AXIOM #20.
Never Attend a Meeting
Without Bringing the Agenda.

Finally, being prepared is critical for any successful manager. Studies on how corporate managers spend their working day consistently show that they attend more meetings than anything else. Few come prepared to discuss issues intelligently. Typically there are two outcomes to every meeting. You walk away following someone else's agenda or your own. Which one has the greater appeal?

While there are times that it is safer to be a follower, it is usually better to come with your own agenda. This means coming with it written down and ready to be passed out. Many meetings are called to present a problem or outline a challenge and solicit ideas on how to resolve it. Most people will arrive with an empty note pad at best. By coming in with your own plan, it won't take long before they are discussing your plan. By the end of the meeting, your original plan may be altered, but at least it is still your plan.

As a final corollary, I'd like to offer this idea: *Success doesn't come from how well you manage your organizational box; it comes from how well you function between everyone else's.*

A former boss of mine once commented when I came to him complaining about my status within the organization. He explained that real power, and therefore a manager's real success, comes from an ability to effectively maneuver outside the formal limits of an assigned position. As we all know, there are two organizations within any company: the formal one and the informal one. The latter can be far more influential and effective when it comes to achieving your aims. Relationships make things happen. A subordinate can affect the outcome of a situation as much as a superior or a contemporary. So when I hear a security director lament that he was the last to hear about something, I question the manager's ability to adroitly maneuver through the organizational maze.

LIPPLE'S 9 BASIC PRINCIPLES FOR SUCCESS

Recently, Horizons Institute of Deltona, Florida, under the direction of security consultant, Steve Keller, produced a management tape entitled "Nine Principles of Successful Protection Management." (40) Featuring another highly respected security professional, Ernie Lipple, the two of them discuss basic approaches to developing an effective security program. These basics serve as building blocks for all other successes.

While they represent a set of standards that can be found in any primer on business management, they serve a purpose here. Namely, success begins with the basics. Building a program based on an established foundation allows managers to leverage other strategies for greater achievements. Lipple, too, believes that success is a planned result. It is built on a blueprint, designed in advance, and adjusted as the need arises. A quick review is therefore appropriate.

Principle #1: Hiring Qualified Staff

Appropriate and effective hiring tops his list. This is true at every level in the organization. To do so requires an ability to attract competent employees, which means more than a competitive compensation program. It also means providing professional working conditions and the necessary basic tools.

Principle #2: Promoting Your Staff

For Lipple, promoting is a twofold process. First, it is the promotion of staff from one grade level to another. Second, it means advocating for them. Provide them with the necessary support to get their job done efficiently. Give them an opportunity to showcase their work with your boss and other executives. A simple strategy could be having each staff member take turns attending a weekly status meeting between you and your boss or updating them on the status of a particular project. Similarly, establish a special meeting where your boss can talk one-on-one with selected staff members. Sometimes promotion may mean helping your people succeed by finding them better jobs outside an organization.

Principle #3: Knowing the Three Basic Goals of Protection

Basically, every security department has three fundamental goals: reduce property loss, reduce injuries, and reduce conflicts. According to Lipple, everything else should be built around these three elements. Decisions relating to staffing, systems enhancements, and operating procedures should reflect one or more of these targets. If senior management wants to place other responsibilities upon the security department for reasons of efficiency, Lipple says that is appropriate, but a clear distinction should be made that such add-ons are separate and apart from the protection program. Resource allocation shouldn't compete with the department's primary functions. If they do, the overall quality of the program will suffer.

Principle #4: Setting Measurable Objectives

Goals are only as good as the objectives that are developed. Good objectives allow goals to be accomplished. Each goal needs to be fashioned in a way that is both measurable and achievable. They must challenge the staff and still bring about a sense of pride after successful completion. Objectives can vary among various organizational levels; there is a need for consistency, however, to provide clarity of purpose and keep the whole department focused.

Principle #5: Training

Lipple contends that training is only training when it is well thought out, written down, and evaluated for its effectiveness. Many security departments claim they have training, but on closer examination, it is more of an informal on-the-job exercise totally dependent on the availability of a supervisor. To be effective, it must be comprehensive, covering the four basic forms of training: Initial Officer Training, On-The-Job Training, Advanced Officer Training, and Specialized Training. Each program should consist of learning objectives, instructor criteria, detailed learning media, evaluational instruments, and a record of the training and test results for each employee.

Principle #6: Supervision

While Lipple would prefer to use the term coaching, he compares the activity to that of a police sergeant, or shift supervisor. Nevertheless, he means that your staff is only as good as its leader. Supervisors/coaches need to be on-site and actively working with the officers and other subordinate staff. Left on their own, inexperienced security officers can, and do, make mistakes. Given the settlement levels associated with negligent security cases, a successful department manager is judged by the caliber and extent of supervision provided.

Principle #7: Professional Development

Professional development covers a variety of activities, such as attending conferences, special briefings, subscribing to professional journals, seeking appropriate credentials, and networking with other professionals. It also involves developing contacts with external support services such as local law enforcement, underwriters, vendors, and educators. Professional development can mean serving on association boards, preparing special reports, providing testimony, speaking with journalists, and representing the department at important functions.

Principle #8: Adapting to Change

The next principle is rapid adjustment to change. The experienced manager understands the dynamic nature of asset protection and the fluid part of organizational life. Each day can either be measured in terms of forward progress or backward movement. The objective is to have more forward days. As Lipple observes, "You're either progressing or you're going backwards. There's never a day, though I wish that there was, when I can put my feet up on the desk and say, well, 'I'm here, I can just relax now.' That doesn't happen."

Goals may not substantially change—nor should they, but circumstances may require a continual adjustment to your objectives. One has to make sure things are going the way they should; you have to be ready when it's necessary to change and not resist it. Equally important, he stresses, is the need to critique what you've done and make sure that it's done right. Keller agrees, noting that one of the greatest shortcomings he observes among managers is that they get a pet project and don't know when to quit. They don't recognize when an idea, even though it used to be good, becomes old and needs to be replaced.

Principle #9: Review and Evaluate

The ninth principle is the end of the success loop. It reviews each of the preceding principles and measures ongoing relevancy—an activity that collects data and feeds the results back to the manager. The review assesses hiring and promotional practices, training, supervision, goal and objective development, professional development, and the department's adaptive skills. Lipple suggests that budget setting is an ideal time to conduct such an evaluation, though he suggests that it should be done more frequently throughout the year. Still, budget time is a good opportunity to ask why are we really doing the things we are.

Keller notes that an effective review and evaluation process addresses even the basic operational level. "You're not just reviewing and reevaluating your objectives, you're reviewing and reevaluating the means to those objectives. You're critiquing your response to situations, your handling of situations. You're critiquing your way of doing things. You're critiquing whether you're being as efficient, as effective, as cost-effective as you can be. You're looking at the very fundamental concepts that we all take for granted in security management and asking: 'Does it really work here, does it still work today?'"

MEISENHEIMER'S FIVE WAYS TO BEAT THE COMPETITION

Leading management consultant, Paul Franklin of the National Training Institute in Portland, Oregon, interviewed Jim Meisenheimer of G.M. Associates, a sales training firm in Libertyville, Illinois, to discuss Meisenheimer's five strategies for beating the competition. Although Meisenheimer's comments are directed at consulting companies and sales forces, his five points, I believe, have a direct application for business unit managers and are in keeping with the axioms and principles that we've discussed above.

Strategy #1—Outbid

In competition with other department heads for limited capital and operating monies, the object is not to demonstrate that your programs may cost the company less. The truer objective is to demonstrate that your programs have, or will bring, increased value to the organization on whole. The best way to win approval is to present the program's features and benefits as something clearly valuable to the decision-maker. Meisenheimer suggests that these added values should be placed strategically in any presentation requesting funding—just before the cost of the program or requested capital expenditure is identified.

Strategy #2—Outdistance

Meisenheimer suggests that the successful manager is one who is prepared and willing to do the work. He says there's no easy way to go the extra mile. If it were easy, everyone would be doing it. By putting in that extra effort, you immediately differentiate yourself from other department heads.

Strategy #3—Outlast

Remember that a large part of business management is the competition for limited resources; therefore, persistence is important. Many managers give up too early or run from resistance, because they can't bear to hear the word no. Meisenheimer suggests that those who persevere tend to be the winners in the end.

Strategy #4—Outfox

Successful managers take seriously the notion of thinking like their customers think. It is also important to think like your competitors think. In doing so, you're more apt to outfox them, especially in very competitive situations. Essentially, to assist you in achieving your end result, ask yourself how the competition has reacted in the past, who was involved, and why they considered certain options. In most organizations, the same department heads come to the capital planning committee or meet each other in the budget process on an annual basis. Invariably some department heads are perpetual winners, while others leave shaking their heads, suggesting that "maybe next year it will be my turn." Those who are consistently successful know the tricks of the game and how to play it.

Strategy #5—Out-of-Step

Meisenheimer says that the quickest way to disinterest decision-makers is to begin with an explanation of your services instead of identifying their problems. Corporate executives make decisions based on the problems currently facing them. They're not necessarily interested in buying a total service package. Most executives want effective solutions to the challenges facing them. If your programs are perceived by them to address their needs, chances are very high that approval will be given. In short, the challenge is to get into step with senior management and align yourself with their needs. Meisenheimer suggests the following, "If you want to finish third, show your customers how little you offer. If you want to finish a close second, place a priority on extra effort. If you want to win, strive to outbid, outdistance, outlast, and outfox your competition, and never be out of step with your customers." (41)

INTERNAL CUSTOMER, R.I.P.

You may recall in Chapter Five, when looking at the issue of TQM, Oren Harari presented a fairly strong argument about the shortcomings and failures of this latest management approach. Harari offers us a second challenge when writing for the June 1993 edition of *Management Review*. "Like a vampire who refuses to die, the 'internal customer' continues to rear its ugly head. I still get letters and documents from individuals who argue that the goal of customer satisfaction applies to both internal and external customers, and that the road to delighted external customers is paved with the satisfaction of internal ones. I admit that the theory sounds rosy, but like some other theories in management, this one has little basis in reality and in practice is downright dangerous."(42) He admits that these are fairly strong words, but they're intended to underscore a serious concern he has about the tendency for large corporations to develop equally large back office support operations, which tend to distract executives from the true nature of their business.

Although I strongly believe in the internal customer concept, I think it's important to include a discussion of Harari's concerns to provide a balanced approach for the business manager intent on achieving success for his program and departmental aims. The bottom line for Harari is that large back office support operations can and do often take on a life of their own. So much so that in an effort to sustain their own existence, they deflect needed resources away from the ultimate aim of the organization—customer satisfaction and established profit margins.

Harari's concern is that in today's business environment, where competitive pressures for cost efficiency, innovation and real-time responses are critical, most companies can no longer afford the luxury of large and cumbersome support units who identify themselves as internal customers. "Companies can no longer afford to carry the overhead of jobs and functions that are buffered from external customers. Neither can companies afford to continue subsidizing a chain of departmental pass-offs, so imminently logical on paper, but in reality so inherently riddled with inefficiencies, blaming, backstabbing, and the creation of self-protecting jobs."(43)

It appears that the message is twofold. One, corporate security directors must recognize that their programs need to reflect a balance between a safe and secure environment and the protection of corporate assets for employees, vendors, and customers. This simply means that programs need to be defined in their broadest terms, with little differentiation between protecting the rights of those who are within the corporation and those who are external to it. The astute security manager will recognize that his department's goal is to provide protection for everyone equally.

The second part of Harari's message is the explicit denunciation of those programs that have become irrelevant to the overall mission of the organization. For security directors, the challenge is to assure that they are providing service in the most cost-effective and efficient manner. Harari offers three alternatives for senior management's consideration.

Consideration #1

Insist that people in all traditional support functions reconfigure their jobs to help serve the external customer directly. The suggestion is for security managers to redefine their department's mission and establish strategies that are more external customer-oriented than internally focused. This should be fairly straightforward for most asset protection managers since the ultimate mission is to protect everyone.

If programs are developed with the external customer in mind, the benefits of those efforts should accrue to internal end users as well. An escort service intended to provide reasonable assurance that people get from their office to their vehicle after-hours, for example, is just as reasonable for an employee as it is for a client. The point is that an escort program should be developed with the understanding that such a service is ultimately in the company's best economic interests.

Consideration #2

Subcontract jobs and functions that do not directly address your core competencies for the external customer. In the following chapter we analyze the notion of creating strategic alliances with external business partners. Harari contends that any internal function not directly tied to the company's core competencies should be minimized and, if possible, outsourced to external suppliers whose own core competency is to perform that function. As Harari observes, "Outside vendors do it better and cheaper. The conventional thinking of vertical integration and 'keep it all under one roof' is being replaced by another philosophy, akin to: let's get ourselves lean, creative and flexible by keeping only what we do best and finding external partners who are experts in what we don't do best, so we can all work in collaboration for mutual benefit."(44)

As we will see in the chapter ahead, the competitive nature of today's American business marketplace underscores the need for security managers to seriously consider using external resources. This does not necessarily preclude an integration of both proprietary and external staffs. For some organizations, maintenance of a proprietary operation may be the best choice. The challenge is to confirm that proprietary operations are as streamlined as possible. Equally important, contracting out services is only valid if there are quality service-oriented suppliers. In some locales, this simply isn't the case.

Consideration #3

If you insist on keeping people who serve internal customers, then insist that they charge those internal customers for their services. In Chapter Five we looked at ways in which you, as a provider of internal services, can offset the associated expense by generating revenue complementary to the aims of your department's mission. For purposes of this discussion, however, Harari presents an interesting challenge. He suggests that accountants, trainers, maintenance engineers, etc., run their own profit centers with their own profit and loss statements. Allow them to charge internal customers at prevailing market rates. They should be allowed to sell their services to people outside the organization, he says. At the same time, however, break in-house monopolies by allowing internal customers to scan the marketplace to see if they can buy better services at better prices.

This idea is not as far-fetched as it seems. Several leading companies have already discovered the value of this approach. AT&T, for example, competitively bids its internal real estate management group's services against external competitors. The business unit manager decides if the real estate price and value offered by AT&T's proprietary staff is better than that which can be purchased in the open market. For the real estate management group this has meant winning some contracts and losing others. This approach is being tried within the ranks of internal security departments as well.

ELVIS IS ALIVE AND WELL
IN CORPORATE AMERICA

Mary Woodell of Anderson Consulting has created the acronym ELVIS to describe a troubling and disruptive phenomenon within many corporations today. ELVIS stands for Executive Level Vicious Infighting Syndrome. In keeping with the theme of this chapter, it's appropriate to briefly review Woodell's concerns about how ELVIS affects the asset protection manager's attempt to achieve a successful administration. In an article published for the American Management Association in January 1993, (45) Woodell explains that infighting is a reflection of human nature. It is born out of a struggle for ascendancy and power that emerges when two or more people are brought together. When department heads start infighting, it's easy for those around them to get sucked into the same vicious type of activity. Being responsible for the company's security department does not make one immune. It's important to recognize disruptive behavior because it can quickly sidetrack (and often derail) you from achieving the goals set forth in your mission statement.

Woodell explains that there are two broad categories of ELVIS. The first is the opportunistic ELVIS. This emerges when the company finds itself in a state of flux, brought on by any number of variables, including charges of criminal liability, bankruptcy, loss of assets, or unethical conduct. The opportunistic ELVIS generally engages those who want to divorce themselves from any accountability or suggestion of culpability.

The second broad category is the institutional ELVIS. This type of infighting is so endemic within the organization's culture that such phrases as "watch your back," or "careful, he's a back stabber" are commonplace. Such institutionalized infighting can be found at all levels of the organization and across business unit lines. Often the term "healthy competition" is used, but in reality, it is a euphemistic expression for underhanded and at times immoral behavior.

Despite the seriousness of her message, Woodell maintains a lighter side when she identifies the different types of ELVISs commonly found in American businesses. Among them are the hydra-headed ELVIS, the ELVIS A-Go-Go, and the retroactive ELVIS.

In the first case, the style of infighting is characteristic of a multi-headed monster, as each manager puts on a different face trying to deflect criticism or blame. Some will act with righteous indignation, while others react with outright delight at the misfortunes of others. Still, some will present a face of shock and horror, while many either attempt to hide or disavow any knowledge of a charge of wrongdoing.

ELVIS A-Go-Go generally results when there's a shakeup at the top of the organization and loyalties are reshuffled. I recall the case of one former security director who worked for an executive vice president of a large financial services company. The executive vice president had a great deal of disdain for another executive vice president and often used the director of security to make life difficult for the other. The security director took great delight in watching the executive squirm and dutifully reported the results of his actions to his boss.

One day the security director was asked to come to a meeting where it was announced that his boss had been forced to resign and that the other executive vice president had been promoted to the company's presidency. The security director, not missing an opportunity, immediately went up to the new president at the conclusion of the meeting, extended his hand to congratulate him, and said without skipping a beat, "I'm sure glad you're in charge now. You can't believe how bad I felt about all of the things that so and so made us do." You might recall at the beginning of this example, I used the word "former" to describe this security director.

The retroactive ELVIS emerges after a disaster or crisis strikes the organization and members of the management team rally around trying to resolve the situation. During this first phase of crisis management they pull together in a spirit of cooperation and resolution. Once the crisis has been resolved, however, the retroactive ELVIS begins affixing blame, as opposed to fixing the problem.

After a serious fire nearly destroyed the headquarters of a major corporation, several key executives from different business units worked together to restore operations as quickly as possible. To the surprise of many, particularly those in the investment community, the corporation was back on line in record time, and a potentially catastrophic economic loss was averted.

Once the round of congratulatory remarks had been made, the process of fixing blame began almost immediately. The security director blamed the safety director for not having an adequate fire evacuation plan. The safety director, in turn, blamed the facilities manager for failing to approve the installation of an adequate detection and suppression system. Similar infighting occurred when the human resources director began blaming the operations manager for failing to provide adequate staffing during critical business hours. The operations manager countered by blaming both the HR director and the security director for their failure to properly staff enough security officers to sufficiently handle the initial stages of the fire. Woodell notes that "whether chronic or episodic, ELVIS—like an oncoming train—frequently can be seen coming, which means you might consider getting off the tracks." (46)

She offers us several different ELVIS indicators. The first she calls the leading-indicator ELVIS—when the level of infighting gradually sneaks up, for example like some kind of unforeseen financial trouble. Her second indicator, termed the pernicious ELVIS, is manifested by infighting that is triggered by a specific event or situation. The third indicator, trickle-down ELVIS, is usually a reflection of individual personalities and management styles. The fourth is the kinder, gentler ELVIS, which is just as mean-spirited as the others, but is cloaked with the team spirit mask and interdepartmental rivalry. Woodell also says that there are ELVIS impersonators who, in an attempt to establish themselves high on the pecking order, find creative and sometimes surprising ways to advance themselves to the discredit of others. Finally, she describes the faux ELVIS, which is the outcome of gossip and rumors that are often deliberately planted in an effort to embarrass or discredit another.

Woodell concludes by suggesting that the successful manager is one who can not only see these indicators, but also adopt a management style that is intolerant of such activity. She offers five quick steps to avoid becoming part of the ELVIS team. First, she suggests standing up to ELVIS and recognizing the infighting factor. Second, lead by your good example. Third, pick your battles. Fourth, just say no. And finally, remember that ELVIS is a bottom-line issue.

SEEING THE HANDWRITING ON THE WALL

Just as Woodell explains that there are clear ELVIS indicators for those looking for them, managers who monitor their own style can see if they're on the path for success or not. On many occasions I've had security directors tell me that "they never saw it coming," referring to either a demotion or their requested resignation from the company. Unfortunately, often there is an actual brick wall that's plain and visible to anyone looking for it. If one is oblivious to the existence of the wall, however, it's understandable that they may not, in fact, see it. More importantly there are certain indicators that can send the security manager a clear message about the status of his programs and how his personal management style is being received.

- Management Signs
- Organizational Signs
- Budgetary Signs
- Personal Signs
- Exterior Signs.

Management Signs

Earlier, we discussed the concept of new team/old team membership. One of the clear signs for measuring the effectiveness of your program and management style is to ask if you are perceived as a member of the old or the new team. We found that if you are, in fact, part of the new team, that's a healthy indicator. Conversely, if there is a perception, rightly or wrongly, that you're a member of the old team, as we discovered, the options are fairly straightforward. You either change team membership or seek a career opportunity outside the organization.

A second management sign is the willingness of those around you to advocate on your behalf. Do you find that your employees speak with pride to other members of the organization about the added value associated with your programs? Does your boss push hard to gain acceptance of your programs? Do your contemporaries support you either in staff meetings or with other business unit managers? The level of support, or lack of it, is one of your strongest indicators, and yet, one that is most often overlooked.

Another management indicator is found within the company's rumor mill. While it is generally accepted that most rumors are groundless, staying tuned into what is currently being rumored can give you some indication how others perceive you within the organization. If you find that you're continually the subject of one rumor or another, this should suggest something to you, particularly if the rumors reflect your ascendancy within the organization—or your descendancy.

A fourth management sign that's reflective of Woodell's ELVIS typology is what I call "the duck and weave" style of management. I attended a meeting once with my boss and his boss. At one point the discussion turned to the considerable amount of infighting that was going on at the company. My boss's boss said, "If nothing else, we've become masters at ducking and weaving." On the surface this was somewhat humorous. On reflection, however, it became evident that while my boss's boss was ducking and weaving, he was leaving both my boss and myself exposed to a number of organizational punches to the face and body. When senior managers are engaging in ducking and weaving, there is little opportunity to advance programs and achieve satisfactory resolution.

Finally, when your manager and other department heads begin treating you differently, or engaging in what might be termed aberrant behavior toward you, this is a sign that suggests that your star may be falling. When you walk away from your boss asking yourself, "I wonder what he says about me when he is talking to his boss?" Or if you find that trusted colleagues don't return your telephone calls or have excuses not to attend your meetings, these are signs that your credibility is spiraling downward and probably out of control. Conversely, if you're being allowed greater autonomy in running your department and others seek both your advice and support on issues unrelated to security, then these are signs that you continue to maintain their respect and confidence.

Organizational Signs

When a company reorganizes, the clearest indicator of whether your programs and personal management style are highly valued or not depends on where you end up. If prior to the reorganization you reported to a senior level person, and now you find yourself reporting to someone one or two levels below, that should tell you that senior management does not consider your department as important as it had previously.

No matter the explanation, the end result can be a loss of influence and therefore an ability to directly control the outcome of your programs. Often security directors hear the argument that the reorganization was no reflection on them or their abilities. They will be told that the reorganization really entailed increased responsibilities on the security director's boss, who therefore had to pare down the number of direct reports in an effort to assume these new responsibilities. If your new reporting relationship is at a par equal to or greater than your former boss, it is a sign of organizational ascendancy. Unfortunately, security directors more often complain that the reorganization netted them a reporting relationship below their prior status.

The next organizational sign is circumvention. This occurs when one business unit or a group of managers deliberately attempts to circumvent the security department, arguing that the security director obstructs more often than assists them. Many security directors complain that they had no prior knowledge of or involvement in the introduction of a particular product or major construction project prior to its start. Consequently, project costs rise when the manager attempts to address the appropriate security concerns after the fact. As often happens, the appropriate security precautions and checks are neglected altogether because the program is too far downstream.

Circumvention is either a deliberate attempt to ignore the asset protection manager, or a consequence of benign neglect and organizational ignorance. If the security director has not been active in marketing both his services and the need for certain controls, business unit managers will often complain that the security head is not doing a sufficient job. Otherwise, they would have gladly built in security precautions as part of the planning process. Circumvention, then, is directly related to the director's ability to develop an effective marketing plan similar to what we discussed in Chapter Three.

The "Snicker Test"

As its name suggests, this activity is usually done behind the security director's back. It unfolds when a protection manager introduces a particular program or solicits other managers' input on an anticipated new project. After the security director presents the plan, some managers suggest that they take the program under consideration. Or, they may offer constructive criticism, make suggestions, or diabolically, in some cases, offer verbal support. After the security director has left, the manager snickers and says something like, "I wonder where this guy's coming from. He certainly doesn't understand the reality of this organization."

Back-stabbing is not only dangerous from an organizational perspective, but it also erodes the credibility of both the security director and the security program in general. Avoiding the snicker test is largely the obligation of the security director. To avoid falling victim to this management tactic, security decision-makers should first seek feedback and reactions from those within their own department, contemporaries (other security managers) from outside the organization, or even their own bosses. Whenever a new program that may be perceived as radical is advanced, the security director may want to actively send up a few "organizational balloons" to see how well they'll be accepted. This, too, can be accomplished by solicitation from within or outside the company, or by carefully advancing the idea to a few trusted department heads: "Say, I have an idea here that sounds a little bit off the wall, but I'd like to get your reaction. How do you think this would be met by the rest of the organization? Do you believe that this is too far-fetched and would actually be seen as something without merit? Or, do you think that others would view it as a value-added service?" A request like that is more likely to receive a direct and honest response. The solicited manager feels more free to render a candid opinion knowing that if the idea sounds questionable, their comments will not offend the security director.

Not Listening Intently

A security administrator told a group once that he had been operating under the impression, for some time, that those outside his immediate department had a great deal of respect for his ideas and, consequently, he enjoyed a significant level of credibility with them. He used to brag to his department and management staff that since he had come to this company, he never once had a program denied. Staff members in turn, he said, should take pride in their security department. A couple of weeks later one of his managers approached him and asked, "Do you think people are still taking you as seriously as when you first arrived?" The security administrator, somewhat puzzled, asked a question of his own, "Why do you ask that? What's the reason behind such a question?" The manager responded that he had attended several directors' meetings recently, and it was his observation that the people attending were not paying complete attention to him. He cited various examples of inattentive behavior at meetings, and was simply questioning the level of actual listening. The director found this observation troubling but also extremely insightful. He took this early warning sign to heart, recognizing that when people stop listening as intently to you as in the past, there is a suggestion that your importance, power, and influence are on the wane. Because of this conversation, he reassessed his own approach and made adjustments accordingly. To him, this observation by his subordinate was a necessary wake-up call to which he was indebted.

BUDGETARY SIGNS
Cost Centers Take the First Hit

Security, as a back office support unit function, is generally defined as a cost-center operation. By this we simply mean that the company spends money on the operation and does not, under normal circumstances, generate any type of revenue or profit from it (a profit center). For a security manager interested in measures of success, it must be understood that when hard times befall a corporation, cost centers typically are the first to be hit. After all, executive management rationalizes, controlling expenses usually means reducing cost center operations. It is better to live without a certain level of back office support than jeopardize profit centers designed to generate revenue. Security programs, and entire departments, are in jeopardy. According to Harari, such reduction in cost center management may be exactly what the organizational doctor ordered. Astute business managers will understand the opportunity when asked to reduce. They know well that performance will be awarded based on their contributions to maintaining the bottom line, as opposed to empire building, or expanding cost center operations.

Delaying New Programs

Waiting until the next fiscal year to initiate a new program does not necessarily guarantee success. As more emphasis is placed on competition, senior management typically takes a harder look with each passing year. Unless a compelling business case can be presented (reflecting both capital/operating budget requirements and near-term organizational value), more often than not, new programs will be delayed. This is especially true as the business cycle swings downward and any type of recession is either anticipated or experienced. A security manager who relies on a new program to measure success is running the fiscal risk of never having the program launched in the first place. Strategies for long-term success can, therefore, be in serious jeopardy.

Curtailment of Existing Programs

Just because a particular project is funded for the current fiscal year, there is no assurance that the program will ultimately transpire. As senior management reassesses profitability reports, cost center managers are often asked to either curtail or altogether eliminate existing programs. In the public sector, once a program has been approved, it is typically implemented. In the private sector this is not necessarily the case. For security administrators, especially those coming out of the public sector, what's important to realize is that existing programs are just as much in peril as new programs when economic times are hard.

Consolidation

Consolidation of services is the current way of corporate life. It is not uncommon to hear about entire levels of middle management getting eliminated as companies consolidate two or more departments under a single middle manager's control. Security departments are no exception. Many have been consolidated with facilities management or a collection of general services departments, including food services, reprographics, transportation services, and mail services. Still, for other organizations, consolidations have meant security merging with corporate safety and/or risk management. For others, consolidations with auditing, legal, and human resources have netted reductions in management expense and administrative overhead. In short, security directors who continue to specialize in asset protection may be limiting themselves to such a narrow field of expertise that they may be working themselves out of a job. Today, the successful manager demonstrates a breadth of management skills that can be applied across multidepartmental lines. It makes sense that senior management will look to those who demonstrate a broad-based skill set—the unit heads capable of managing a variety of tasks, leaving the technical aspects to be performed by line personnel or experienced third party partners.

PERSONAL SIGNS

When It Is No Longer Fun to Go to Work

Many books have been written (some of which are included in the bibliography) on the importance of maintaining a "fun" perspective about your job. Unless you believe that there is an intrinsic enjoyment that comes from working for your company, and that you generally welcome the opportunity to go to work each day, you will not be able to achieve the full potential of what you or your job has to offer. Unless you're having fun, the job will be a burden, and therefore, affect your overall morale. This, in turn, has a direct impact on the morale of those working for you, and is readily picked up by your contemporaries and senior management. When the job becomes drudgery, any creativity you might otherwise have had diminishes, and your overall effectiveness declines significantly.

This is not to suggest that there will never be dog days when you don't want to go to work. We all have down days. The point here is, however, that when depression sets in regularly, the notion of going to work can sometimes make you physically ill. Maintaining mental health is just as important as physical health when it comes to succeeding on the job. This can be particularly troublesome for a security director who's been given the responsibility of protecting both the assets and people of an organization.

Making Their Agenda Your Agenda

Commonly, when a security director begins administering an asset protection program, there is a tendency to introduce a variety of new agendas. Every new security head wants to make his mark. After all, he reasons, he's been hired to run the security program based on his new ideas and abilities. There is nothing wrong with this line of thinking, but beware of an inherent trap here.

If the security director's agenda is either contrary to or foreign to that of other business unit heads, support likely will be difficult to obtain—if not outright impossible. A technique I have found particularly successful is for the asset protection manager to approach business unit managers and ask them about their particular security concerns. I call this the "empty note pad" approach. It goes something like this: A targeted executive is contacted, generally through the secretary, for an appointment with the security administrator. At the time of the meeting, the executive will certainly question the nature of the meeting. For that matter, many will ask their secretaries to call ahead under the guise of preparing for the meeting. It's important for the security director to advise that the meeting's purpose is to solicit the manager's input, ideas, impressions, and concerns about security. At the meeting it's particularly important for the security director to walk in and simply say that he's looking for new ideas, new approaches, issues, and concerns that might be relevant to the business unit manager and unknown to the security director. At this point, and admittedly with some showmanship, it's particularly important for the security director to take out an empty pad and announce that he's there to solicit the manager's input with no preconceived ideas or strategies. Say that this is an opportunity for the business unit manager to tell the security director what is relevant to the unit's scope of responsibility. This approach may sound familiar because it also serves as a major marketing strategy for winning advocacy on new programs.

The Gunslinger

When I was growing up there was a favorite television western called, "Have Gun Will Travel." The show was built around the concept of a hired gun who was paid by a small town besieged with bad guys and in need of assistance. Invariably, each week's episode started off in a barber shop or in the back room of a bar with the city council huddled together, coming to grips with the fact that their town had been overrun by desperados.

In the next scene the townsfolk would realize that to rid the town of the bad guys, they needed their own good "bad guy"—Paladin. In the following scenes, Paladin would ride into town, confront the bad guys, and warn them if they weren't out of town by sunset, they would face his six shooter. Of course, each week the desperados ignored Paladin's warning and we'd watch the inevitable shootout on Main Street. Before long, the street would be littered with the bodies of desperados, and many times, unfortunately, innocent townspeople drawn into the crossfire. At the show's conclusion, Paladin rode off into the sunset, and townspeople emerged to clean up the mess.

Today, organizations in many ways mirror this classic TV show. New managers are brought in at the request of shareholders to rid the organization of the perceived bad guys. The new management team, the gunslingers, systematically go about their business of shooting the rascals under the guise of organizational turnaround, and then, within a fairly short time, they move on to their next assignment, leaving the organizational survivors to clean up the mess.

The message for a security director is to assess whether they are one of the gunslingers or one of the townsfolk. In either event, it's their obligation to assure that few, if any, innocent bystanders are caught in the crossfire. If they're successful, whether they opt to move on to the next challenge or stay, their legitimacy will remain intact; otherwise, they will be perceived as nothing more than a hired gun.

EXTERNAL SIGNS

When Recruiters Start Calling You

One sign of success is when your reputation begins to extend beyond your organizational limits. One note of caution, however, success is not measured on whether you receive such notice or not. It's merely one of many possible indicators. As people call, you should realize that your ideas and accomplishments are being recognized, and they're perceived as bringing added value.

Those who will call you most often are other security directors soliciting your feedback on programs and ideas that they're considering for their firm. Another group of people who call may be magazine editors or freelance writers seeking your ideas on an article they are writing. A third group of callers may be professional recruiters attempting to find out if you're interested in working for another organization. These people will have either heard about you by a direct referral, read about you in a magazine or newspaper article, or solicited you because of your position within an organization known for its successes.

You Feel Good About Your Professional Stature

When you begin to feel good about who you are and what you've accomplished, this is an indication of the degree of success you're having. While you may not have initiated many programs that have gained widespread recognition outside your company, you know yourself that you're bringing added value to the total organization. This can be supported by other department heads and letters of commendation from clients, vendors, members of the public, or senior management.

The Family

What happens in the office is commonly carried home with you. When you've had more successes than failures, both your body language and mental state are conveyed to those at home. Family members are quick to pick up when things are going well at the office and when they're not. As noted earlier, this isn't to suggest that everyone doesn't occasionally have a down day. When down days become the pattern, however, it's the family who can serve as a valuable source of feedback. We've all heard the adage, "Sometimes it's better to go home and just simply kick the dog" when things in the office are not going as well as we would like. Perhaps you should watch the dog's reaction the second time you come home when things haven't exactly gone your way. You're more likely to find the dog cowering in a corner, hiding behind the couch or under the bed. Whether we like to admit it or not, our attitude is displayed in both our physical actions and verbal comments.

CONCLUSION

As I said at the outset, this is my fun chapter. We began by looking at a series of twenty axioms that I've come to realize are not only true in the everyday life of a security manager, but can also serve as a set of strong indicators to measure one's level of success. We also had an opportunity to look at a number of principles offered by Ernie Lipple, that serve as a basic cornerstone for developing a successful security program. Next, we reviewed five strategies outlined by Jim Meisenheimer on how to out-perform your contemporaries to achieve the success that you desire.

We explored a rather light, but serious, discussion on corporate infighting written by Mary Woodell. As she termed it, ELVIS may be alive (and unfortunately) more well than we would care to have him in the halls of corporate America today. Finally, we looked at five indica-tors—or types of handwriting on the organizational wall that can help us measure how successful our programs and personal accomplish-ments are within that organization.

Thus far we have looked at a variety of success strategies ranging from developing an internal marketing program to availing ourselves of a variety of new management strategies, such as benchmarking and quality improvement programs. As we've learned in this chapter, there are some pragmatic strategies available to us as well. Each of the fore-going has helped to set the stage for still another major management tool, namely, the resources available to us from external sources.

7

Outsourcing—Your Strategic Partner

INTRODUCTION

As the 1990s unfold, the trend toward replacing a company's internal security force with one provided by a third party contract agency continues to grow. Today, the U.S. Department of Labor estimates that nearly 60 percent of all companies using security forces rely heavily, if not exclusively, on contract providers. How long will the trend continue? It depends on several factors, not the least of which is the contract industry's ability to rise to the new demands associated with strategic outsourcing.

In Chapter Five we introduced the concept of strategic partnering. We learned that it is one of many management tools used by decision-makers as a way of improving an organization's efficiency and effectiveness. The aim of this chapter is to examine in detail how security executives are coming to terms with this new concept and the more traditional approaches to outsourcing. Before doing so, however, it's important to note that while many security directors and owners of contract companies are beginning to talk about the value of strategic partnering, few are actually implementing such relationships. Some suppliers claim that their concern for quality service has lead to partnering alliances. In reality, this is more marketing hype than anything else. For the most part, none of the top twenty-five security companies in the United States today can be characterized as committed to strategic partnering. Most remain content with the more traditional approach to buyer/seller relationships that we will examine later in this chapter. Some of the reluctance is theirs, a great deal is not. Nevertheless, if the trend toward strategic outsourcing is to continue, both sides need to work out a plan to accomplish this new relationship.

If outsourcing was strictly based on achieving lower operating expense, the trend of displacing proprietary staffs would continue indefinitely. In reality though, healthy performance transcends solely economic profit-loss considerations. It also entails a myriad of legal, ethical, human resource, and other business issues. Each of these issues fuses to make the decision to use in-house staff or contract suppliers less than clear cut. While the debate continues, the evidence suggests that the answer does not come from whether a proprietary force is better than an outsourced staff or vice versa. The answer is found within the specific needs of a particular organization. What is best for one organization rests more with measurable business-related issues than with professional ideologies.

Historically, contract security officers were used instead of a proprietary staff as a direct means of controlling costs. Companies sought low-paid officers to act as night watchmen or guards with little understanding of the nature of asset protection. Today, many organizations are looking for more. As outsourcing has become a way of life for them in all sectors of their business, they need the assurance that their security provider is more than a risk buffer.

Other organizations have yet to fully accept the partnering relationship that mutually benefits both. They are willing, though, to establish preferred-vendor relationships with specific suppliers. Still others continue to look at security providers as little more than guard companies in business to help them keep the bad guys at bay—and then at the lowest possible cost.

In this chapter we are going to examine new and traditional approaches to the client-vendor relationship. The intent is not to endorse the use of contract staffing over a proprietary operation. As a valuable management tool, however, a security decision-maker should have a thorough working knowledge of outsourcing. We will look at strategic alliances as a way for both parties to share in the risks and rewards of asset protection. We will examine the business reasons for considering a contract supplier or using a proprietary staff. We will also review the downsides. Our analysis begins with a discussion of the myths surrounding the use of contract forces and the four distinct types of contractor-client relationships. As we move through this analysis, we'll look at what some third-party suppliers are doing to enhance their added value to their clients. We'll also look at what the industry is doing to actually distract from this contribution.

THE MYTHS

In January 1993, *Security Management* magazine published an article I wrote entitled "Contract Labor: The True Story," where I discussed three popular myths. A review here of these myths is appropriate since they often stand as obstacles to serious consideration of third party suppliers.

When the question comes up regarding the use of a proprietary versus contracted forces, security experts tend to define their positions along adversarial pro-con lines based largely on a number of myths. The consequence of such debates pits the merits of one against the other, spinning the dialogue into a highly emotional discussion. Often they focus on factors that may have been true once but are not necessarily so today; consequently, they miss considering the merits. The challenge is in the decision-maker's ability to determine whether having a proprietary or a contract force is most advantageous for their organization. Such appropriateness must be based on sound business principles that survive the scrutiny of those beyond the security department. The asset protection manager must clearly see the reasoning associated with using a proprietary force over a contractor.

The decision to employ a third-party or an in-house workforce should be based on economic imperatives, corporate culture, and operational synergy. Unfortunately, among security professionals I find that these three dynamics are often set aside for other sacred cows that cannot be justified with empirical data. This is particularly true for the proponents of proprietary operations who are quick to conclude that contract service is less than adequate because of three factors:

- Quality of the workforce
- Loyalty of the workforce, and
- Turnover of the workforce

Let's briefly examine each of these three myths.

Quality of the Workforce

I find the issue of quality particularly interesting since it assumes that there must be two or more labor pools to draw from. For proponents of proprietary workforces, the implication is that contractors somehow recruit from a less-qualified group. The fact is there is only one labor pool from which all employers choose. They obtain the quality they demand or can afford. To say that contractors use lower-paid, lesser-experienced staff as a matter of routine is to underplay the root cause for such usage. Contractors would rather pay their employees more; particularly when their billing rate—and therefore their profitability—is directly tied to an employee's base hourly compensation. Regrettably, organizations intent on lowering operating costs typically focus on labor costs and require lower-paid, lesser-experienced individuals. Not only is it unfair, but it borders on absurdity for a manager to ask for such employees and then claim that outsourcing provides a lower level of service due to inadequate staffing.

Generally speaking, it is fair to say that quality is linked to compensation. While exceptions can be found, experience has shown that as the compensation package goes up, the ability to draw quality performers goes up. As the adage goes, "You get what you pay for." Quality reflects what is prescribed and is not an inherent trait of one workforce over another.

There is always the exception to every situation or rule. Pay is not always directly related to performance. Many times you find an individual who is not motivated solely by compensation. In any size workforce, you are likely to find one person, or more, that looks for other motivators: an intrinsic work ethic, pride in a job well done, a desire to help others, or any other number of factors. There is the case of Ed C., for example.

Ed was a security officer for a large bank. He also happened to be a master silversmith. A former freedom fighter during World War II, his aim with a pistol was as accurate 40 years later as it was during the conflict. Ed had one of those personalities you immediately liked. Low key and unassuming, you knew he was more interested in helping someone else than he was in helping himself. A true gentleman.

He was a proprietary security officer for a large bank when the decision was made to convert the force to a contract supplier. He was given the opportunity to go with the contractor, although this meant that he would suffer a 30 percent pay cut. He chose to go with the contractor because he enjoyed being a security officer. For him, the pay was secondary.

Ed represents one of the few who seek other motivators. Even though compensation may not be the overwhelming reason most people seek a particular job, worker motivation seems to be correlated to the degree of base compensation. In other words, the higher the hourly rate, the more likely you will find a highly motivated workforce.

Loyalty of the Workforce

Like the issue of quality, the concept of loyalty is equally misrepresented. Whether an organization uses contract labor or not, loyalty is built on trust, acceptance, and integration. Each of these can be effectively administered without breaching the issue of joint employment. Astute security managers can provide opportunities for the supplier's employees to develop a strong identity with their client's organization.

Developing the loyalty of a contract employee is both easy and inexpensive. Here's a quick test to determine the level of success: When asked for whom do you work, does the contract employee say the client first or the contractor? Through a series of properly managed target incentives and activities, contract employees can develop a strong identity with the client organization and therefore a high level of loyalty.

Offering dinner certificates through the supplier to a medium-range restaurant (e.g., $35 for dinner for two) for completing a training program or recognizing a special anniversary or event, goes a long way. Want to go an extra step to secure a deeper sense of loyalty? Include an extra $15 to pay for the evening's baby-sitter. For $50 you've just created a very loyal individual. Similarly, tickets to sporting events for the officer and the officer's family are another inexpensive way of showing recognition beyond the typical lapel pins, certificates, and other awards offered by most contractors. Loyalty is directly related to an organization's willingness to include outsiders. If the corporate culture distances itself from vendor employees, then the blame lies squarely with the organization, not the contractor.

Turnover of the Workforce

Finally, there is the myth that security suppliers have a higher turnover rate. This apparently is not true. The 1992 National Private Security Officer Survey suggests turnover is less than 60 percent annually. Previously, estimates have ranged from 200 to 300 percent. Whatever the percentage used, turnover need not be an issue if the force is properly managed. Contract language can specify a turnover rate comparable to that experienced by the organization's own back-office support functions. Failure by the supplier to hold to a preset level (generally 35 percent annually after the first 60 days of operation) triggers a financial penalty. Conversely, if the supplier can hold turnover under the established rate, an appropriate incentive is paid.

The Economic Trap

Moving beyond the myths, there is another issue that surrounds the debate of proprietary versus contract labor forces, specifically, the issue of reduced operating expense. This deserves special attention since it is one of the driving forces behind many of today's conversions from in-house operations to outsourced agencies. It is not unusual for a conversion to a contract supplier to yield savings in excess of $1 million annually. Clearly, such conversions are strong arguments in favor of contract staffs. Yet, there is a catch.

Once the proprietary staff has been replaced, the new staff begins the climb up the compensation ladder. This means that for every year they are on the payroll, their salary will likely escalate at the rate of inflation. In four to five years they are above the midpoint of their original salary range. Since contractors typically tie together their total billing rate, incorporating their officers' salaries to inflation, it isn't long before the client could actually do better by replacing the contract staff with its own proprietary staff at a lower starting wage. The cycle begins again. Within another five years it will again be more economical to replace the proprietary staff with a contracted force. This is why the proprietary-contract phenomenon is so cyclical; the proverbial pendulum is always in operation. With each swing new variables arise, as we will see below, yet the basic pattern holds. If this is so, then, the logical question to ask is: Why convert? The answer lies in the fact that there are other things besides immediate economic gains to consider.

DEFINING OUTSOURCING— FOUR STRATEGIES

Today there are many different types of external sourcing. There is smart sourcing, multi-sourcing, co-sourcing, and outsourcing. We will only focus on the latter, which comprises four distinct strategies:

- The Traditional Vendor Relationship
- The Preferred Vendor Relationship
- The Strategic Partner Relationship
- The Strategic Alliance Relationship

The Traditional Vendor Relationship

In Chapter Five we discussed the Shamrock Organization concept. As part of that discussion we briefly looked at the use of contractors. Third party suppliers were mentioned as a critical variable because the core of professional workers rely on their technical expertise. The traditional vendor relationship, sometimes referred to as the "buyer-seller" relationship, is the most common type of arrangement—particularly in the security industry.

In this association, the external provider is cast into a subordinate role and the communication channel is largely one-way. The buyer (client) dictates terms and conditions and the seller (supplier) is expected to fall into line. The relationship is well defined within a passive context. The supplier has to continually react to the wants and needs of the client. Little opportunity exists for the third party to assist in the management or operational control of day to day affairs.

The vendors provide little added value since they are only an extension of an otherwise myopically defined security program. Traditional roles are performed—standing post, conducting prescribed rounds, and running errands. Another characteristic is the "closed book" approach to the bidding process. The vendor typically suspects that the client wants to hold their profit margin to the lowest possible level. They are very reluctant (and sometimes outright refuse), therefore, to open their books for inspection. Their suspicions may be well grounded; this type of relationship is often more adversarial than cooperative.

The buyer-seller relationship can only offer standard products and services. The security supplier may set a lower than desired billing rate in order to get the business. For them, the client may be a loss leader to gain a foothold into a certain market. Or, they will hope to use the name recognition of certain clients to influence other customers to contract their services. Either way, the total relationship suffers because the supplier becomes a reluctant party that doesn't want to spend more than it has to—it is already operating at or near a loss.

To control costs the vendor will offer only the usual and well-established services. They have no desire to develop new products or offer extended services since this may entail a developmental cost that may not be recaptured. For the client, this can be very frustrating because they may have special training needs or other requirements. The suppliers typically respond that the client pays for what he wants. Add-ons are an extra expense. In short, the relationship is primarily driven by price.

A final aspect of the buyer-seller relationship is the limited amount of communication between both parties. Previously we talked about the one-way nature of client-supplier communication channels. It is further limited by the amount of time spent communicating. The client will typically be satisfied with a minimum number of dealings with the supplier's account representative. Weekly status meetings are rare, often scheduled monthly or quarterly. More frequent communication is generally marked by the client complaining about some officer's failure or shortcoming, delayed billings, or other administrative snafus.

The traditional vendor relationship is still the norm in today's client-supplier relationships. Most security decision-makers are still driven by all of the wrong reasons. Their focus on price causes low wages with minimum benefits, if any at all. Staffing is held to a minimum and undue risk-taking is a de facto reality since adequate resourcing is often neglected in an effort to save money. These kinds of buyer-seller relationships promote the myths that devalue the use of external resources. An insidious situation—the client demands the low-road approach and the supplier acquiesces, complaining all the way.

The Preferred Vendor

The second type of outsourcing strategy is a preferred-vendor relationship. Here companies seek a supplier and assure them of a higher level relationship because of the vendor's reputation, pricing strategy, or another business reason. The preferred vendor earns some measure of trust based on previous experience or, quite often, a personal relationship. Regardless of the cause, the client wants a prolonged relationship and is willing to sign a multiyear contract. The preferred vendor is perceived as having added value. This may be because there is no in-house capability or the supplier is known for a particular service. Some organizations, for example, may want the supplier to provide a number of services. To this extent, larger suppliers such as Borg, Pinkerton, and Wackenhut have an advantage. Their sheer size and diversity of services allow them to provide domestic and international security, specialized investigations, and executive protection. Many smaller firms provide an equally qualified level of basic security service, but fall short due to their limited offerings.

The preferred vendor is expected to continually improve and develop (if not already on hand) various quality programs. First Security, a large regional company in the Northeast, offers a Quality First Focus Program. Many of their client associations are as preferred vendors because their longstanding relationships are nurtured by this program.

Situational Case # 22: The Quality First Program

The Quality First Program was begun in 1989 by First Security's founder, Bob Johnson. The program's aim is to keep First Security positioned as a New England-area leader that offers a variety of quality programs. Perhaps he best summarizes the thrust of the program himself: "Quality First Focus is not simply a project or a program of limited duration and scope, it is an embedded philosophy of our management culture and a permanent commitment and continuously developing and improving principal management objectives." The program cuts across all levels of the organization and extends into the client's environment. As part of the program, each manager, supervisor, officer and client representative is asked to provide their own definition of quality service. From there a consensus is developed that allows First Security, as a service provider, to custom tailor a quality-driven program for each client.

Unique to this program is First Security's commitment to providing each client with documented evidence of their performance successes and shortfalls that require responses from First Security's management. Also documented are quality improvement initiatives. They have developed internal standards and related measures for each aspect of their operations at the client location. This is supported by standing committees or councils at each level of the organization. Local managers report and present their findings at monthly meetings at the corporate office.

What is perhaps most interesting about First Security's approach was the timing of their initiative. In New England, 1989 was a time of economic downturn. First Security saw this as an opportunity to impress on their clients that through delivery of quality programs, the client could achieve higher value even when under pressure to reduce operating expenses. As Johnson notes, "Our continued and enhanced focus on quality service operations will assure our success even in these, what might be considered opportune times for intensified low-bid marginal quality competition. We have seen the reality of this statement in numerous instances where we have retained accounts who, in the midst of economically driven cost reduction efforts, have decided to continue our services even though in receipt of significantly lower bids. These decisions were clearly based upon their confidence in our ability to continue to provide quality service."

Such a statement reflects a preferred vendor-oriented company that is moving up to the next level of supplier-client relationship—the strategic partner.

Strategic Partner

In a partnership, the old adversarial style is clearly recognized as being ineffective. Developing a closer relationship is the norm. The supplier is involved in a multitude of tasks, including program design. The client recognizes that their core business interests allow them to provide less than half of the resources necessary to meet their asset protection needs.

Often a partnership relationship is confused with an alliance relationship, the highest form of client-supplier integration. A partnership is defined as the arrangement between two or more companies seeking a long-term working relationship that provides shared benefits to the mutual satisfaction of the parties in terms of creating value, long-term business growth, continual improvement, problem resolution, and information access. The similarities between a partner and a preferred vender are also similar and therefore confusing. This is because a partnership serves as the bridge between preferred vendor status and the strategic alliance.

With a partnership there is mutual respect based on a recognition that each has a core function uniquely its own. The client may be a manufacturer, a retailer, or a financial services company in need of asset protection. The security supplier, as a partner in the relationship, has a core competency of protecting the manufacturer's assets, the retailer's goods, and the banking center's securities. Together, their partnership ties the core competencies of each into an overall asset protection program.

The partnership is characterized by an open, sharing environment. As Alan Serbus, senior vice president for Continental Illinois Bank, notes: "You come to love them as your brother. Just as sometimes you want to strangle your brother, knowing all along you love him and can't live without him, so too, it is with a strong partner." This may be a little dramatic, but it underscores the intensity of the partnership relationship. It highlights a mutual need and dependency. Also underscored is another valued characteristic: the opportunity to engage in both formal and informal communications.

Within the partnership there are shared expectations. Each party shares responsibility for successes such as the resolution of a major fraud, a timely response to a life-threatening situation, or something as simple as a letter of commendation for a job well done. They also share the failures. Each works with the other to improve, learn from mistakes, and accept responsibility for failures or breakdowns. There are no pointing fingers.

The exchange of information becomes a valued resource. There is a recognition that through information sharing, better quality service is the logical outcome. Open communications allow for constructive differences of opinion. Whether the communication is in the form of a project status report or a more informal briefing, it is valued as a key resource to problem resolution.

One of the key differences between a buyer-seller or preferred vendor relationship and a strategic partnership is the implementation of world-class concepts. Both the client and the supplier are familiar with best-in-class practices and strive to meet them. Together, they realize that this can only be accomplished through mutual effort. These best-in-class practices may involve setting security policies and practices to be followed by employees or adherence by other contractors to strict specifications.

The partnership planning process is focused on long-range targets. The client may ask the contractor for a two- to three-year plan, complete with time and action plan. As part of this process, the supplier's capital budgets may have to be presented to a planning committee. This requires a higher-level manager than typically assigned to a customer account. To be successful, the supplier must provide a business-oriented manager, not just an operational supervisor or lead security officer.

Another key expectation is a dedication to continual improvement. As noted above, First Security is one of those firms that is transitioning from a preferred-vendor strategy to a partnership. As evidenced by their Quality First Focus program, this is more than a long-term commitment to quality improvement. For them, as with true partnering relationships, the concept of continual improvement is part of the corporate fabric. Likewise, in a partnership, traditional barriers between companies break down. The notion of co-employment becomes passé and each accepts a proportionate share of the responsibility for providing security services.

Other barriers to partnering include limits on financial record access. Each company needs to be sure that a certain profit margin is achieved. After all, if one of the partners starts acting like a reluctant warrior, the success of the mission will be jeopardized. Therefore, each should know the other's financial breaking point and support them to keep profit margins buoyed at a safe and reasonable level.

Situational Case #23: The Diebold Story

Strategic partners can be found in both the service and product sector. One such product company is Diebold Incorporated of Canton, Ohio. This 135-year-old security company is a leader in asset protection products. In 1993 their sales exceeded $620 million—a 15 percent increase over 1992. To service their customers more effectively they have developed a strategic alliance (discussed below) with IBM. They seek strategic partnerships with as many of their customers as possible.

To demonstrate their added value, they have developed a TQM program dedicated to delivering defect-free products and services on time. A Corporate Quality Council supports this mission by instituting quality measures, training, employee recognition programs, and publications based on the Juran Quality Improvement process.

Among a variety of service offerings, they have developed a Field Automated Control and Tracking System (FACTS) to monitor equipment performance, service calls, and service activity analyses. Moreover, they have started a customer response center and alert system. Supported by an 800-telephone number, the customer center is designed to provide rapid response to customer needs. The alert system tracks a customer's system when it is out of order. After it's down for four hours, a technical specialist is called in to aid the service team. After eight hours the customer's system is placed on a national alert system that triggers corporate-level resources to work on returning the system to full service as soon as possible.

Diebold equips field service personnel with hand-held computers tied to the company's national parts distribution center. These computers also keep technicians informed about up-to-the-minute announcements. With the hand-held computers, Diebold can track parts and replenish inventory automatically. Service reports for each site are made a part of the customer's history. Using a next-call system, the location of service personnel is easily identified and assignments are changed quickly to address high-priority situations.

Going one step further, Diebold allows their customers (partners) access to their Central Service Dispatch system via a Diebold terminal installed at the partner's location. Called DECAL (Diebold Electronic Customer Access Link), customers receive estimated and actual arrival times and service call completion information. Additionally, one can immediately access equipment lists by product ID, location, equipment type, and serial number.

To demonstrate their commitment to being a true business partner, Diebold developed a unique customer satisfaction guarantee that begins with the customer determining the level of satisfaction. If a customer is dissatisfied, Diebold will correct the problem to the customer's satisfaction and reimburse one month's service fee for the applicable equipment.

Diebold describes the way in which it works:

- The customer calls 1-800-DIEBOLD and says that they want to invoke the guarantee.
- After taking the necessary information regarding the customer and the nature of the dissatisfaction, sales and service personnel are instructed to work together to resolve the problem.
- The customer is then called to determine their satisfaction with the problem's resolution.
- If the customer is not satisfied, telemarketing may decide that the guarantee goes into effect. A check will be issued to the customer account for one month's service on the affected equipment.

This type of comprehensive service offering positions Diebold as a strong strategic partner.

Strategic Alliance

The highest form of outsourcing is the strategic alliance. Some progress has been made by a handful of contract security companies to develop alliances with a few clients. This number is not particularly surprising since the concept of strategic alliance is still fairly new. Very few inroads overall, however, have been made to date in the security industry. Nonetheless, it is important to analyze this form of outsourcing since many companies are developing these relationships for other back office support functions. It is only a matter of time before they begin looking to security managers for the same type of relationship. Many writers and practitioners define the strategic alliance as the way businesses will be routinely run before the end of the century. If so, now is the time to begin developing strategic alliance relationships, lest we find ourselves, as we have in the past, in another defensive position.

An alliance is different from the others described since the parties seek a cooperative arrangement to integrate commercial and technical aspects of their business. To add greater value than the sum of the individual parts, the relationship is long-range in scope and endorsed by each respective level of senior management. Each alliance partner recognizes the risks and opportunities of such a relationship, believing that in working together more stands to be gained than lost.

As the definition outlines, an alliance requires both companies to do more than lower barriers. Sometimes, there may be a need to open each other up for the good of the alliance. This means that a supplier trusts that the client is serious about helping them achieve profit margins and provide the highest quality service. Unfortunately, few are willing to risk such openness and demonstrate such trust, especially if the account is not a large one. Yet, herein lies the irony.

Alliances seek to provide reasonable profit margins. It is acknowledged that volume is not a true indicator of profitability. The alliance relationship discourages the supplier from engaging in loss-leader activities, with the knowledge that it is better for the third party to secure a reasonable margin than to take on a prestigious account based on the reputation of the client's name alone. A Fortune 100 company once sent a notice to its service providers demanding a 12 percent rebate on all contracts. They claimed that their reputation as a client alone meant as much as a 12 percent increase in market value for any contractor. When challenged to prove this, they said that one of their vendors told them that their sales increased 12 percent simply from having them as a customer. The Fortune 100 company, in turn, concluded that their name alone had a certain value to a vendor, therefore believing that any added sales monies should be shared. For the security provider, a 12 percent rebate meant the difference between a profitable account and a money-losing account. Although the account represented more than twelve hundred weekly hours of service, they told the Fortune 100 company that they intended to terminate the contract. At first, the client balked, but then they reluctantly backed away from the demand.

This example illustrates the importance of both parties understanding the needs of the other. While this was not an alliance relationship, the supplier understood the difference between profitable accounts and high-profile accounts. SpectaGuard Security, based in Philadelphia, takes this position with all of their accounts. As a company, they have established a set profit margin. They will open their books for any client and show exactly what that margin is and how it was determined. If the account does not meet certain criteria, SpectaGuard will not establish the relationship. They recognize that this corporate policy may result in lower total sales, but the financial caliber of retained accounts will be assured. This then extends to their ability to offer added services.

A strategic alliance is far more than shared profitability. This type of relationship opens the door for both the client and the contractor to assess other markets. The client will make introductions and engage in directed referrals, as will the supplier for the client. Together they understand that their relationship extends to other synergies. In this type of business arrangement, there is a high level of respect between senior managers. Each seeks out the other for ideas, new approaches, and true problem solving. By combining resources, they hope to realize a significant gain.

A strategic alliance is the end result of several other motivators. Both parties are intent on improving quality levels, reducing the client's overall supplier base, and using each other's people, money, and resources to achieve a common goal. At the root of the relationship is the recognition that the client cannot do everything themselves, particularly in these days of downsizing.

Strategic alliances are not limited to big companies using other big companies. For that matter, an alliance can be successful on a small-scale basis because each party realizes the needs and value of the other.

Success can only be achieved if senior level managers agree to pre-scribed goals and are willing to define the objectives of the alliance. Continual interaction is needed by way of established meetings and planning sessions. The strategic plan of each company must be inte-grated into the other.

A strategic alliance is characterized by the following elements:

- Resource sharing to maintain competitive edge opportunities for each within their respective marketplace.
- Integration of new visions that allow each to operate more efficiently and yield higher quality products and/or services.
- Development of world-class operations, assuring the highest level of customer satisfaction.
- Long-range stability by leveraging the resources of the other and establishing exclusivity arrangements.

Earlier we talked about the need for a paradigm shift when it comes to re-engineering your security department. Pursuing a strate-gic alliance is another challenge to traditional security approaches. Starting such a relationship requires another paradigm shift. The rela-tionship should be viewed by both parties in a new way. Cast aside notions of "business as usual" and assume a position of trust and confidence under the umbrella of enhanced quality service.

To better explain the concept of strategic alliances, John Englert, vice president of real estate for Kodak and noted strategic alliance expert, has developed a model based on the work of Prof. J.C. Hender-son at the Massachusetts Institute of Technology. (47) His model is divided into two aspects: The Alliance Context and the Alliance in Action. The former defines the alliance in terms of necessary predis-position on the client's part to engage in the alliance, both parties' com-mitment, and recognizable mutual benefits. Bringing the alliance to fore requires mutual dependencies, an organizational link, and knowledge sharing regarding internal processes. A brief word of explanation about each of these factors will help clarify what is needed to achieve a successful alliance.

ALLIANCE CONTEXT

Predisposition

The alliance must be based on trust and a willingness to work within the context of existing attitudes and assumptions. This doesn't mean that these attitudes and assumptions cannot be changed. Quite the contrary. Over time, it may well prove that the alliance itself is a catalyst for changing strongly held attitudes.

In the 1970s and early 1980s, Continental Illinois Bank held steadfast to the attitude that only by doing it themselves could they assure themselves that it would be done right. Regardless what "it" was, the bank's attitude strongly supported a proprietary perspective. With the conversion of the security workforce, employees and managers alike saw that quality of service could not only be maintained, but actually enhanced through the intervention of a third party. It was only after the initial conversion proved successful that a predisposition for the eventual acceptance of a strategic alliance relationship could evolve. We all know that trust is earned. It is based on the track record of both parties and results in personal relationships. These relationships can then be expanded and integrated into the company's competitive marketing strategy.

Commitment

To sustain the relationship, a commitment by both parties is necessary. This requires a common mind-set where goals are mutually developed and shared. This, in turn, allows both to equally negotiate solutions in areas where conflicts occur. Commitment also requires the development of incentives and a legally binding agreement. The incentives reinforce the structure of the goals and the contract clarifies expected benefits and identified shared goals. Note that Henderson and Englert both say that the contract, over time, usually becomes increasingly less specific but often serves as an important symbol.

Mutual Benefits

The alliance creates a synergy between the partners that allows benefits to accrue to both that would not otherwise be possible independently. A true alliance fosters an environment that promotes pooling talent and resources from each company. They share market knowledge and process information in a way that allows them to innovate. Conversely, an alliance creates a partnership for assuming greater risks. The shared risk is a mutual benefit that defuses negative impacts resulting from any one or more identified risks.

ALLIANCE IN ACTION
Mutual Dependencies

Moving from the world of ideas to the world of implementation, strategic alliances require certain skill sets and information resources from both parties. Each must have market knowledge, management skill sets, and experience. When combined, the partnership will be led along mutually developed strategies. Should errors occur, one's strength may offset the other's weakness. Should both miscalculate, however, the alliance will likely end. For both in the end, even this is positive.

Organizational Linkage

To bring the alliance into action requires a linkage of three facets: process integration, information integration, and social networks. *Process integration* is the intermixing of the partners' actions and activities. The client, for example, may allot the contractor a designated space designed to carry out the needs of the client—an office; an operations center with shower facilities and briefing/training room; and a central monitoring console. Process integration also embodies those functions associated with a supplier and client working together to develop the most effective overall approach to each assignment. Together they identify minimum staffing requirements and work toward balancing capital with operating procedures and practices.

Information integration refers to the exchange of data necessary to carry out the objectives of the alliance. Since the issue of co-employment is set aside under a strategic alliance, for example, development of post orders and directives can be generated on both sides to better equip security officers for handling specific incidents. Payroll and time-keeping information can be exchanged to provide more effective and comprehensive monitoring. Moreover, management planning can be enhanced with an exchange of information and perspectives from each party.

The organization is linked by the personal and *social relationships* that develop; they should be encouraged at all levels and reflect actual business processes essential to supporting the partnership between companies. From allowing the supplier to be part of intercompany athletic teams to cafeteria privileges, these networks may extend into day-to-day interactions involving meetings, planning sessions, or common office space. The key to success is the development of relationships tied directly to the actual business processes that are critical to the partnership.

Shared Knowledge

Keeping the alliance active requires an interchange, or sharing of knowledge about the cultural nuances of each organization. Included are corporate culture, the processes that support various functions, and any restrictions or limitations placed on either company. A security company intent on enforcing after-hours access control procedures needs to know if there are exceptions for certain organizational levels and what they are. Likewise, the security partner needs to generate reports that reflect the language of their client/partner. Banking partners may have different requirements than a property management company or a light manufacturer. It is incumbent on the security provider to ensure that the alliance partner understands the latest changes in law or judicial rulings that affect the control of people or assets. Similarly, changes in corporate policy need to flow naturally to the supplier-alliance partner just as they would for any other employee group.

Summary Table of Vendor Outsourcing

Having discussed each of the four strategies for outsourcing, the following table summarizes each major component within a client-supplier relationship and how it is manifested within each strategic approach.

CHARACTERISTIC	BUYER SELLER	PREFERRED VENDOR	STRATEGIC PARTNER	STRATEGIC ALLIANCE
RESPECT	LACKING	REQUIRED	CRITICAL	CRITICAL
TRUST	LACKING	REQUIRED	CRITICAL	CRITICAL
CONFIDENCE	LACKING	REQUIRED	CRITICAL	CRITICAL
COMMUNICATION	ONE WAY	TWO WAY	TWO WAY	INTERACTIVE
SR MANAGEMENT COMMITMENT	MINIMAL	DESIRABLE	REQUIRED	CRITICAL
RESOURCES	LIMITED	DESIRABLE	SHARED	SHARED
RISK/REWARDS	LACKING	LIMITED	SHARED	SHARED
STRATEGIC PLANNING	LACKING	LIMITED	REQUIRED	CRITICAL
POTENTIAL GROWTH	LACKING	LIMITED	DESIRABLE	SHARED
PROBLEM SOLVING	MINIMAL	LIMITED	REQUIRED	CRITICAL
ADDED VALUE	LACKING	DESIRABLE	REQUIRED	CRITICAL
QUALITY DRIVEN	MINIMAL	DESIRABLE	CRITICAL	CRITICAL
PROGRAM DESIGN	LACKING	MINIMAL	REQUIRED	CRITICAL
SHARED EXPECTATIONS	LACKING	MINIMAL	REQUIRED	CRITICAL
SHARED RESPONSIBILITY	LACKING	MINIMAL	REQUIRED	CRITICAL
BEST-IN-CLASS ORIENTATION	LACKING	DESIRABLE	REQUIRED	CRITICAL
PRICING ORIENTED	HEAVY	MEDIUM	MEDIUM	MINIMAL

BUSINESS REASONS FOR CONSIDERING OUTSOURCING

Despite the advantages of strategic partnering and alliances as a concept, both are some time off from becoming the norm. As noted earlier, the security industry is an evolving profession. Most current relationships are limited to buyer-seller arrangements. Some have ascended to the preferred-vendor status, however, in time the industry will grow and focus more on the higher relationships. The evolution, however, may be slower than needed. This is natural and should be resisted. The security industry, despite its current evolution, is a mature industry. As such, it is naturally slow to change. Dynamic industries realize much quicker new potentials and opportunities. The more mature the industry, the more difficult it is to embrace change—even if it is necessary.

Until then, the more pragmatic question is: "What needs to be done now?" Since most client-supplier relationships are defined within the scope of the buyer-seller relationship, our assessment will be based on this platform. We begin by asking a more basic question: "Is contract security appropriate for my organization?" You may argue that "It doesn't matter, I'm already using one." Regardless, whether your company uses a proprietary force exclusively, a contractor exclusively, or a combination of both, there are four basic criteria that set the stage for any business-oriented discussion on the use of external suppliers. Once these have been adequately assessed, all other business rationales follow.

THE FOUR-LEGGED STOOL

The decision to use contract labor requires the presence of four fundamental opportunities. To best illustrate the necessity of each, imagine a four-legged stool. Designed as a four-legged sitting instrument, it becomes difficult to maintain balance for a sustained period if one or more of the legs are missing. Similarly, for a successful contractual relationship to exist, each of these four "legs" must be present. Once one or more disappear, the time may be ripe for a change. This may be as simple as changing contractors, or it might involve conversion from an external workforce to an in-house staff.

Economic Gain

The first leg is the obvious economic gain to be achieved. To justify a true need for a third-party vendor, we must demonstrate that significant savings will be achieved. For large organizations this can mean more than $1 million in annual savings. For smaller companies, the value may be interpreted in terms of percent of net profit, added sales, manufactured units, and assets. Whatever measure is used, the significance should be apparent to everyone. We noted earlier that the use of contract workforces and in-house staffs is economically cyclical. Left to its own, as salaries (or billing rates) escalate, there will come a point where it is economically advantageous to make a change. Laws and other safeguards are in place that prohibit companies from making capricious decisions to change based solely on economics. Once that threshold approaches, however, serious consideration is in order.

Transfer of Risk

The second leg is the transference of risk. As with any other business decision, the cost of doing business involves accepting a certain level of nonreimbursable loss. Couple this with the associated insurance premiums, and the decision to pursue one course of action over another can be more than worthwhile. The business of asset protection is inherently risky—particularly when a security force is armed. Unfortunately, we live in a litigious world. Since security deals in the realm of people's rights, property protection, limiting access, and environmental safety, it is easy to fall victim to civil suits and cries of criminal negligence. The mere existence of these risks means an organization could incur large costs either defending or insuring against such actions. Consequently, any time exposure can be shifted wholly or partially away from the organization, while keeping security's overall aims, it is prudent to consider it.

Security is characterized by the courts as a nondelegable duty, meaning that the organization cannot transfer its duty to provide a safe and secure environment wholesale to a third party. The company is obligated to meet its duty directly. An arm's length relationship can be developed, however. This allows a company to shift a considerable portion of its financial burden onto another party by way of contractual language that creates a hold-harmless and indemnification obligation on one party for the other. Under a buyer-seller relationship or preferred-vendor agreement, this arm's length relationship can be sustained. Under a strategic partnership or strategic alliance the issue becomes cloudy. The former two can be constructed to avoid claims of co-employment. The latter two encourages an active interaction, thus bringing into question the matter of joint employment. Although contractual language can be developed that differentiates a supplier's employees from those of the client, the courts may view the active interface as an extension of the client's employment responsibilities.

Assuring Quality Service

The third factor is the issue of quality service. The decision to make a change should be based on the assurance that the quality service is not going to be lessened. There should be real evidence to suggest that the change will enhance the quality of service. This is one of the most sensitive issues in the decision-making process and by far the most subjective. Empirical measures are available, however, that can bring a high degree of objectivity and independence to the process.

Quality service means several things. First, quality depends on education and basic skill levels. These include the ability to respond and adequately handle a multitude of life-threatening situations, in addition to customer relations and employee interactions. Second, quality service involves both verbal and written communication skills. Powers of observation and discretionary decision-making are intricately involved, as are common sense and the ability to follow orders under stressful situations. Throughout this book we have discussed the issue of quality because it is one of the highest concerns for American businesses today. Without assurances that quality will be maintained or improved, a decision to change should be weighed carefully, if not rejected altogether.

Increasing Management Flexibility

The final leg is management flexibility. Like quality service, this, too, can be subjective and difficult to empirically defend. Criteria are available, however, to objectively measure the degree of flexibility achieved. As either a condition of an existing agreement or past practice, for example, security personnel may be able to pick their assignments and shifts. This can have a direct and overburdening impact on management's ability to provide adequate and qualified staffing at lesser desired posts or unpopular shifts.

At times, other rules and requirements may directly conflict with such an arrangement. Hiring requirements may require a balanced mix of employees based on race or sex on a shift basis. Practices or agreements that allow senior employees to draw preferred assignments can inadvertently create discriminatory practices, the onus of which falls on management. Several other issues are incorporated in this last criteria. Among them are hiring and supervisory practices, promotions, demotions, and related disciplinary actions, training, assignments, and scheduling. A decision to convert from a proprietary force to a contracted force obligates the supplier to meet these operational issues, thus freeing management to pursue other business interests. Conversely, a decision to move from a contract relationship to an in-house operation means that management must be willing to deal with each of these issues directly.

With the advent of Equal Employment Opportunity legislation, Affirmative Action, the American Disabilities Act, and union requirements, the ability to manage personnel matters with any degree of flexibility is constantly shrinking. By shifting personnel matters such as recruitment, discipline, and separations to an outside source, more time can be allocated to the core constituency staff for other security functions. Experience shows that as much as 10 percent of an entire staff's time can be redirected. This simply means that projects currently on hold and otherwise beyond the reach of the staff can now be accessed.

These then are the four legs:

- Economic Gain
- Improved Quality of Service
- Transference of Risk
- Management Flexibility

OTHER BUSINESS REASONS
FOR OUTSOURCING

One of the earliest to take the concept of outsourcing to its furthest extent is Continental Illinois Bank (now in merger talks with San Francisco based bank of America). This large Midwestern financial institution once ranked among the top 10 until its near collapse in the early 1980s. As part of its reorganization, it began to look for smarter ways to conduct its business and control expenses. One strategy was to outsource support functions.

Outsourcing began with the conversion of its security force in 1985. In direct response to runaway labor costs out of line with the marketplace and restricted management flexibility, the idea to convert to a unionized contract force was born. The net result was an increase in quality performance and a million dollars in annual savings. The bank was also able to transfer a part of the risk associated with an armed security force.

When the new chairman saw the reductions in operating expense, he encouraged the expanded use of outsourcing. Soon food services was converted (at its height, Continental Bank was the largest daily food server in Chicago). This was followed by a conversion of the entire legal staff. New ground was then broken when they converted their entire computer operations department. The properties management function was also converted and security was transferred to the third party supplier of facilities services.

For Continental Illinois, outsourcing was the result of pushing the organization into a new way of doing business. By reducing corporate staff, new ideas and approaches could be aimed at enhancing efficiencies and effectiveness. The idea of outsourcing entire back office operations requires a change in mind-set—a true paradigm shift.

The Continental Illinois experience also shows that costs can be lowered when you charge all expenses back to the requesting unit. Departments will be more selective in their requests and not call for unnecessary service. As Serbus notes, "After the successful conversion of the guard force and food services, managers found that the company had not faltered. This created a platform for other conversions. After that, there was never any assumption other than it could be done, and it could be done successfully. The only question to be asked was: 'Who do we turn to as a provider? With whom do we feel comfortable as our provider?' The result has been one of the most comprehensive, extensive outsourcing programs in corporate America. Serbus makes several noteworthy observations about choosing a provider:

- Look for a provider who has an attitude and aspirations that you can work with.
- Look for someone who has been around for a while, someone with an established local office. Just because they are a national firm doesn't mean they are experienced in your marketplace.
- Outsourcing requires a certain leap of faith. You must recognize that in dealing with third-party relationships, especially those based on strategic partnering, there are few established rules.
- Volume levels can provide greater economies and therefore better position an outside supplier than an in-house operation. Pricing incentives, discounted rates, and caps can hold costs in line.
- Since all expenses should ultimately flow to the business unit, outsourcing can better reflect a variable cost structure. To be effective, this may mean allowing the supplier to make fiduciary decisions. As a means of control, however, appropriate check points may be required, such as weekly status meetings and/or monthly reports.
- Outsourcing requires centralized accountability for determining end-user limits and requests. Left unchecked, the internal customer can easily go around the process, especially in a decentralized organizational environment.
- Outsourcing requires patience and understanding. Former employees may initially believe that they want to join the contractor's ranks only to discover that the fit is wrong. This is not the supplier's fault. Similarly, the service provider may not bring the right people into your organization 100 percent of the time. The process of outsourcing requires a certain degree of trial and error.

Continental Illinois is not alone in its widespread use of third party suppliers. The Travelers Insurance Company, AT&T, and IBM are other prime examples. Travelers notes that outsourcing is sometimes confused with *out-tasking*, which is a mild form of outsourcing that does not necessarily require the displacement of an entire workforce. Out-tasking generally refers to the use of third-party vendors for specific tasks or series of tasks. You may elect to outsource a particular investigation or type of investigation, for example, due to location and degree of complexity. Or, you may be responsible for the organization's disaster recovery and business resumption program and need a level of expertise beyond that of your staff. These types of specific tasks can be contracted out. They generally have a designated beginning and end unlike true outsourcing, which is designed to provide ongoing daily service.

Englert and Henderson join with Tomasko in noting that today we are discovering many more business-based reasons to consider outsourcing:

- A desire to ally with a recognized world-class partner. The security industry now surpasses $40 billion annually, and as with nearly every other sector of the business community, it is a global industry. Foreign companies have made inroads into the American marketplace just as our own companies have penetrated their arena. New levels of competition arise and recognition follows that some companies are considered the global standard. Outsourcing allows individual companies to take advantage of this competition to assure that they are getting the best value for their dollar.
- Possible access to other markets by leveraging your relationship with the external provider. Drawing on the resources of an external partner, a company can take advantage of security organizations who may have made inroads into former inaccessible markets. This is particularly true when dealing with a security firm owned by a non-U.S.–based company.
- A realization that no one company can truly do everything themselves. In the past, many companies believed that only they knew

what was best for themselves and therefore had to do everything themselves. The end result was the creation of their own investigative services operation, guard operations, and security systems design unit. This resulted in internal competition for scarce resources. Support units competed with one another as opposed to working together for the common good. Outsourcing allows a more equitable distribution of resources.

- Use of another company's money and resources. Often this is one of the most overlooked advantages to any outsourcing endeavor. Money paid in wages and related benefits, along with expenses associated with training, uniforming, vehicle leasing, and occupancy can be diverted or defrayed. Monthly invoicing can give a company more extended use of its own money.

- A realization that the work to be performed is not critical to the competitive success of the company. Businesses need to maximize their efficiency by focusing on their own core competencies. Bankers should focus on financial services, retailers should focus on selling activities, and manufacturers need to concentrate on production. By directing valued resources away from these core activities, the company becomes less efficient. They are not as effective in meeting their asset protection requirements as a company whose core business is security.

- A favorable market exists to supply the services. A need or strong desire to use a third-party supplier does not necessarily mean a company ought to outsource. Not all security companies are equal in their ability to meet the needs of every business. Even companies with offices scattered across the country cannot guarantee every need will be met in every locale.

- The company stands to gain more than it risks. Security has been determined by the courts to be a nondelegable duty for a company. No company can ever totally transfer to a third party its responsibility to provide a safe and secure environment. Even so, it can mitigate the likelihood of absorbing 100 percent of the liability costs by using an external partner. Outsourcing can be an effective way to lessen the risk.

- The work to be performed is temporary or cyclical. Many times a need arises requiring skills that may not be available within the security department such as a special type of investigation or training in workplace violence or drug abuse recognition. These skills can be acquired through a contractual relationship with an external provider. Similarly, design assistance may be necessary for installation of a new security system or extra help needed for a specific event such as a corporate outing, board meeting, or public event sponsored by the company. These one-time or infrequent events warrant outsourcing as opposed to retention of a full-time resident staff.
- The company can manage the external relationship. Just as there is a need to conduct a cost analysis to determine economic value and market analysis to ascertain the capabilities of vendors, there is also a need to conduct a management analysis. Outsourcing the security function is only successful when there is an internal accountability established to manage the external relationship. Many managers believe that they can off-load the responsibility for asset protection to a third-party supplier. While it may be reasonable to pass along the daily operation of security, there is still the need to oversee the supplier. This assures that the core values and aims of the company are properly addressed. Absent this, outsourcing can be tantamount to corporate Russian roulette, only in this game the chamber has three bullets instead of one.

THE DOWNSIDE OF OUTSOURCING

Training and Promotions: Proprietary security departments typically do a much better job of training both the asset protection staff and other employees. They can often draw on the support of their company's human resource department or other corporate-sponsored programs. Moreover, it is not unusual to find a resident training specialist within a proprietary security operation.

Similarly, I have found they do a far better job with performance evaluations and have clearly articulated criteria for promotions. Most contract agencies spend little time training their management staff on how to properly identify and promote leaders. Typically, the person with the most seniority is promoted. For an account with high turnover, this is particularly disturbing since the most tenured person may have less than two years' experience and suddenly be promoted to a level of considerable responsibility. Promotional exams are rare in the contract industry.

Corporate Acceptance: Proprietary staffs tend to be more in tune with other corporate units. Business unit managers are more apt to look to an internal operation for advice and assistance. Regardless of how well the contractor attempts to integrate their security operation into the client's, there is a natural resistance. The "we-they" syndrome is invariably an operational stumbling block for the supplier. On whole, in-house staffs have the advantage for meeting a broader set of operational needs.

The Potential for Overbilling: Lacking proper automated systems and staff support, third-party suppliers can overbill by as much as 10 percent due to human error and/or failure to provide adequate information for proper processing. The answer lies in choosing a contractor with a proven system in place. But this may be easier said than done. Overbilling can occur for a variety of reasons. Account managers may create ghost billings to hide a deficiency in staffing caused by their own inability to maintain a preapproved turnover level. Or they innocently overbill because they are not diligent in tracking their own employees' time. One officer may check-in and be assigned to a remote location, for example. The officer will then leave for several hours or go home knowing that inadequate supervision means he likely will never be discovered. Meanwhile, the account manager bills the officer's time, assuming the officer worked a full shift.

Contractors May Misrepresent Their Real Capabilities: Some companies say that they are fully insured to the level required by the client. They produce certificates of insurance showing a level of coverage in excess of the requirement. For the unsuspecting security manager, the certificate may not accurately reflect the true value of the coverage. For example, some say that they have more than $25 million in coverage for general commercial liability or for errors and omissions insurance. In fact, they may have an umbrella policy that on the surface seems adequate, but in reality is limited.

Similarly, contractors may not have the amount of staff previously reported. Relying on part-timers or occasional staff, they can lead a security manager to believe that they are larger, and therefore capable of meeting call-up requirements, when in fact they cannot. In the discussion that follows on contractual agreements, there is mention of "shortfalls," "shortfills," and "double banking." These terms, borrowed from the Standard Government Contract for Canadian Contract Services, speak to other misrepresentations or unacceptable staffing practices that need to be addressed by the astute business-oriented security manager.

Lack of Qualified Suppliers: Many security providers promote themselves as "can do" suppliers. They contend that they can provide security for just about any type of organization and point to their diverse client base as proof. In their attempt to be the jacks-of-all-trades, they often diminish their effectiveness and, therefore, the quality of service they provide. Many national and large regional companies present themselves as being able to meet your particular needs since they provide a like service in another part of the country. Their marketing objective is for you to consider them viable in your area since they say it is not difficult to open a branch near you. In either case, there is a significant trap. Proven local management is the key to any successful outsourcing relationship. When assisting clients in the selection of a qualified contractor, I use a weighted average, ranking local management as the highest. While there may be several legitimate reasons to consider establishing yourself as a test site for a contractor, it's you, the decision-maker, that will be held accountable for the success or failure of the experiment. Typically, most organizations do not want to be on the leading edge of a service-related opportunity. Rather, they want proven track records. Given the nature of your business and your location, there simply may not be a qualified provider in your area. Although there are more than six thousand guard companies in the United States, not every locale is covered and certainly not every type of business can be served.

Acquisition Mania: Another drawback to finding qualified contract security providers is the result of what I call "acquisition mania." Mergers and acquisitions are commonplace in the private sector. Security suppliers are no exception. The firm your company contracts with today may not be the same tomorrow. Ironically, the acquiring company may have been one that you rejected previously. This may mean another change or a reluctant willingness to allow the new supplier to take over the account.

Only within the recent past have security company owners wanted to actually reinvest in their own companies. Many are merely in the business for the profit. More than once contractors have confided that their primary aim is to build their account base to a certain level and then sell it to the first bidder. This type of profiteering not only fosters unprofessional management, but also plays directly into the widespread instability of smaller guard companies.

Dual Masters: The biblical adage that says no man can serve two masters has equal relevance when considering an external supplier. A good contract requires that vendors meet prescribed callbacks within specified periods. Depending on the size of your account, you may or may not receive the level of service you expect in case of an emergency. Larger, more valued accounts will receive priority service. If you are a smaller account, your needs may not be met in a timely manner.

As an offset, for security managers charged with the responsibility of what might be considered a small account (less than 400 hours per week of coverage), consider the concept of shared resourcing. By joining with other organizations to form a consortium, you can achieve not only a volume-based discounted rate, but also gain more attention and services from the contractor. Recently, in Washington, D.C., five Class A multi-tenant high-rises merged their security programs to create one larger program. Each property was owned by a different corporation. By joining together under a single supplier, however, individual costs were reduced while each site was assured of dedicated on-site management and more interactive training. The smallest property with eight security officers could demand the same service as the largest property with thirty-seven officers. Instead of bidding on five separate contracts, the supplier provided a dedicated workforce that could be cross-trained and assigned as needs warranted. Each property had an equal voice in operational issues, especially as they applied to their own circumstances. The supplier found this relationship advantageous as well since it reduced overhead and allowed them a singular source to direct staffing and related operations.

Assuring a True Hold Harmless and Indemnification: Even when an organization believes it has the appropriate level of coverage, there is no absolute guarantee. What if a legal settlement exceeds the insured amount? Can you recover by going after the contractor's asset base? Often the contractor is protected by limits on liability. Even then, there is little an organization can do if the contractor files bankruptcy and walks away—something more common than is widely believed.

Equally troubling is the relationship between the supplier and their underwriter. Just because an organization has a hold-harmless and indemnification clause, there is no assurance of financial protection. Once a significant claim has been filed against the contractor's insurance carrier, the carrier will likely attempt to show a joint-employment relationship in an effort to disallow the indemnification and/or hold-harmless clauses. The client must be well versed in how to be a contract administrator and not a contract manager. This is a very important issue that should be reviewed closely by corporate counsel. A resident staff certainly places accountability and liability squarely with the organization when things go awry. Using a third-party provider to mitigate liability is possible, provided it is managed with tight contractual language. If your corporate culture does not allow considerable latitude for discretionary decision-making by outsiders, a proprietary force is far more beneficial. Similarly, unless your company is large enough to be self-insured, fidelity bonding requirements may preclude the use of contract labor when dealing with highly valued commodities or securities.

The Survival Factor: Last, but far from least, is the issue of those employees who are not outsourced. While there is little the contractor can do to lessen how others feel about their introduction into the organization, your management will need to address this phenomenon directly and forthrightly. Employees need to know the reasons behind the change and be assured that their safety and well-being will be protected. Equally important, they need to be assured that their jobs are secure. If this isn't so, the organization needs to be up-front and honest with employees. Today's employees don't necessarily view long-term relationships with organizations as a major priority. What they value more is an employer who is fair, up-front, and honest in dealing with them. Sadly, I find many senior management teams incapable of dealing adeptly with this issue. The consequence has been lawsuits filed by employee groups, a sudden run-up in stress-related disabilities, and large-scale employee turnover.

To ease the sting of conversion, some organizations have sought to have a mix of proprietary and contract officers. If your company is considering such a move, one critical variable needs to be addressed. There should be uniform standards—the same hiring, training, management, and performance requirements should be followed for both forces. Failure to do so places the organization at risk. If there is a difference, employees protected by the lesser group could claim unequal security coverage and challenge their protection on the grounds that the organization knowingly allowed a double standard to exist. Again, this is an issue warranting legal review.

If senior management is inexperienced in dealing with displacement issues and their impact on those who survived the conversion, retention of a proprietary force may be more favorable. Given the level of uncertainty and impact on morale, without proper handling, productivity can suffer, litigation can result, and credibility can be damaged.

DEMONSTRATING ADDED VALUE

As noted earlier, many security company owners are committed to bringing added value to their clients. They recognize that part of their success depends on the degree of perceived value they bring to the total company. Security decision-makers need more than just guards on duty. For many external security providers this is proving to be both a challenging and exciting expectation. For purposes of this discussion I've chosen three service companies that are doing something to demonstrate their worthiness to partner with their clients—a national company, a large regional firm, and a small security organization. My purpose in choosing each is to illustrate that company size does not need to be an obstacle to success. Each is headed by an individual with proven professional experience.

The Pinkerton Story

In 1988 California Plant Protection (CPP) took the security industry by surprise by purchasing Pinkerton Security and Investigation Services. Since then, under the direction of Tom Wathen, Pinkerton has expanded into new markets across the United States and several other major countries around the globe. Today, this nearly billion-dollar company is one of the largest and most well-known private security companies in the world.

With other acquisitions under their belt, Pinkerton offers one of the most extensive service offerings of any security company. This is advantageous because they can legitimately position themselves with a client as a full-service security provider. With services ranging from consulting to systems design to guard services, they offer a full complement of investigative services ranging from background checks to the most sensitive inquiries. Pinkerton also has expanded beyond the service sector, offering products that include one of the industry's most respected honesty testing screening tools. Other products include training materials for clients, model operating procedures, and model bid specifications for guard service.

Besides positioning themselves as a turnkey provider, Pinkerton takes pride in their management academy. One of the few such programs in the security profession, Wathen believes it is the oldest, dating back to when it was offered by CPP. "We began this program when my operations manager, Minot Dotson, began offering it to our field service representatives out of the trunk of his car. He would circulate among them, making sure that they understood the basics of good account management." (48) Today, under the Pinkerton banner, the program is a formalized three-week course of study. The company dedicates a full training facility to the program and candidates are prescreened. "Not everyone makes the cut," Wathen adds, noting that selection to attend is something earned by the manager.

Another unique characteristic of Pinkerton is their commitment to quality. Though some of their competitors are also committed to quality, for Wathen, the quality manager is an integral part of the overall senior management team. He notes that the quality manager's office is located right next to the chairman's by design. While other companies seat the head of operations, personnel or finance in a similar position, for Pinkerton, the message is strongly seen and heard by virtue of the office's proximity to the ultimate decision-maker—the CEO. For clients, this is a strong selling point, especially in today's quality-driven climate.

The company is also one of the very few to work with several of their clients in developing tailor-made TQM programs. At AT&T, Pinkerton developed one of the security industry's first programs. The impact of this program has been felt in many sectors of the AT&T organization. So much so, that other departments look to security as a model for their own needs. Similarly, Pinkerton actively embraced the need to develop quality programs for Solectron in Milpitas, California. This small high-tech firm was awarded the Baldrige Award in 1992 for their commitment to quality customer service. As a part of Solectron's success, the security manager developed a Baldrige-process program with Pinkerton's assistance for internal customers. This same idea was later carried over to another Pinkerton client, AMP Inc. of Harrisburg, Pennsylvania. AMP is the world's largest electronic connector company, with sales six times greater than their nearest competitor and operations in 32 countries.

Another value-added contribution developed by Pinkerton is their automated inter-branch network. For clients, this is seen primarily as a scheduling tool. In truth it is much more. Known as PARS for Personnel Automated Reporting System, it is a computerized payroll and personnel assignment system that matches their employees' qualifications with the needs of the client. It assures that only those possessing certain skills are assigned to specific accounts. Individual training accomplishments are tracked with the system and it serves as a master personnel administration file for management. PARS also tracks security-related incidents and generates trend analysis reports and other management decision-making tools. Through its corporate-wide interconnectivity, PARS allows even the remotest branches to communicate with and draw upon the resources of other Pinkerton branches across the company's network.

The sheer size of Pinkerton allows for volume buying without loss of quality. From uniforms to automobile leases, the vastness of the company means they can offer their services at highly competitive rates without affecting the individual officer's compensation. Profit margins can be squeezed tighter without impairing the branch manager's incentive because there is more room for negotiation. Setting price aside, Pinkerton's volumes allow the client to receive greater value through increased insurance levels, broader benefits for officers, and access to other markets. For Pinkerton, size has its advantage. They can outgun the competition in many areas. Even so, the smart client isn't going to make a final decision based solely on cost or Pinkerton's vast offerings. Clients want qualified local managers committed to taking care of them. That's where Pinkerton's management development program is critical. As Wathen notes, "If the area manager can demonstrate business know-how and has the basic management ability, they will win relation-ships. Everything else Pinkerton has to offer is really for our account managers. If they can show the client that they care and have access to all we have here at corporate to support them, Pinkerton should be around for some time."(49)

Wathen says that, as an industry, security companies are prone to respond to weak specifications offered by potential clients. This serves only to prevent many companies from offering truly quality-driven pro-grams. Trying to win the contract at any price, these companies put undue burdens on others. By being willing to bid on less than definitive specifications, they often force a low-bid situation. This, in turn, only exacerbates an otherwise frustrating situation because low-bidding only reinforces the stereotype of an industry driven by low cost and low quality. Wathen concludes that the single greatest challenge facing third-party suppliers is a willingness to set standards and accept the responsibility of policing themselves before they are forced to do so by outsiders who may not understand the nuances of the profession. I agree.

The SpectaGuard Story

Without a doubt, a strong argument can be made for considering a national company for your outside business partner. But an equally strong argument can be made for considering a strong regional supplier. One such company is Philadelphia-based SpectaGuard, a privately held company affiliated with the SpectaCor Company. SpectaCor's business largely focuses on arena management; they own and/or operate some of the country's largest sports and entertainment arenas. As an outgrowth of this business, they formed a proprietary security company to offer security service at many arenas. Since its formation, however, Specta-Guard has become a major regional security provider along the North-east corridor, competing with not only the major nationals, but also several well-established local companies.

SpectaGuard is a unique regionally based security provider, offer-ing both quality-driven programs and local hands-on management. Contrary to many regionals who have attempted to demonstrate an increase in annual sales, SpectaGuard recently took a different approach. "We are not intent on being the biggest, we just want to be the best," says SpectaGuard's president, Bill Whitmore. As a demonstration of their commitment, they recently analyzed each of their accounts and examined both residual value and profit margin. They then defined what they believed to be a reasonable market value for each of their clients and defined a profit margin aimed at meeting business objectives. Clients that fell outside established parameters were notified and given the opportunity to respond. This type of vendor-directed approach allowed them to tell their clients that they place a value on the relationship and expect that basic business principles are met in order to sustain an ongoing partnership. The net effect was the loss of several accounts. Whitmore notes, however, "We claim to be a quality-driven company. If so, how can we maintain that quality if we are expected to perform at a level below what it takes to produce that quality. For us, it simply didn't make sense. Rather, we want our clients to be proud of our service. In order to achieve that, we had to make some hard business decisions. Simply put, there's a cost associated with quality. We don't want to be known as just another 'also ran.' We want our clients to take pride in the relationship they have with us. To do so means cutting away those accounts, regardless of the name of the client, that work against our ability to maintain quality service. In short, we'd rather be known as the best supplier in our marketplace, not the biggest."(50)

This type of attitude exemplifies the challenge most national companies face today. A well-managed regional will do well in the bidding process, even against the largest suppliers if they can demonstrate an ability to provide local quality management. Just as Pinkerton's Wathen notes, in the final analysis, the truest test is local management. Whitmore would no doubt agree.

SpectaGuard separates itself in many other ways. They have developed an interactive Quality Audit program that is used as a basis for improving specific client performance and identifying new approaches for other accounts. This program takes seven months to complete and is applied to all current accounts. It begins with the identification of an audit team consisting of at least one senior manager from the home office's quality assurance and training department. A set of standards is first identified for each account, followed by a questionnaire to each account representative and a site visit.

The questionnaire asks for a rating of the service provided and dedicates a section to suggested improvements. The on-site visit is operationally oriented, consisting of a review of SpectaGuard's files, post orders, and a formal face-to-face with the client's representative. What typically emerges is an evaluation of how well the local management team is doing in meeting the client's expectations. The audit serves as the backbone for future improvements that can be applied across as many accounts as possible.

SpectaGuard also takes pride in its computer-based training program. The results to date have been a key factor in their overall success. Having spent more than $500,000 to develop the program, it is broken into three segments. The first, Pro Step I, focuses on basic security operations required of all officers. The second, Pro Step II, is industry specific, meaning that an officer assigned to a health-care client is trained in the specifics associated with a medical facility. Similarly, retail assignments have retail-specific training and financial services have their own training program. In this way the client is assured that the officer receives the basic training necessary to address the particularities of their profession. The final phase, Pro Step III, is designed to meet specialized areas, including hazardous material training, handling infectious people or materials, nuclear site security, explosive ordinance disposal, etc.

The computerized training is more than an officer interacting with a specific training program in front of a PC. The program is designed to test the officer's knowledge of a specific topic. If the officer fails to answer correctly, the program forces the student to return to that specific section for material review. Unlike other programs that allow officers to seek the correct answer and continue, SpectaGuard's program tallies the number of times an officer misses a specific question and adjusts the final score accordingly.

Once the officer misses one question, he or she can never obtain a perfect score. Their final correct answers represent a cumulative score and a final grade is awarded. Even though the officer may eventually get every answer correct, a separate score is maintained that identifies potential weak areas that need to be specifically monitored by the officer's supervisor. Most other programs allow the officer to repeat wrongly answered questions over and over until the correct answer is given. In this way, they can claim that their officers received perfect scores. For SpectaGuard, this is deceptive and does not advance the real issue of ultimately assuring quality service.

Another program is their three-part Guarantee Plan that involves three client-directed assurances. First, SpectaGuard's corporate management visits each site at least twice a month. The company goal is at least three such visits; however, if they fail to meet a minimum of two monthly visits, the client is reimbursed for one full-day's service. As Whitmore notes, for their larger clients, this could mean as much as $15,000. Second, client telephone calls are promised to be returned by the close of the business day. Finally, SpectaGuard pays for any false alarm that they monitor. This assures the client that SpectaGuard will maintain their equipment in proper working order and respond with qualified officers.

Whitmore argues strongly for the regional approach, citing several advantages. He contends that a regional company can more tightly focus on the client relationship since the owners have more at stake than a national firm. A regional company is quicker to respond to a client's needs since there is less bureaucracy and a greater likelihood that the supplier's senior management has more knowledge of the local market and its resources (e.g., law enforcement, other businesses, and local government officials). This, in turn, creates a stronger partnership with clients. He believes that well-managed regional companies consistently display a stronger can-do attitude.

Wathen, by comparison, might agree. He says that a major challenge facing his senior management team is the development of programs that keep his local managers sufficiently motivated. As with any large organization, unless continually nurtured, there is a tendency for field operations to lose sight of and identification with corporate goals.

Whitmore also believes that a strong, professionally oriented regional company places more emphasis on tenure and can provide a better career path for aspiring employees. He also believes that regionals, unlike smaller local firms, are less likely to be bought out and can therefore provide more assurance to their client base that they will be around for the duration of the contract. This may or may not be so. Given the current merger mania that is widespread across all of America, Whitmore's point is not to be taken lightly. In general, regionals tend to become megaregionals rather than a part of a larger national firm.

Whitmore offers a few insights into why many suppliers fall short of the mark in providing true professional service. He contends that contractors are short-sighted when it comes to their own financial thinking. Like Wathen, Whitmore believes that most of today's contractors opt to low-bid the competition instead of presenting their true costs and profit margin. In an effort to win, they sacrifice an ability to offer quality workers and service. Although they may be offered more contracts, these suppliers are soon having trouble pleasing their clients. The end result is that they soon lose the assignment and the industry takes another jab to the chin.

Whitmore additionally believes that most national companies suffer from an inability to be long-range thinkers due to their public status. By this he means that there is the ongoing pressure to appease stockholders each quarter. Driven by the need to show continuous profitability to hold the value of the stock, Whitmore says that the publicly traded companies put an undue burden on local managers to win contracts. A boomerang effect occurs insofar as local managers accept contracts outside of their specialty just to show a positive earnings stream. Since most regionals are privately held, they can afford to be more selective, thereby assuring more personalized attention to their clients. The challenge for those within the publicly traded sector is to develop a long-range business plan that stretches beyond the traditional quarterly framework for measuring success. Such non-security giants as IBM, RJR-Nabisco, Chrysler, and Kodak have proven the validity of such an approach.

Whitmore makes three additional observations. First, security companies need to break away from the low-wage, no-benefits mentality. Wathen agrees. Security suppliers who continue to purport that wage and benefits have little impact on productivity are simply missing the point. Of the more than 500 companies I have reviewed over the past 15 years, there is a consistent lack of sustained quality performance associated with those who offer low wages and little or no benefits. Granted there are exceptions, but as a group, those who concentrate on low labor costs tend to offer the least to their clients. Unfortunately, these companies still tend to win more than their share of the business because of most clients' shortsightedness.

This leads to Whitmore's next point—most security suppliers are reluctant to push their clients in a positive way to improve the lot of the security personnel assigned to their location. He cites cold lobbies as an excellent example. Property managers intent on reducing operating expense opt to shut off the heat in their lobbies during nonbusiness hours. Officers are forced to wear heavy coats or huddle in front of space heaters. The client then complains that the officer does not present a professional image.

My personal favorite is the client who clears a space in the boiler room or basement, calls it the security office, and then has the nerve to complain that security is less than professional. What do they expect? I've often suggested that management move their office to a similar spot then report to me on how professional they feel. It constantly amazes me how many security suppliers roll over on this issue, lamenting that they are powerless. Let me ask, how many auditing departments, human resource departments, or food service managers are subjected to similar abuse? Until more security providers are willing to demand better working conditions for their employees and clients are willing to respond, the issue of quality service will remain largely an academic discussion.

Finally, Whitmore concludes with a somewhat Zen perspective by saying, "It is the wise person who bears the end in mind." Security decision-makers ultimately hold the key to their own success. By bearing in mind the desired end result, the manager and supplier can define what is ultimately judged a quality-oriented program. This requires a focus on the longer range ideal and a willingness to work through near-term shortcomings.

The Arko Executive Services Story

So far we have looked at a large national company and a regional supplier. What set them apart is their willingness and foresight to break away from their contemporaries. Let there be no mistake, both are not without their critics. Neither is close to being perfect. The same can probably be said for our last example, Arko Executive Services. Located in Atlanta, Georgia, this company has one additional office in Denver, Colorado. With less than $10 million in annual sales, this company would be classified as a small security company. Its approach to business, however, is remarkably similar to the big guys, largely owing to its founder and current president, Bob Arko. He has more than 30 years experience in the security industry, having held senior management positions with two large national firms. His experience is the result of having learned the business as he rose through the ranks. In other words, Arko knows what drives a client.

He emphasizes bringing highly qualified business managers into the security profession. His own acumen drives him to understand that clients need more than a business partner willing to provide guard service. Through personal commitment to providing quality customer service, he has established one of the country's most comprehensive private security libraries, and he makes it available to his clients at no cost. This extensive facility houses a wide assortment of periodicals, texts, studies, and papers. Training videos and other media are also available to teach his clients and employees about the latest issues in asset protection.

Because his business is small, Arko emphasizes the personal touch. For his clients, he personally assures that Arko places client concerns squarely in the president's office. His personal reputation is at stake. He can't hide behind the screen of "well, you know it's those guys at corporate...." For Arko, small means being effective and taking responsibility for your company's work product. By taking this position, Arko offers stiff competition to the larger security companies. As he says, "Sometimes I feel like David going against Goliath. It can be intimidating at first, but then I remember that it was David who won."

Like Wathen and Whitmore, Arko, too, believes that success is directly tied to local management. With more than 160 combined years of management experience surrounding him, he is careful to point out that small companies need to have breadth of experience to assure competitiveness. Many security expert wannabes attempt to make their marks as local entrepreneurs, offering a variety of security services. Some emphasize a particular minority advantage with hopes of gaining an inside edge. In the final analysis, though, it is a local company like Arko's that sustains many challenges because of their commitment to quality service.

Arko's success is rooted in his own business knowledge. Having been affiliated with the majors, he understands how the business ought to be run and the weaknesses of his big time competitors. For him, quality is directly tied to three variables: 1) Make a promise and deliver, 2) Move fast, and 3) Think like the big boys. This last point is particularly crucial since it allows him to anticipate how they will respond to a particular request for proposal and then posture his company similarly. It also allows him to think of ways that he, too, can demonstrate added value. Making his library available is only one such technique. Arko also provides consulting services when he knows that he will not be competitive in a bidding process for security officer services. He has borrowed management techniques from outside the security service to improve his own ability to stay informed. Using a method known as the 5-15 Report, he requires his staff to fill out daily reports that take less than five minutes to read and analyze and take less than 15 minutes to complete. This allows him to stay in touch with every aspect of his business without creating an overwhelming burden on the executive staff.

Arko believes that demonstrating technical proficiency means more than field experience. He pushes every staff member to complete a level of academic excellence, including achieving the security industry's Certified Protection Professional (CPP) program. Besides having six certified administrative staff members, another nine have either a bachelor's or master's degree. While the CPP has its critics, Arko's point is that clients want to know that their property and assets are in the hands of professionals. The CPP designation is one way of demonstrating such competency. This is particularly insightful since most other professions are now developing similar certification programs, including financial services, retailing, property management, data processing, and engineering.

Taking full advantage of commercially available desktop publishing programs, Arko can generate professional documents on a par with his regional and national counterparts. This allows him to remain competitive throughout the proposal process and gain entry when other small firms are excluded. He also relies on his experience to define certain jobs as something other than a traditional security officer, thus lowering his insurance costs and making his bid more competitive without loss of quality service or lowering wages and benefits. He can directly pass the savings on to his client, thus giving him an inside advantage over his larger competitors.

Due to the size of his company, Arko can assure his clients that every officer will be evaluated once a month. He takes pride in likening his company to a jack rabbit—able to respond rapidly and decisively, something most larger companies cannot claim. He cautions, however, that many small companies tend to overextend themselves. To secure higher profits, there is always the temptation to take on accounts that are out of the reach of a small company. Arko's experience has taught him to avoid such traps.

CONCLUSION

In sum, there is no one answer. The decision to use a smaller company over a larger, international firm depends on the perceptions of each client. Operating expense, quality of service, management flexibility, and liability depend on the security company's culture and business aims. Choosing the most appropriate provider can only be defined within this context.

As noted at the outset, outsourcing is a critical tool for today's success-oriented manager. In a world of downsizing and searches for more effective resource utilization, consideration of external partners is essential. As we have seen, however, it is not a simple process. Outsourcing has its myths, not the least of which are questions of worker loyalty, unacceptable turnover rates, and reliance on lower caliber workforces. As a strategy, there is typically one of four approaches available. Your measure of success depends on determining which one is best for your organizational needs. We've learned that outsourcing is an evolving management approach running from a traditional buyer-seller relationship to one that very few security managers are trying—strategic alliances.

There are many proven business reasons for considering the use of a third-party supplier, ranging from an ability to draw on a broader scope of resources to more efficient cash flow management. We also learned that like any other tool, there are downside risks, including effectively integrating two cultures into one and the possibility of a supplier overstating their capabilities.

Finally, we examined three current suppliers and their approach to helping organizations with security-related issues. A large national company, a regional company, and a small local concern were chosen to illustrate that size is not necessarily a deciding variable in making the correct selection. The true value of a supplier is rooted in their ability to deliver quality services that complement your organization's needs. These three represent what I call the new breed. With experienced and dynamic leaders, each company has committed itself to professional standards and serves as an example of what the industry has to offer.

8

In Pursuit of Excellence

INTRODUCTION

Security is a non-codified industry. Unlike rules governing fire and safety professions where one finds a plethora of local ordinances and state mandates, there are no comprehensive laws covering the security profession. Today there are still more than a dozen states that do not regulate private security services. Despite past and current attempts to pass national standards—which have been and continue to be operationally impotent—the United States remains behind Australia, nearly all of Europe, most of Latin America, and the Far East in regulating the security guard industry. Given the high military presence in third world countries, even the cynic could rightfully claim that the United States is behind most in prescribing rules of conduct for private security workforces.

The purpose of this chapter is to define the current state of private security's quality performance standards. Operating largely in an unregulated environment, legal, ethical, and smart business practices should compel us to police ourselves and establish appropriate guidelines. Even if the current effort to introduce nationally legislated standards succeeds, we will still have a long way to go. Below we will discuss what is commonly known as the Martinez bill and briefly compare it to laws in other countries. We will also examine three other alternatives that not only drive current efforts to upgrade officer performance, but will likely remain the driving forces over the next several years.

I hope that by concluding this book with such a discussion, security decision-makers will take note that their individual success is grounded on assuring high standards. One theme has remained consistent over the course of this text, namely, organizational success is linked more to business management practices than to the technical aspects of asset protection. These management practices are deeply rooted in quality performance standards. Without them, there is no excellence. It's as simple as that.

"Standards" vs. "standards"

Before beginning our discussion it is important to clearly define what I mean by standards. Unfortunately there are standards with a small *s* and there are Standards with a capital *S*. The difference is critical since many organizations assume that because they have taken the time to articulate standards for themselves that they, therefore, have Standards. This is not necessarily so. They may have defined criteria for their company to follow, but these are not Standards. To have Standards, one must follow a set of criteria that has universal acceptance. These Standards are easily recognized and rarely subject to debate—unless someone is attempting to define a new Standard.

Take for example my model contract in Appendix A. Prior to its introduction there was a "Standard" guard contract written many years ago by an attorney for a third party supplier that over time became universally accepted. The contract has become so commonplace that today one can go into many business supply outlets and purchase a copy. The Model Contract also included here, on the other hand, is emerging as the new Standard. It was written from the purchaser's perspective and offers a number of performance criteria not found in the conventional guard contract. Even though each of the top 10 service providers and literally dozens of smaller firms do not present it as their contract when asked, they all operate under it because of their clients' counteroffer of it as the agreement they wish to govern the relationship. Given its broad appeal, many professional writers and corporate security administrators have adopted it. In time, it will likely become the new Standard.

Another example is known as ISO 9000. Sponsored by the International Standards Organization, ISO 9000 lists detailed criteria for many products and services. It has become the European Standard for excellence and commonality and is being widely adopted by American firms. ISO 9000 is also becoming the Standard for most other countries as they attempt to position themselves in the global community. In the U.S. there is also the U.L. Standard, or the Underwriters Laboratory sign of approval. Other Standards include those developed by federal agencies such as the Food and Drug Administration (FDA), the Department of Alcohol, Tobacco and Firearms (ATF), the Department of Defense (DOD), and the American National Standards Institute (ANSI) which is widely used by computer users, manufacturers, and banking organizations to develop and publish industry standards ranging from data proessing and encryption to product development and protection.

Standards, with the capital S, serve as the basis for establishing quality performance. They define minimums and set expectations. They also underscore basic assumptions. Lacking such a solid foundation, it is easy to understand why so many so-called security programs fall short of the mark. The absence of universally recognized minimums is clearly holding the security industry back. The Safe Streets Act of 1968 created basic standards for law enforcement. Born out of the President's Crime Commission recommendations on how to improve law enforcement, this act set forth basic criteria for the hiring, training, and equipping of police agencies. That was nearly thirty years ago. Yet, today, the private security industry finds it difficult to get legislation passed for even the slightest baseline performance criteria.

THE GORE AND MARTINEZ BILLS

In 1991 Al Gore, as a senator, introduced Senate Bill 1258 (51). This proposed legislation was later killed for lack of support and objection from a variety of lobbying groups, not the least of which were from the police lobby. Its defeat was largely the result of political infighting by vested interests. Nonetheless, it was an attempt to introduce the most basic hiring and training standards for the security industry. In 1992 Representative Martinez from California sponsored H.R. 5931 (52). Like the Gore Bill, this legislation also called for minimum hiring and training requirements.

Known as the Security Officers Quality Assurance Act of 1992, the Act is based on nine points:

- Rapid growth within the industry,
- Opportunity for employment for entry level applicants,
- A demand for qualified, well-trained security officers,
- Allowances so employers can screen applicants,
- New-hire training requirements,
- State requirements vary widely,
- Public safety would be improved if appropriate screening and training were required,
- States should enact regulations imposing minimum standards that are the same nationwide for screening and training, and
- "State security officer regulation should apply to all security personnel whether employed by security contractors or other employers."

The last point is a direct quotation from the bill because I want to underscore its significance. If passed, it will have a profound impact on the industry. Note that it says: "whether employed by security contractors or other employers." Any organization employing their own proprietary security workforce will be obligated to adhere to these same standards—a radical departure from all previously proposed legislation. It drives the concept of hiring and training Standards across the entire business and governmental sector. Anyone employed for the purpose of providing asset protection will be required to meet basic requirements.

In essence this seems like an excellent bill, but it is also a potential political bombshell. The Martinez Bill was drafted by the contract security industry; the last principle is self-serving. The implication is that organizations will opt to outsource their security workforce to the "experts" as opposed to incurring the added burden of assuring that every officer hired and trained is according to regulatory mandates. In truth, however, if the bill is passed as is, the total impact will likely be negligible at first because the Standards are so minimal. The real test will come when new and more stringent regulations are added. The adage "beware of letting the camel gets its nose under the tent" comes to mind. Once passed, the likelihood that more rules and requirements will be needed, with their associated costs, is great.

But is this all bad in the long run? Certainly proponents of strategic partnering and alliances would strongly argue in favor of the bill. They would say such a move is consistent with sound business practices. Others would say that the need for Standards is overdue and that there should not be a double standard—one for contract providers and one for proprietary staffs. For both reasons, I agree that some form of the Martinez Bill should be passed.

Note, I say that "some form." I have trouble with many proposed sections because they fail to go far enough. (I suppose that in a former life, I may have been a very large camel.) Since the purpose of this chapter is not to debate this piece of legislation, I will not enumerate my concerns. I do believe the bill needs more teeth if we hope to take a serious bite out of the current levels of neglect, dereliction, and incompetence often found in our industry's hiring and training practices. As we shall discuss below, companies of all sizes are currently requiring their security business partners to provide two to four times the initial and annual number of training hours than what is being proposed. Requiring a minimum of eight hours of initial training, four hours of on-the-job training, and four hours of annual training is woefully insufficient. By comparison, the New York Security Guard Act of 1992 requires eight hours of initial preassignment training and forty hours of on-the-job training—ten times more than that required by the Martinez Bill.

Equally disturbing is the lack of attention given to business asset protection techniques and customer service. Neither is even addressed in the proposed bill, yet both are critical components of any private security program. The bottom line is straightforward: this type of Standards setting is fairly impotent.

Many states are now beginning to address this issue from a variety of directions. In California, for example, Assembly Bill 508 (53), passed in 1993, is directly targeted at the health-care industry. It requires hospitals to provide a security staff, train all emergency and trauma department personnel in security topics, and provide specific training to security personnel in emergency room conditions such as the characteristics of aggressive and violent patients and victims. The law also covers:

- Obtaining patient histories from those with violent behaviors,
- Verbal and physical maneuvers to diffuse and avoid violent behavior,
- Restraining techniques and strategies to avoid physical harm,
- Appropriate use of medications as chemical restraints, and
- Critical incident debriefing and available employee assistance programs.

These types of minimum requirements put organizations on notice that security-related issues are serious business. Failure to adequately address them will have equally serious consequences. Despite the fact that eighteen states have yet to even address the issue of security standards, there is a clear indication that many others are ahead of the nation at-large (54).

As a minimum, it seems to me, any attempt to legislate Standards nationally should begin with stipulating levels of performance commensurate with the risk at hand. While such a level may be debatable, few would disagree that eight hours of classroom training designed to cover more than a dozen topics is inadequate. Unless more is required, I fear what remains are only political rhetoric and public policy.

THREE ALTERNATIVES

If national and local regulations fall short, what then can be done to assure the establishment and adherence to quality performance? It appears that there are three forces at work to fill part of the void:

- Judicial decisions,
- Establishment of measurable performance criteria that are directly tied to merit raises, management incentives, and disincentives, and
- Strategic quality management.

Since the previous chapters provided a detailed discussion of the latter, we will concentrate essentially on the first two in this list.

Alternative #1: Judicial Decision-Making

Lacking mandated Standards, the courts have taken an active role in enforcing accountability measures, particularly in the area of premises liability. Forensic consultant Chris McGoey notes that the first major award for an inadequate security claim was reported in 1965 for $25,000. By 1982, the average jury award involving inadequate or negligent security had risen to $921,696 (55). Today, it is not unusual to find jury awards exceeding $2 million.

An Ohio jury awarded $2.1 million against the owners of a previously crime-free parking lot because of negligent security (56). In another case, a New York City jury awarded a teacher $5.2 million when a security guard allowed the brother of a reprimanded seventh grader to go directly to the teacher's classroom (57). The award was based on the resultant injuries received from an assault by the brother. The legal ruling was predicated on negligent security. In Beaumont, Texas, a jury awarded a store clerk more than $16 million after she was raped twice in one week. The store owner didn't do anything between the two incidents. The jury rejected the notion that not enough time had elapsed, citing that at the very least, management could have temporarily transferred her after the initial assault (58).

These examples, and dozens like them, are commonplace. They underscore the fact that if management does not establish a clearly defined security program and enforce it, then the courts will hold them financially, and in some cases, criminally liable. The end result is de facto establishment of security performance Standards. Another way of viewing this is to say that if owners and their agents (managers) are not going to establish criteria, then the courts will.

Unfortunately such an approach is far from perfect. Because there is no uniformity among various judicial entities, inconsistent approaches prevail. On one hand, the courts are demanding basic rules to allow more judicious decision-making. On the other hand, absent such criteria, they are left to their own interpretations. Over time, however, courts will create an umbrella for basic Standards simply because with each ruling, they are currently constructing such an envelope. The question that remains is whether such judicial "Standard setting" will ultimately be in the interests of everyone. Reasonableness, though the objective of each court review, is not always so clearly achieved.

As an illustration, two court decisions handed down in 1993 by the State of California will both no doubt affect the issues of premises liability and inadequate security. The first, *Nola M. v. University of Southern California* (59) involved the case of a woman who was raped while en route to the school's credit union. She filed suit based on inadequate security. The second, *Ann M. v. Pacific Plaza Shopping Center* (60), was likewise a charge of negligent security after the plaintiff was raped shortly after opening a photo processing store in the center.

In both cases the plaintiffs and their experts contended that the owners should have provided better security measures, including the presence of officers. In the first case the court reaffirmed the notion that liability can only be assessed when there is a direct link between the injury and an owner's lack of providing "reasonable" security. Citing several previous decisions, they challenged the notion that security programs and the extent of their effectiveness should be left to the opinion of so-called experts (which, it is reasonable to conclude incorporates both consultants and security managers). Rather, they conclude that effective crime prevention must be tied to some measurable factor. If it cannot, then it is at best an "opinion" and therefore not particularly binding on a landlord or its agent.

In the second case, the state Supreme Court reversed a former landmark ruling (*Mervyn Isaacs et al., v. Huntington Memorial Hospital, et al.*). In *Ann M.* the court essentially held that the landlord's duty to provide security guards is limited to either prior similar acts on the property or the surrounding area. Under the *Isaacs* ruling, property owners were obligated to assume a duty based, in part, on the foreseeability of a particular crime. In doing so, they were required to develop security programs accordingly. In other words, anticipate what likely could occur if improper or inadequate measures were not instituted. There, the court defined a new Standard, saying that there must, in fact, be evidence of prior similar acts.

These types of judicial rulings underscore our contention that they are defining the umbrella of Standards. The courts and juries are attempting to define what is reasonable and what should have been an appropriate security program prior to any given incident. If left on their own, judges and juries will define boundaries. The real question is whether security decision-makers, and those whose interests they represent, will find this acceptable. Unless the security industry takes a more active role in defining what should be sound asset protection strategies, they will be forced to live with the outcome determined by others.

Alternative #2: Establishment of Measurable Performance Criteria

Judicial rulings set a much needed framework for establishing what should be considered a reasonable Standard. But they cannot be expected to engage in definitive operational measures. This burden must be placed elsewhere. As we have seen above, legislatures and city councils do not appear ready to seriously assume this responsibility, either. The onus, therefore, falls directly where it should be in the first place—on the security decision-maker and corresponding executive management team. Lacking prescribed Standards, those responsible for asset protection can take solace in establishing moral, ethical, and legally prescribed practices that reflect a commitment to quality customer service. This, then, is the link. By articulating a program committed to meeting customers' needs, security managers can go forward with a reasonable assurance that their programs, if tested, will be judged against a backdrop of qualitative standards.

I believe a Quality customer service requires the development of performance criteria that are relevant and easily measured. ~~Can such criteria be developed? The answer is yes.~~ Let's begin by looking at the standards of performance delineated in the model contract. We start there because these criteria should be constant for the security industry, whether comprised of a third party–supplied workforce or an in-house staff. *(Dalton 1995)*

At the officer level, quality performance criteria (QPC) begins with the basic step of developing responsibilities relevant to the specific assignment. These should be a combination of position descriptors common to everyone in the particular classification, specific professional responsibilities, and personal development challenges. *(Dalton, 1995)*

Position descriptors are often associated with job descriptions. These *will* range from entry-level positions to managers. ~~Article 8 of the Model Contract illustrates the differences and can be applied to any type of workforce.~~ *Dalton, 1995)*

A. Entry Level Performance Objectives (an officer's first 90 days of employment).

- Ability to demonstrate a working knowledge, via paper/pencil testing, on-site observation by their supervisor and actual performance, of the following:
- Emergency response plans, bomb threats and fire/safety evacuation plans.
- All systems, checkpoints, and conditions of normalcy associated with roving rounds.
- The responsibilities associated with after-hour employee escorts to parking facilities.
- The duties and responsibilities as outlined in their job description.
- Submit written reports that are grammatically correct and able to be presented for management and/or attorney review.
- Further, each entry-level and experienced security officer shall demonstrate an ability to maintain those skills required as part of their initial hiring.

B. Every Permanent Security Officer (those with more than six-months) assignment to CLIENT) shall demonstrate, via paper/pencil testing, on-site observation by their supervisor and actual performance, the ability to:

- Respond to and control emergency situations, as defined within the scope of their responsibility.
- Teach and guide new hires in the performance of their duties to assure that job responsibilities as defined by post assignments are carried out according to stated objectives/instructions.
- Perform according to the objectives as set forth for all entry-level security officers, including adherence to the duties and responsibilities as defined by the established job description.

C. Every supervisor and manager shall demonstrate an ability, via paper/pencil testing, on-site observation and actual performance, of the following:

- The ability to meet each of the performance objectives as outlined for both the Entry Level and Permanent Security Officer stated above.
- The ability to train and serve as a positive role model for entry-level and permanent security officers in meeting the requirements of this assignment.
- The ability to insure compliance with the rules, regulations, duties and responsibilities by each assigned subordinate officer.
- The ability to assist in the orientation and training of new and experienced officers.
- The ability to provide assistance and guidance to all officers on matters of policy and operating procedures and personal matters by:
  - Discussing account/departmental matters.
  - Answering questions by subordinates.

- Advising subordinates of changes in procedures.
- Informing the client of questions, concerns or matters requiring further clarification and direction.
- Scheduling personnel to meet post assignments under normal and emergency conditions.

These ~~three~~ *four* levels demonstrate a commitment to meeting basic job duties. One level serves as the building block for the next. Common to all three is a means of measuring performance. In this example, performance is measured based on the development of three measures. The first is an actual written test that requires the response to a series of questions, statements, and/or situations that test the individual's knowledge of the job. This measure is complemented by on-site observation and actual performance. The first requires the individual's supervisor to observe and record specific outcomes. Quality specialists would say that this is an excellent opportunity to engage in coaching and one-on-one training in areas noted as deficient. Actual performance is also a measure that can deliver quality service. Simply stated, until one is exposed to each basic facet of the job, the individual will not know how well they can perform (Dalton, 1995)

Each of these measures may appear to be basic, but it is surprising how often they are overlooked. ~~This is especially true among contract providers who have traditional buyer-seller relationships with a customer.~~ It has been my experience that proprietary operations pay more attention to individuals when they are just beginning their careers. These operations too, however, generally fail when it comes to developing specific performance criteria. This is partly due to the lack of clearly articulated departmental goals and objectives, ~~which we will discuss below.~~

As noted earlier, developing basic job criteria is only the beginning. Each position needs to reflect specifically defined criteria. Such criteria should reflect three elements: 1) a specific action or activity; 2) some measurable criteria; and 3) progress within a defined period of time. ~~Here are a few examples.~~

Example #1: Dispatch Center

This year, console operators working the day shift will answer telephone calls by the third ring 90 percent of the time, answering by stating that this is the Security Department, stating their name, and in a courteous manner asking how they can be of assistance.

In this example, the time frame is one year, which sets a time limit to determine if the console operators are meeting their objective. The measurable activity is the ability to answer the telephone by the third ring 90 percent of the time. The quality measure is answering the call in the courteous manner detailed. (Dalton, 1995)

Inherent within this objective is the assumption that it is realistic in the first place. Management needs to assure clients that the console room is adequately designed and staffed for the particular shift. It may be that this objective is achievable for the afternoon or evening shifts but due to activity levels, will need to be adjusted upwards or downwards for the day shift. Performance objectives shouldn't be thought of as having universal application. Each shift is different, and therefore, may require different measures. (Dalton, 1995)

Example #2: Investigators

Fraud investigators for this year will maintain an average caseload of 20 incidents. Each case will be opened according to the established case management criteria and be closed only when a final recommendation is forwarded to the policy and procedures analyst.

Here the objective is limited to fraud investigators. The period of time is defined as the current year, which allows management to establish annual averages since at any time the investigator's caseload may be above or below 20. The quality performance criteria are inherent in the requirement of following prescribed opening procedures and a special note that a case is closed only when a recommendation is forwarded to a third party.

These two examples illustrate that nearly every aspect of a security person's job can be reduced to measurable performance criteria. But a third component is equally important in achieving quality performance, namely, the opportunity to develop specific skill sets for the individual. Despite the criteria established for initial hiring or promotion, it is unrealistic to assume everyone will have the same performance level. Some people are better writers than others. Some have more developed social skills. Likewise, some display their leadership skills differently than others. The end result is that each person needs to be evaluated by their own skills set and how it affects their personal performance. The assessment should determine what areas need development, what areas are strong enough to offset other areas, and lead to a career development plan tailored specifically for the individual.

In the case of a security officer, we may find that she needs to improve her report writing skills and radio annunciation skills. As a part of her performance skills assessment, she may need to attend and successfully pass two courses within a prescribed period of time. When added to the basic job requirements noted above and coupled with specific assignment criteria, her total performance is a measure of how well she accomplishes all three. To pull all three together, let us assume that she is an experienced officer. As such, her performance objectives might look like this:

> For the calendar year, Officer Smith will demonstrate via her performance and as measured by the department's established testing and evaluational criteria the following:
>
> - When dispatched or through her own observation, will respond to and control emergencies according to established procedures, such actions to include rendering first aid as required, calling for assistance, directing and controlling crowds as reasonably as possible until help arrives.
> - As assigned by her supervisor, teach and guide new hires in the performance of their duties to assure those job responsibilities, as defined by post assignments, are carried out according to stated objectives and instructions.
> - Perform according to the objectives as set forth for all entry-level security officers, including adherence to the duties and responsibilities as defined by her job description.

- Complete her assigned patrols 90 percent of the time within the prescribed times, noting safety deficiencies, reporting security problems, and taking corrective action.
- As the primary lead on the day shift lobby console, will handle access control requests and visitor passes, issuing each 85 percent of the time in less than one minute.
- Will complete the department's report writing training module within 90 days, with a passing score of at least 70 percent.
- Will complete the department's approved external radio communications course within 60 days, with a passing score of 90 percent, and maintain effective annunciation and code adherence for the balance of the year.

These performance criteria reflect departmental standards for quality service. They demonstrate that security has taken the time and effort to establish criteria that it believes are achievable and reflect customer care. Quality performance is tied to more than individual officers, however. It is also linked to the department's established goals and objectives. For that matter, it is the development of the department's goal and associated objectives that sets the tone and parameters for individual performance.

In the case of the console operators being required to answer the telephone on the day shift within three rings, this should be tied to the department's overall objective of assuring quality customer care. In other words, if the goal is to provide a high level of quality, then how it is to be accomplished needs to be articulated in measurable terms. Each function needs to be analyzed and objectives generated which complement the goal. Therefore, if rapid telephone response times are considered a measure of quality, then the department should establish objectives to achieve this. The actual assurance that the objective is being met is reflected at the officer level. In short, quality performance criteria are set at the top and then passed down successively.

Accomplishing each objective results in the officer, supervisor, and manager receiving a merit performance increase to base compensation and/or bonus. As opposed to receiving an automatic pay increase, under a system of pay-for-performance, the increase is earned. Incentives and disincentives can also be calculated into the final formula. In the case of employee turnover, for example, a set rate can be established (i.e., 25 percent on an annualized basis). If the manager can hold the rate below 25 percent, an incentive of $100 for each percentage point can be paid directly to the manager. Conversely, for every percentage point above the established rate, $100 is deducted from the potential merit increase or bonus pool. Whatever system is used, the important point is that a system needs to be put in place. Studies on performance consistently have shown that while compensation is not the only factor influencing quality outcomes, it certainly plays a significant role.

Alternative #3: Strategic Quality Management

In the previous chapters we discussed the concept of strategic partnering and alliances in-depth as agents for change. We saw that despite their limitations, far more advantages are achieved. Strategic Quality Management (another way of describing TQM) is by its nature a way of establishing performance criteria. It operates on the premise that quality is an outcome, not something that can be defined in a vacuum and acquired for a price. It is earned. It is the end result of doing things right. When asked by my clients what are the basic quality-driven performance criteria to look for in security programs, I outline six factors.

Factor #1: Management

The key to any successful customer-driven program begins with the management team. Whether the management team responsible for the security program is internal or drawn from an external supplier, success requires an experienced team. Experienced means that the management group needs to be proven in your industry, in place, and willing to take bold actions. Although they may occasionally experience operational setbacks, their successes will far outnumber their slip-ups. Proven management ability is by far the most important ingredient.

Factor #2: Supervision

Right behind management is demonstrated skill in proper supervision. If management sets the tone, then supervisors must have the proven skills set to lead their staff. This includes coaching, prodding, encouraging, showing by example, and advocating. Supervision is the critical link that moves the abstract into reality. Simply stated, it is the connector.

Factor #3: Hiring

You cannot win a horse race without horses. The same is true in meeting the objectives of the security program. Whether your company employs an in-house or contracted staff, or assigns this responsibility to others, successful performance depends on those charged with the responsibility of protecting assets. This requires established criteria designed to attract and retain the best. Quality hiring begets quality performance. While not everyone will eventually measure up to the standard, most will and that is what drives the final outcome.

Factor #4: Training

Even the best cannot be expected to do their best without guidance and training. They need to be shown what is expected of them and given the opportunity to hone their skills. Relying solely on on-the-job (OJT) training falls short. As we have seen, training requires a program of initial officer training (IOT), on-the-job training (OJT), and advanced officer training (AOT) typically conducted once a year, followed by specialized officer training (SOT). These four uniquely defined programs are designed to assure that established skills are continuously tested and security personnel are exposed to new ideas, requirements, and techniques.

Factor #5: Administrative Support

The success of any program is directly linked to the level of support received from its infrastructure. Whether one is considering an external partner or drawing on internal resources, there is a need for support, including clerical, professional, technical, and administrative assistance. Each provides a link in the success chain that may involve reviewing documents, generating management reports, analyzing new approaches or data, or meeting payroll. Together they serve as the underpinning for the overall program. Here is a simple example. Take your favorite sports team. Throughout the season they travel to other locales. On game day they emerge onto the field, court, or rink fully equipped, uniformed, refreshed, fed, and ready to play. How did all of this occur? They had a support structure in place. The same holds true for a security program. Support is critical.

Factor #6: Cost

To be successful your program needs to be cost-effective. To sustain continued acceptance, it must be worth the price paid or expense incurred. When value (the outcome) is less than expected or perceived, the cost is immediately challenged. Success requires that the value received is complementary to the associated expense. No one likes to pay more than they feel is necessary. Cost should be an important driving factor.

In the wake of the World Trade Center bombing and the increase in workplace violence, executives are asking what is necessary to protect both their assets and people. They are not willing, however, to provide blank checks to their security decision-makers. Today's managers are asking the very tough question of what is reasonable. They are willing to accept that there are risks associated with doing business. The challenge of asset protection leaders is to provide value at a cost that is consistent with other company support services. Hence, success is based again on bottom-line performance.

Practicing strategic quality management, then, is a means of assuring that value can be achieved without the existence of uniformly accepted Standards. Such practitioners can be reasonably assured that they will reduce the likelihood of a serious legal challenge or lawsuit because they have defined what is a reasonable risk in advance and designed their programs accordingly.

CONCLUSION

I think it is fitting that the conclusion of this chapter is also the conclusion of this book. In a real sense we have come full circle. We began with the premise that today's successful asset protection decision-maker is foremost a business manager. As such, they are concerned with developing a program that truly brings value to the organization. To do so requires a commitment and open mind to do things boldly and differently. Unfortunately, security is not an industry that is easily judged against a set of ordained Standards. Yet, we know that value can be achieved through the application of strategies and techniques apart from the technical aspects of private security.

We have seen how our success is directly tied to becoming a full partner in meeting the profit and/or service motives of our organization. To prove value we need to have technical expertise resident within the program, be it a staff person or a proven external partner. We also need commitments from those outside our immediate control. As we have seen, this is what we call mutual ownership. We know that our success is directly linked to the success of our programs. Without the ability to maneuver through the maze of organizational dynamics, we have seen that both our subordinates and colleagues can become quickly mired down. The result, it seems to me, is that success comes to those who transcend the common definition of a security professional and see themselves as a corporate administrator.

Appendix A

CONTRACTUAL TERMS AGREEMENT

By and Between

_____

and

_____

This agreement is made and entered into this _____ day of _____, 199__, by and between _____(hereinafter CLIENT), a property managed by _____ organized and existing under the laws of _____ having its principle place of business at _____and, _____ (hereinafter CONTRACTOR) a corporation organized and existing under the laws of _____ and having a branch office located at _____

WHEREAS, CONTRACTOR engages in the business of providing uniformed security services, and is willing to provide these services to CLIENT under the terms and conditions hereinafter set forth; and

WHEREAS, CLIENT desires to have CONTRACTOR furnish uniformed security service for CLIENT at its location; and

WHEREAS, CONTRACTOR agrees to furnish such service on the terms and conditions set forth below;

Now, THEREFORE, in consideration of the mutual covenants and agreements herein contained, CLIENT and CONTRACTOR agree as follows:

ARTICLE 1. CONTRACTOR'S GENERAL DUTIES

During the term of this agreement CONTRACTOR shall furnish CLIENT with up to (INSERT NUMBER) fully-trained and qualified uniformed security officers, (INSERT NUMBER) fully-trained and qualified uniformed supervisors, one (1) full-time account manager and one (1) full-time assistant account manager. The Account Manager shall be responsible for the direct supervision of CONTRACTOR'S officers and supervisors furnished to CLIENT pursuant to this Agreement and shall be available at reasonable times to consult with CLIENT or its designated representative regarding the services rendered or to be rendered under this Agreement. The duties and responsibilities of CONTRACTOR'S officers, supervisors, account manager and agents shall be those specified herein; in particular, but not limited to, ARTICLES 5 through 11. CONTRACTOR'S employees assigned under this Agreement shall conform to such rules and regulations and shall perform such other duties as may be mutually agreed upon in writing from time to time by CONTRACTOR and CLIENT.

ARTICLE 2. TERM OF AGREEMENT

The term of this agreement shall be for three (3) years effective (MONTH, DAY & YEAR), through (MONTH, DAY & YEAR), subject to performance by CONTRACTOR in providing timely uniformed security service as specified herein and in the attachments.

ARTICLE 3. RELATIONSHIP BETWEEN PARTIES

The relationship of CONTRACTOR, its security officers, supervisors, and account managers to CLIENT shall be that of independent contractors. The CONTRACTOR'S officers, supervisors and account manager furnished pursuant to this Agreement shall be employees of CONTRACTOR, an independent contractor. CONTRACTOR shall exercise complete and exclusive control over all aspects of their employment and conduct. Such control to include evaluation, and the resolution of complaints and grievances.

CONTRACTOR shall pay all payrolls, payroll taxes (including but not limited to, Federal Social Security Taxes, Federal and State Unemployment Taxes, and State Workmen's Compensation Taxes), insurance premiums, license fees, fingerprinting costs, outfitting expense, and all other expenses of CONTRACTOR or such employee in performing this Agreement.

ARTICLE 4. LICENSES

CONTRACTOR, its employees and all others acting under its direction and control, shall be duly licensed and will obtain all necessary permits to perform services where service is to be performed. Costs for all licenses and permits and background and screening costs are the sole responsibility of CONTRACTOR. Throughout the term of this Agreement, CONTRACTOR shall maintain current licensing. Potential for license suspension, revocation, or limitation must be reported to CLIENT within ten (10) days of notice from State, County or City licensing boards.

ARTICLE 5. COVERAGES

CONTRACTOR will provide a minimum of (INSERT NUMBER) uniformed security hours per year, inclusive of supervision. Actual assignment of hours per shift will be mutually agreed upon between CONTRACTOR and CLIENT prior to such assignments. In addition, CONTRACTOR will provide (INSERT NUMBER) hours of management by providing a full-time, fully dedicated Account Manager and a full-time assistant account manager.

ARTICLE 6. STANDARDS OF CONDUCT

CONTRACTOR'S employees assigned to this account will have personal contact with customers, employees, visitors, and vendors of CLIENT and, though independent contractors, may be deemed by some customers, employees, visitors and vendors as direct representatives of CLIENT. Accordingly, it is agreed that said CONTRACTOR employees shall meet high standards of appearance and demeanor, and shall at all times treat customers, employees, visitors, and vendors of CLIENT with the utmost courtesy and respect, all as is appropriate to the environment and business of CLIENT.

It is understood that CONTRACTOR'S employees may have access to areas which are restricted to CLIENT customers, employees, visitors and vendors, provided CONTRACTOR'S employees have met the requirements as set forth by CLIENT in accordance with CLIENT'S standards for procuring and maintaining such admissibility requirements.

ARTICLE 7. DUTIES AND RESPONSIBILITIES

Customer service is a critical component of CLIENT'S business strategy. Security is an integral part of accomplishing this objective. Therefore, the primary responsibility of each officer, supervisor, and the account manager will be to provide quality customer service. Typical duties will involve providing directions, assisting CLIENT'S customers, tenants, visitors, employees and vendors. Occasionally, escorts may be required. Answering telephone inquiries and serving as a central or visible source of information is a significant part of the security officer's job. To this end, each officer, supervisor, and the account manager must exercise courtesy, respect, and professionalism. In addition, CONTRACTOR will assure CLIENT that each of its assigned personnel will comply with the following added duties and responsibilities:

a. Provide security, as defined by CLIENT, for its customers, tenants, visitors, employees, and vendors.
b. Respond to all alarm conditions and enforce all access control procedures through identification of personnel and control of entry and exits to CLIENT'S facilities and vital areas.

c. Enforce control over removal of CLIENT property, documents, or any vital material as identified by CLIENT.
d. Use reasonable effort to deter, or only when absolutely necessary, detain persons observed attempting to gain or gaining unauthorized access to any of CLIENT'S facilities.
e. Respond to suspicious incidents and take reports. When necessary and deemed appropriate, follow incidents to their conclusion, including court appearances.
f. Cooperate with and assist law enforcement agencies in connection with crimes committed against CLIENT, including maintaining the scene of a crime to protect possible evidence in accordance with established procedures.
g. Respond to and provide assistance in security- and/or safety-related situations, demonstrating common sense and good judgement and in compliance with CLIENT'S policies and practices.
h. Assume additional responsibilities, though not specifically enumerated herein, as may be set forth in CONTRACTOR'S special orders or manuals and procedures issued by CLIENT.
i. Maintain training and certification of those items, skills, concepts, and other requirements as outlined above and defined through mutual agreement by CLIENT and CONTRACTOR.
j. Maintain knowledge of appropriate federal, state, and local statutes and ordinances, and regulatory requirements, including periodic updates provided by CLIENT.

ARTICLE 8. STANDARDS OF PERFORMANCE

As a condition of this agreement the following standards will be required of CONTRACTOR. All personnel assigned to this account will:

a. Possess proof of having met the requirements from the State/District of _____ for Private Security Guards.
b. Possess a high school diploma, GED, or equivalent training or job experience.
c. Demonstrate the ability to read and write in English equivalent to a high school graduate. Have the ability to verbally communicate in English; particularly in emergency situations requiring clear

and definitive articulation to assure confidence, control, and safety of those involved.

d. Have the ability to demonstrate psychological stability under a variety of conditions as illustrated by passage of appropriately administered testing consistent with national standards.

e. Pass an annual physical fitness examination, including drug and alcohol testing, by a licensed physician which demonstrates an ability to meet the requirements of this account.

f. Possess CPR and First-Aid certification as set forth by the American Red Cross or equivalent association.

g. Pass a test on Customer Service Relations, to be set forth by mutual agreement between CLIENT and CONTRACTOR and undergo periodic training as agreed to from time to time by CLIENT and CONTRACTOR.

h. Receive a 24-hour course of advanced officer training annually, the curriculum to be mutually agreed upon between CLIENT and CONTRACTOR, reflecting changes in law, customer relations, corporate policies, etc.

In addition, CONTRACTOR shall:

i. Assure CLIENT that no security officer, supervisor or manager will be assigned, reassigned, disciplined, promoted or transferred within or away from the account without CLIENT'S prior notification.

j. Assure CLIENT all staffing will be in compliance with established EEO standards for the geographic area.

k. Provide annual testing of all assigned personnel on CLIENT'S emergency procedures plans.

l. Assure that all personnel assigned to operate a motor vehicle or other such equipment requiring special licensing shall have such certification and appropriate levels of insurability.

m. Assure CLIENT that all assigned personnel pass a comprehensive pre-employment background/reference check.

(ALTERNATIVE LANGUAGE)
CONTRACTOR shall submit to CLIENT, within seven (7) days

before the commencement of service or concurrent with assignment, a background investigation report for all personnel assigned to CLIENT under the terms of this agreement. The background investigation report will include, but not be limited to:

- Police Record Check
- Credit Check (if permissible)
- Confirmation of Previous Employment
- Verification of All Application Information

CLIENT reserves the right to fingerprint and photograph all personnel assigned under terms of this agreement. If CONTRACTOR receives an unsuitable report on any of CONTRACTOR's employees subsequent to the commencement of service, or CLIENT finds a prospective incumbent CONTRACTOR employee unsuitable or unfit for assigned duties, the employee will not be allowed to continue work, or be assigned to work, under the terms of this agreement.

n. Provide CLIENT with a Letter of Affidavit on each person assigned to the account certifying that the individual has met all of the hiring and training requirements as set forth in this Agreement.

CONTRACTOR will also assure that:

o. All services, equipment or material furnished or utilized in the performance of services and quality of service provided by CONTRACTOR shall be subject to inspection and testing by CLIENT without notice. Such inspections and testing will be conducted in a manner so as not to unduly interfere with CONTRACTOR'S ability to carry out the terms of this agreement.

Should CLIENT determine, as a result of these inspections and testing that services and/or equipment or materials used by CONTRACTOR are not satisfactory, CLIENT shall inform CONTRACTOR in writing. CLIENT reserves the write to: (a) require CONTRACTOR to take immediate action to bring such matters into compliance with the terms of this agreement; and (b) impose monetary deductions in accordance with a schedule to be mutually agreed upon between CLIENT and CONTRACTOR prior to the initiation of this agreement.

Should CONTRACTOR fail to take necessary measures to ensure conformity with the requirements of this agreement, CLIENT reserves the right to (a) procure or furnish services as required by CLIENT and charge CONTRACTOR any cost that is directly related to the performance of such services; or (b) terminate this agreement for default in accordance with the terms set forth in Article 26 governing Termination of Agreement.

p. Further, within 60 days of the initiation of this agreement, CONTRACTOR will develop a set of measurable performance objectives. These objectives will be developed for each position assigned to this account. Personnel assigned to this account must satisfactorily complete each of the performance objectives in order to be eligible for an increase in base wages. Performance objectives will be evaluated on an annual basis and be responsible for 75% of any consideration for an increase in wages. The balance of the performance evaluation will be based upon the officer's compliance with general orders, absenteeism, personal bearing and professionalism.

Each security person will receive an interim evaluation every 90 days, to be administered by the selected contractor. This evaluation will be a brief overview to allow the officers to know and understand the quality of their performance. A thorough review of performance will be conducted every 180 days. For the term of this contract and in addition to those objectives mutually agreed upon between the client and the contractor, the following performance objectives will serve as measurables for all security officers:

A. Entry Level Performance Objectives (an officer's first 90 days of employment).

- Ability to demonstrate a working knowledge, via paper/pencil testing, on-site observation by their supervisor and actual performance, of the following:

- Emergency response plans, bomb threats and fire/safety evacuation plans.
- All systems, checkpoints, and conditions of normalcy associated with roving rounds.
- The responsibilities associated with after-hour employee escorts to parking facilities.
- The duties and responsibilities as outlined in their job description.
- Submit written reports which are grammatically correct and able to be presented for management and/or litigative review.
- Further, each entry-level and experienced security officer shall demonstrate the ability to maintain those skills necessary to insure initial hiring to this account.

B. Every Permanent Security Officer (those with more than six months assignment to CLIENT) shall demonstrate, via paper/pencil testing, on-site observation by their supervisor and actual performance, the ability to:

- Respond to and control emergency situations, as defined within the scope of their responsibility.
- Teach and guide new hires in the performance of their duties to assure that job responsibilities as defined by post assignments are carried out in accordance with stated objectives/instructions.
- Perform in accordance with the objectives as set forth for all entry-level security officers, including adherence to the duties and responsibilities as defined by the established job description.

C. Every supervisor and manager shall demonstrate, via paper/pencil testing, on-site observation and actual performance, the following:

- The ability to meet each of the performance objectives as outlined for both the Entry-Level and Permanent Security Officer stated above.

- The ability to train and serve as positive role models for entry-level and permanent security officers in meeting the requirements of this assignment.
- The ability to insure compliance with the rules, regulations, duties and responsibilities by each subordinate officer assigned to this account.
- The ability to assist in the orientation and training of new and experienced officers assigned to this account.
- The ability to provide assistance and guidance to all officers on matters of policy and operating procedures and personnel matters by:
  - Discussing account matters.
  - Answering questions by subordinates.
  - Advising subordinates of changes in procedures.
  - Informing the client of questions, concerns, or matters requiring further clarification and direction.
- Scheduling personnel to meet post assignments under normal and emergency conditions.

ARTICLE 9. STAFFING AND ASSOCIATED PENALTIES

A. OVERTIME

CLIENT will pay for only that overtime it authorizes. CLIENT will pay CONTRACTOR a rate of one and a half times the base rate of pay for each person assigned on each of those calendar days designated as CLIENT holidays. Overtime requests for special events or times of the year which require in excess of 40 hours per week of additional service will be billed at the normal base rate, provided CLIENT gives 30 days advance notice.

B. OVERFILLS

Overfills occur when CONTRACTOR supplies too many individuals, or individuals for longer periods than required, or at a higher level—as defined by a schedule mutually agreed upon by CLIENT and CONTRACTOR at the outset of this Agreement or anytime thereafter in advance of such overfills. CLIENT will pay for only the services requested.

C. SHORTFILLS

Shortfills occur when CONTRACTOR supplies unqualified personnel. CLIENT reserves the right to refuse CONTRACTOR'S personnel whom CLIENT determines not to be qualified. Overtime will not be paid to CONTRACTOR to compensate for shortage of personnel.

D. SHORTFALLS

Shortfalls occur when the required services are not supplied at any post or work site. CLIENT will pay for only time actually worked. If a security officer arrives late for work or leaves early for any reason, overtime will not be paid when CONTRACTOR fills the vacancies so created. Moreover, the absence of a security officer at a post or work site without a replacement constitutes a shortfall for a portion of a shift and a proportional reimbursement will be charged.

E. DOUBLE BANKING

Whenever it becomes necessary to assign or reassign an individual to a post for the first time, CONTRACTOR shall arrange, at its expense, to have the new individual "double bank" with an experienced employee prior to having the inexperienced individual take over any post on their own. CONTRACTOR will bear the associated expense for this double banking.

F. TURNOVER

Turnover is the number of security personnel hired to replace those leaving or dropped from CONTRACTOR'S workforce. For purposes of this account, the turnover rate will be expressed in terms of the actual number of hired replacements. Turnover will be calculated on an annual basis and a turnover rate in excess of the established rate will be considered unacceptable and may be cause for the termination of CONTRACTOR'S services. The acceptable turnover rate for this account is (INSERT PERCENTAGE) or less of total number of personnel assigned to this account.

G. INCENTIVES AND PENALTIES

(As a part of the final contract terms, the selected contractor and client will agree upon a mutually acceptable surcharge that may be assessed if the contractor has an excessive amount of shortfills or shortfalls. The client will also credit the contractor $100 for each percent below the acceptable turnover rate that is achieved on an annual basis. For example, should the established turnover rate be set at 40% and should the contractor achieve a 30% turnover, a credit of $1000 will be given by the client. Conversely, the client will assess a $100 surcharge for every one percent over the established annualized rate.)

ARTICLE 10. ADDITIONAL PERSONNEL
CONTRACTOR shall assure CLIENT that CONTRACTOR will maintain a fully trained cadre of (A NUMBER WHICH REPRESENTS A REASONABLE LEVEL OR PERCENTAGE TO BE NEGOTIATED) backup personnel ready to assume assignment at CLIENT'S location(s) on request by CLIENT. By fully trained it is meant that such personnel will meet CLIENT requirements.

CONTRACTOR shall maintain manpower levels capable of meeting the call-back requirements mutually agreed upon between CONTRACTOR and CLIENT without regard to any riot, war, act of God, the enactment, issuance, or operation of any municipal, county, state or federal law, ordinance or executive, administrative or judicial regulation, order or decree, or any local or national emergency, or any other similar cause outside of the control of CONTRACTOR.

ARTICLE 11. LENGTH OF DAILY ASSIGNMENT
Normally, no security person will be allowed to work more than 12 consecutive hours. Only CLIENT can declare an emergency and authorize CONTRACTOR to hold their security personnel beyond the 12-hour requirement. Nor shall any security officer report for duty with less than 12 hours off from having worked a previous shift, unless such reporting is necessitated by an emergency. Further, no security person may be assigned to work a post or work site by themselves without first having been tested and successfully demonstrating a comprehensive knowledge of the job functions and responsibilities.

ARTICLE 12. UNIFORMS AND EQUIPMENT
CONTRACTOR will supply all uniforms and assure that they are continuously cleaned and maintained. The cost will be borne by CON-

TRACTOR and is reflected in the stated billing rate outlined in Article 13 below. CONTRACTOR will not require their employees to purchase uniforms, nor assume the cost of cleaning.

CLIENT will furnish the necessary office space and supporting equipment necessary to service this account (telephone, copier, desk and chair, basic supplies, radios, etc.). CONTRACTOR will supply, at its expense, all-weather gear, leather gear, flashlights, pagers, and other equipment as is mutually agreed upon between CLIENT and CONTRACTOR, in order to meet the requirements of this account.

CONTRACTOR will assure CLIENT that CONTRACTOR will replace or repair at its cost any CLIENT-owned equipment (such as but not limited to communications equipment, fire and safety equipment, and locks and keys, access control systems, CCTVs, etc.) damaged or lost through abuse or neglect by CONTRACTOR'S personnel. Use of CLIENT'S telephone system for personal use is prohibited. CONTRACTOR will be either billed or the cost of such usage will be deducted from the monthly payment, at the discretion of CLIENT.

ARTICLE 13. CONTROL OF PREMISES
It is hereby understood and agreed that CLIENT, as owner of its property and facilities, has the exclusive right to control and deny access to same to any individual including, without limitation, an employee or agent of CONTRACTOR.

ARTICLE 14. BILLING RATE
SEE REQUEST FOR PROPOSAL FOR SPECIFICS
—ALSO INCLUDE LANGUAGE FOR BENEFITS—

ARTICLE 15. METHOD OF PAYMENT
CONTRACTOR shall submit a monthly invoice for services rendered in accordance with the terms and conditions of this Agreement. The invoice shall be accompanied by originally signed timesheets and other attachments, as may be necessary on occasions, demonstrating proof of purchase for items needed and approved prior to such purchase by CLIENT.

Said invoice and relevant documentation shall be mailed or delivered to such office as directed by CLIENT and are payable by CLIENT at the address specified on the invoice within 30 days of receipt. Should CLIENT contend any such invoice as incorrect, CLIENT shall notify CONTRACTOR in writing within said 30 days and specify the reasons for such contention. CLIENT shall pay the amount mutually agreed upon on settlement of such dispute and shall not be deemed in default.

ARTICLE 16. INSURANCE

At all times while performing the services, and for two (2) years after the cancellation or termination of this Agreement, CONTRACTOR shall maintain, at its sole cost and expense, at least the following insurance from insurance companies and in a form satisfactory to CLIENT with limits of liability not less than stated below. CLIENT shall have the right to inspect and review the policies and shall be provided with copies upon request. Certificates of Insurance shall be in the name of CLIENT and each such certificate shall list CLIENT and MANAGER as additional insureds. Certificates of Insurance shall be delivered to CLIENT ten (10) days prior to the inception of the Agreement and any change or cancellation shall not be valid without thirty (30) days prior written notice to CLIENT. CONTRACTOR shall provide to CLIENT, promptly upon receipt by CONTRACTOR, renewal notices regarding such insurance policies.

A. Commercial General Liability Insurance
- Combined single limit for bodily and property damage of not less than $5 million for each occurrence and annual aggregate providing:
- Broad form property damage coverage
- Broad form contractual liability coverage
- Products and completed operations coverage
- Personal and advertising injury coverage
- Such policy to include Owner and Owner's Agent as additional insureds for all activities arising out of the performance of the services. This policy shall be primary for all purposes to other insurance coverage, whether such other

insurance is stated to be primary, contributory, excess, contingent or otherwise.

B. Comprehensive Automotive Liability
  • Combined single limit for bodily injury, death, and property damage of not less than $1 million per accident.

C. Workers' Compensation and Employer's Liability Insurance
  • With limits of liability for workers' compensation, of not less than those required by law, and;
  • With limits of liability for employer's liability, of not less than $1 million each accident, $1 million disease-policy limit, $1 million disease—each employee.

D. Contractor's Third Party Fidelity Bond
  • In the amount of $50,000 for each occurrence covering all employees of CONTRACTOR.

CLIENT will not be liable for the payment of any premiums or assessments with respect to the coverages described above. Further, CLIENT, it's officers, agents and employees shall be named additional insured as respects the named insured's activities on or about CLIENT'S premises. The policy shall be endorsed to provide that this insurance shall be primary and not contributing with any other insurance available to said additional insureds as respects any and all liability, loss, claims, damages or expense arising out of the negligence or alleged negligence of the named insured.

ARTICLE 17. CONFIDENTIALITY

CONTRACTOR understands that during the term of this Agreement, its employees and agents may produce or have access to confidential information, records, data, specifications, trade secrets, customer lists, and secret inventions and processes of CLIENT. All records, files, drawings, documents, or copies thereof, relating to CLIENT'S business, which CONTRACTOR shall prepare or use, or come in contact with, shall be and remain the sole property of CLIENT, and shall not be reproduced, transmitted or removed from CLIENT'S premises without it's written consent, and shall not be disclosed to any persons, or business entity without the written approval of CLIENT. CONTRACTOR shall hold all such information contained in or derived from any of the sources described above in trust and confidence for CLIENT except as authorized by CLIENT in writing. CONTRACTOR agrees to adopt and maintain procedures reasonably calculated to insure that only such employees of CONTRACTOR that have a need to know such information in order to discharge CONTRACTOR'S obligations hereunder have access to such information. Upon cancellation or expiration of this Agreement, CONTRACTOR shall return to CLIENT all written or descriptive matter, including but not limited to drawings, descriptions, or other papers or documents which contain any data or information of the nature described above.

ARTICLE 18. SOLICITATION OF EMPLOYEES
CONTRACTOR will not require its employees to sign any document prohibiting them from seeking employment with another security contractor for any period of time either during or subsequent to their employment with CONTRACTOR.

ARTICLE 19. SPECIAL SERVICES
(Insert language that specifies special services (i.e., escorts, money transports, executive protection, etc. which may be required over and above those responsibilities listed above.)

ARTICLE 20. USE OF CLIENT'S NAME
CONTRACTOR shall assure CLIENT that CONTRACTOR will not, without CLIENT'S prior written approval, publish or use any advertising, sales promotion or publicity matter relating to services equipment, products, reports, and material furnished by CONTRACTOR wherein the name of CLIENT is mentioned or its identity is implied.

ARTICLE 21. INDEMNIFICATION
CONTRACTOR shall indemnify, defend, and hold harmless CLIENT, Manager, and their respective partners, directors, officers, employees, servants, agents, representatives, and affiliates from and against any and all claims, liabilities, demands, actions, suits, damages, losses, injuries, costs and expenses (including without limitation reasonable

attorney's fees) involving any personal injury or property damage suffered or incurred by CLIENT, caused by the negligent or wrongful acts or omissions of CONTRACTOR. CONTRACTOR'S duty to indemnify and hold harmless CLIENT is limited to the proportionate share of such damages, losses and expenses attributable to the aforesaid acts and omissions of CONTRACTOR, its employees, agents or representatives.

It is expressly understood and agreed that the provisions of this Article 19 (i) shall survive the termination of this Agreement, and (ii) shall not be limited by the limits of insurance required in Article 15 of this Agreement.

ARTICLE 22. FORCE MAJEURE

"FORCE MAJEURE" as used in this article shall mean an act of God, industrial disturbance, exclusive of those related to labor disputes, act of the public enemy, war, blockage, public riot, lightning, fire, flood, earthquake, explosion, government restraint, unavailability of equipment, and any other cause, whether of the kind specifically enumerated above or otherwise, which is not reasonably within the control of the party claiming suspension of those services enumerated herein this Agreement.

If either party is rendered unable, wholly or in part, by Force Majeure to carry out its obligations under this Agreement, such party shall give to the other party prompt written notice of the Force Majeure with reasonably full particulars concerning it; thereupon, the obligations of the party giving notice, so far as they were affected by the Force Majeure, shall be suspended during, but no longer than, the continuance of the Force Majeure. The affected party shall use all possible diligence to remove the Force Majeure as quickly as possible. In the event CONTRACTOR is unable to carry out its obligations under this Article, CLIENT may upon thirty (30) days written notice cancel this Agreement in whole or part without any obligations or liability to CLIENT.

ARTICLE 23. EQUAL EMPLOYMENT OPPORTUNITY AND AFFIRMATIVE ACTION

CONTRACTOR represents that it is in compliance with all applicable federal, state, and local laws, regulations and orders with respect to Equal Employment Opportunity and Affirmative Action, and either has previously provided or will provide to CLIENT, the certifications and representations regarding same that CLIENT may require under such laws, regulations and orders.

ARTICLE 24. IRCA COMPLIANCE

CONTRACTOR agrees at all times to remain in strict compliance with all terms, provisions, regulations and rulings relative to the Immigration Reform and Control Act of 1986 (IRCA). All employees of CONTRACTOR assigned to the Properties will have had their identity and eligibility for work within the United States properly verified. Within three (3) days of receipt of a written request from CLIENT or Manager, CONTRACTOR shall provide CLIENT or Manager with copies of the I-9 form or such other documentation as may be appropriate to satisfy CLIENT or Manager as to CONTRACTOR'S compliance with IRCA.

CONTRACTOR agrees to defend, hold harmless and indemnify CLIENT, Manager, and their affiliates and subsidiaries, directors, partners, officers, agents, representatives, and employees from and against any claims, costs, including but not limited to attorneys' fees, actions, suits, or proceedings of any type whatsoever arising out of or in any way connected with CONTRACTOR'S breech of the terms of the paragraph immediately above.

ARTICLE 25. PROVIDING DUE NOTICE

CONTRACTOR shall assure CLIENT all logs, incident and daily reports will be completed and submitted in accordance with the schedule as set forth by CLIENT. Further, CONTRACTOR shall assure CLIENT receives adequate notice of hazards, safety violations, or other conditions that warrant an unsafe condition, as may be discovered by CONTRACTOR'S personnel so CLIENT may take appropriate action in an expeditious manner.

ARTICLE 26. METHOD OF NOTICE

Any notice or other communication provided hereunder shall be given in writing and shall be deemed to have been duly given when delivered by hand, or five (5) days after being mailed, postage prepaid, certified with return receipt requested, addressed to:

If to CLIENT:

with a copy to:

If to CONTRACTOR:

Or to such other address as either party may specify to the other in writing.

ARTICLE 27. TERMINATION OF AGREEMENT

CLIENT shall have the right to terminate this Agreement in its entirety without cause at any time by giving CONTRACTOR thirty (30) days written notice of such cancellation or termination. In the event of any cancellation or termination of this Agreement, the compensation provisions herein specified shall apply only through the date of cancellation.

Each party to this Agreement may terminate this Agreement immediately upon written notice in the event of default by the other party in the payment of any monies due hereunder or in the event at any time during the term of this Agreement there shall be filed by or against the other party in any court pursuant to any statute, either of the United States, or of any State, territory or possession, a petition in bankruptcy or insolvency or for reorganization or for the appointment of a receiver or to receive all or a portion of such party's property, or similar or related relief, or if such party makes an assignment for the benefit of creditors, or if either party shall be approached and accept an offer for sale, merger, or acquisition by another party.

Either party may terminate this Agreement upon written notice in the event of a material breech by the other party of any provision of this Agreement. CLIENT may terminate this Agreement immediately upon written notice in the event of a strike or other labor disturbance against CONTRACTOR by CONTRACTOR'S employees. Further, CLIENT may terminate this Agreement immediately upon written notice if CONTRACTOR fails to maintain insurance coverage in accordance with the conditions of Article 15 of this Agreement.

Termination of this Agreement shall not affect the obligation of either party to the other to pay any fees or reimburse any amounts due and payable at the time of termination pursuant to this Agreement and shall not affect the obligation of CONTRACTOR to indemnify CLIENT in accordance with this Agreement.

ARTICLE 28. PENDING ACTIONS

CONTRACTOR certifies that no lawsuits, legal proceedings, administrative proceedings, or other actions, whether voluntary or involuntary, are threatened or pending against CONTRACTOR or any of its officers or employees which may have a material impact upon CONTRACTOR'S ability to perform this Agreement.

ARTICLE 29. SUBCONTRACTING AND ASSIGNMENTS

This Agreement shall not be assigned or subcontracted, in whole or in part by CONTRACTOR. Nor shall CONTRACTOR assign any monies due or to become due hereunder without prior written consent of CLIENT. Any attempted assignment or subcontracting hereunder without the prior written consent of CLIENT shall be void.

ARTICLE 30. ENTIRE AGREEMENT; AMENDMENTS

This Agreement supersedes all previous agreements entered into between CONTRACTOR and CLIENT and represents the whole and entire Agreement between the parties. No other agreements or representations, oral or written, have been made by CONTRACTOR. This Agreement may not be altered, modified or amended, except in writing and properly executed by CONTRACTOR and CLIENT. Any purchase order or similar document issued by CLIENT simultaneously with or subsequent to this Agreement, and related to the subject matter of this Agreement, shall be subject to and governed by the terms and conditions hereof which shall supersede any conflicting terms or conditions of such purchase order or similar document.

ARTICLE 31. BINDING AGREEMENT

This Agreement shall not be binding upon either party until executed by its duly authorized representative.

ARTICLE 32. NO WAIVER

The failure by either party to enforce at any time any of the provisions of this Agreement or to require at any time performance by the other party or any of the provisions herein shall in no way be construed to be a waiver of such provision or to affect the validity thereof.

ARTICLE 33. SEVERABILITY

Whenever possible, each provision of this Agreement shall be interpreted in such manner as to be effective and valid under applicable law, but if any provision of this Agreement is held to be prohibited by or invalid under applicable law, such provision shall be made to conform to the law and this Agreement shall otherwise continue in full force and effect.

ARTICLE 34. APPLICABLE LAW

This Agreement shall be governed by and construed under the laws of the (APPLICABLE STATE AND/OR DISTRICTS).

ARTICLE 35. SURVIVABILITY

CONTRACTOR understands and agrees that the following Articles of this Agreement survive the expiration, cancellation or termination of this Agreement:

Articles: 6 through 13, 15 through 25, and 27 through 35.

IN WITNESS WHEREOF CLIENT AND CONTRACTOR have caused this Agreement to be executed by their respective duly authorized representatives as of the date first above written.

CLIENT
By:_____
Its:_____

CONTRACTOR
By:_____
Its:_____

Appendix B

For your reference, each situational case is listed and summarized below.

Situational Case #1: Misdirected Advocacy The security director who obtained support from everyone but those who made the final decision.

Situational Case #2: The Improper Response The officer who responded by driving on the sidewalk and hit a pedestrian.

Situational Case #3: The Misguided Security Director The security director who spent more time developing external relationships than internal ones and lost his position.

Situational Case #4: The Trapped Executives Developing international security programs when strong advocacy is not there.

Situational Case #5: The Mounted Patrol Using a mounted horse patrol as an alternative to conventional parking lot patrols.

Situational Case #6: ATM Servicing Integrating the servicing of ATM's into routine patrol patterns as a demonstration of a value-added contribution.

Situational Case #7: Quality Tenant Services Turning internal messenger services into a multiple win-win situation in an effort to improve quality tenant services.

Situational Case #8: Reducing Supplier Costs Identifying ways a manufacturer inadvertently imposes its own bureaucracy to keep production costs higher.

Situational Case #9: The Security Consortium Merging several small guard accounts to achieve greater volumes and more services from one supplier.

Situational Case #10: Redefining Your Workforce By using part-timers, more coverage can be obtained at a lower cost.

Situational Case #11: The Riot that Never Took Place Over-reacting to suspected events can cause excessive expenditures.

Situational Case #12: The LA Olympics Excessive resourcing lessens credibility.

Situational Case #13: The Emergency Response Team Unbalanced union negotiations, over time, can result in inappropriate staffing.

Situational Case #14: Developing Mutual Ownerships By shifting the responsibility for asset protection to unit managers, security staffing can be reduced without loss of quality.

Situational Case #15: The Bank Guard Customer service means going the extra mile. In doing so, surprising outcomes can result.

Situational Case #16: Re-Engineering Security Succeeding in today's organizations may mean redefining security's structure entirely.

Situational Case #17: Three Examples of Security-Business Communication To succeed one needs to learn the importance of thinking and talking in the business one purports to serve.

Situational Case #18: The Promoted Manager A successful manager understands the necessity in meeting the needs of the entire staff, even when accepting new responsibilities.

Situational Case #19: The Internal Auditor Controversy Success means being willing to take a position when it is essential and fighting for it, even if it means your job.

Situational Case #20: Merging Staff & Line Ideas New ideas emerge when staff and line workers come together.

Situational Case #21: The Retiring Executive Our importance is directly related to our association with the organization. After retirement even the best are a fading memory.

Situational Case # 22: The Quality First Program First Security's Quality Customer Service Program.

Situational Case #23: The Diebold Story An example of a strategic alliance between Diebold and IBM.

End Notes

1. Stuart Feldman, "Restructuring: How to Get It Right," *Management Review,* April 1993, p. 16.
2. The "Virtual Organization" concept has become very popular with companies seeking strategic partners and alliances (both of which are discussed in detail in Chapter 7). Its basic premise is to allow one company to focus on its core competencies while transferring many of its support services or targeted markets to another company. To the uneducated outsider, there would be no apparent difference between the two firms. A good example is the relationship between a small commuter airline and a large one. USAir licenses its name and logo to Pennsylvania Air for many of its commuter flights. To the air traveler, there is no outward sign that the two have an alliance; Pennsylvania Air is a virtual organization for USAir.
3. Samuel Martin, "The Perception Gap," *Security Magazine*, November 1990, pp. 57-61.
4. The mall used a mix of media including newspaper ads, flyers, and brochures. On television they ran adds showing long shots of the mall with the horse patrol passing by the front entrance. While no direct mention was made of the horse patrol, the reader or viewer could easily infer their presence.
5. Jay Abraham, *Your Marketing Genius At Work,* Torrance, Ca: Abraham Publishing Group, 1992.

6. Thomas A. Stewart, "Re-Engineering—The Hot New Managing Tool, *Fortune,* August 23, 1993, pp. 41-45.
7. To obtain the latest studies on shoplifting and its associated costs see:
   * *The Price Waterhouse Study;* The Peter Berlin Retail Consulting Group, 380 North Broadway, Jericho, Long Island, N.Y. 11753,
   * *The FMI Study: Loss Prevention Services Dept.,* Food Marketing Institute, 800 Connecticut Ave., N.W., Washington, D.C. 20006, or *The Hayes Study,* Jack L. Hayes, 405 Prevention Way, Stanfordville, N.Y., 12581.
8. Robert M. Tomasko, *Rethinking the Corporation: The Architecture of Change,* New York: AMACOM, 1993.
9. "The Outlook: Economy's Slow Pace Masks Competitiveness," *The Wall Street Journal,* September 13, 1993, p. 1.
10. Farrell Kramer, "Executives Unprepared for Change," *San Francisco Chronicle Examiner,* September 12, 1993, p. E-3.
11. John J. Fay, "Corporate Security: Protecting Assets in an Evolving Shamrock-like Organization," *Security Journal,* Volume 3, Number 4, October 1992, pp. 194-198.
12. *Ibid.*
13. John Fay, "Management: A Security Strategy for the '90s," *Security Technology & Design,* September/October 1993, pp. 38-43.
14. *Ibid.,* p. 42.
15. *Ibid.*
16. Letters, *Management Review,* May 1993.
17. Oren Harari, "Ten Reasons Why TQM Doesn't Work," *Management Review,* January 1993, p. 35.
18. *Ibid.,* p. 37.
19. Donald P. Jackson, "TQM Does Work!" *Management Review,* May 1993, p. 8.
20. This is a proprietary management strategy tool that is used by The Forum Organization. It has been reprinted here with their permission. Any use or application without their permission is strictly prohibited. For further information on P.R.O.G.R.E.S.S. or other quality improvement programs, I would recommend contacting Melinda Gleason in care of the Forum Corporation, Boston, MA.
21. Richard M. Hodgetts, *Blueprints for Continuous Improvement,* New York: AMA Membership Publications Division, American Management Association, 1993.
22. Mark Graham Brown, *Baldrige Award Winning Quality,* Second Edition, White Plains, New York: Quality Resources, 1993.
23. Timothy J. Ogilvie, "Lost In Space: Typical Benchmarking Problems," *Management Review,* September 1993, p. 21.

24. Michael Hammer and James Champy, *Re-Engineering The Corporation: A Manifesto for Business Revolution,* New York: HarperCollins Publishers, Inc., 1993.
25. *Fortune* Book Excerpt, *Fortune*, May 3, 1993, p. 94.
26. *Ibid.*
27. *Ibid.,* p. 95.
28. George Harrar, "How Radical Should Reengineering Be?" *Enterprise,* January 1994, p. 21.
29. *Ibid.*
30. Charles Handy, *The Age of Unreason,* Boston: Harvard Business Review Press, 1990.
31. John J. Fay, "Corporate Security: Protecting Assets in an Evolving Shamrock-like Organization," *Security Journal,* Volume 3, Number 4, October 1992, p. 197.
32. *Ibid.*
33. Commonly referred to as the Atkinson Report, this is a report authored by Stephen Gale, Keith Duncan, Rudolph Yasick, and John Tofflemire, "A White Paper on a Value-Added Model for Security Management," Washington, D.C.: American Society for Industrial Society Foundation, 1990.
34. *Ibid.,* p. 16.
35. *Ibid.,* pp. 16-17.
36. *Ibid.*
37. Richard Buskirk, *Handbook of Management Tactics,* Boston: Cahners Books, 1976, p. 143.
38. Roger A. Golde, *Muddling Through,* New York: AMACOM, 1976, p. 102.
39. *Ibid.,* p. 152.
40. Steven Keller, *Nine Principles of Successful Protection Management,* Deltona, Florida: Horizon Institute, 1992.
41. Jim Meisenheimer, "How To Outperform Your Competition," *The Professional Consultant,* Portland, OR, Issue #1522, p. 4.
42. Oren Harari, "Internal Customer, R.I.P." *Management Review,* June 1993, p. 30.
43. *Ibid.,* p. 31.
44. *Ibid.*
45. Mary Woodell, "ELVIS Stalks the Corridors of Power," *Management Review,* January 1993, p. 58-61.
46. *Ibid.,* p. 59.
47. John Englert, "Strategic Alliances: A Process for Developing Partnerships in Corporate Real Estate," Remarks before the 1993 Industrial Development Research Council, New York City, Dec. 2, 1993.

48. Thomas Wathen, chairman of the board, Pinkerton Security and Investigative Services, personal interview for this book, February 2, 1994.

49. *Ibid.*

50. William Whitmore, president, SpectaGuard Security Services, personal interview for this book, February 9, 1994.

51. Senate Bill 1258, 102nd Congress, First Session, Sponsor: Senator Gore, State of Tennessee, June 11, 1991.

52. House of Representatives Bill 5931, 102nd Congress, Second Session, Representative Martinez, State of California, September 10, 1992.

53. State of California, Assembly Bill 508, California Legislature, 1993-94 Regular Session, Assembly Member Speier (Principal Senate Coauthor: Senator Killea), February 18, 1993.

54. *The Security Letter Source Book,* 1990-1991.

55. Chris E. McGoey, *Security: Adequate or Not,* Phoenix, Az: Aegis Books, 1990.

56. *Doe vs. System Parking,* No. 178051, Ohio Court of Common Pleas, Cuyahoga County, *Security Law Newsletter,* No.94-2, January 18, 1994, p. 3.

57. *Krakower vs. City of New York,* No.13102/89, Bronx County Superior Court, May 13, 1993, 36 ATLA Law Rep. 258 (September 1993), *Security Law Newsletter,* No.93-109, September 1993.

58. *Berry Property Management Inc. vs. Bliskey,* No. 13-91-658-CV, Court of Appeals, Thirteenth Judicial District of Texas, February 25, 1993, *Security Law Newsletter,* No.93-92, August 1993.

59. *Nola M. vs. University of Southern California,* 16 Cal.App. 4th 421; Cal. Rptr. 2d, June 1993.

60. *Ann M. vs. Pacific Plaza Shopping Center et al.,* 93 C.D.O.S. 9323, (Supreme Court of the State of California, No. S030815), December 1993.

Bibliography

Abraham, J., *Your Marketing Genius At Work,* Torrance, Ca: Abraham Publishing Group, 1992.

Albrecht, D., "Total Quality Service," *Global Management 1994,* Volume One, International Edition, New York: Sterling Publications, 1994, pp. 76-82.

Berry, T.H., *Managing the Total Quality Transformation,* New York: McGraw-Hill, 1991.

Blaxill, M. and Hout, T., "The Fallacy of the Overhead Quick Fix," *Harvard Business Review,* July-Aug. 1991.

Brown, M.G., *Baldrige Award Winning Quality, How to Interpret the Malcolm Baldrige Award Criteria,* White Plains, NY: Quality Resources, 1991.

Buskirk, R., *Handbook of Management Tactics,* Boston: Cahners Books, 1976, p. 143.

Byrne, J., "Management's New Gurus," *Business Week,* Aug. 21, 1992, p. 50.

Camp. R.C., *Benchmarking: The Search for Industry Best Practices That Lead to Superior Performance,* White Plains, NY: Quality Resources, 1989.

Conners, R., Smith T., Hickman, C., *The OZ Principle,* Englewood Cliffs, NJ: Prentice Hall, 1994.

Crosby, P.B., *Completeness: Quality for the 21st Century,* New York: Penguin Books, 1994.

Crosby, P.B., *Quality Is Free,* New York: Penguin Group, 1979.

Crosby, P.B., *Quality Without Tears,* New York: Penguin Group, 1984.

Davidow, W. and Uttal, B., *Total Customer Service: The Ultimate Weapon,* New York: Harper & Row, 1989.

Drucker, P.F., *Managing for the Future, The 1990s and Beyond,* New York: Penguin Group, 1993.

Drucker, P.F., "The Coming of the New Organization," *Harvard Business Review,* Jan.-Feb. 1988.

Fay, J.J., "Corporate Security: Protecting Assets in an Evolving Shamrock-like Organization," *Security Journal,* Volume 3, Number 4, October 1992, pp. 194-198.

Fay, J.J., "Management: A Security Strategy for the '90s," *Security Technology & Design,* September/October 1993, pp. 38-43.

Feldman, S., "Restructuring: How to Get It Right," *Management Review,* April 1993, p. 16.

Fromm, B. and Schlesinger, L., *The Real Heroes of Business: And Not One of Them Is a CEO,* New York: Doubleday, 1993.

Golde, R.A., *Muddling Through,* New York: AMACOM, 1976, p. 102.

Handy, C., *The Age of Unreason,* Boston: Harvard Business Review Press, 1990.

Harrington, H.J., *Business Process Improvement,* New York: McGraw-Hill, 1991.

Hickman, C.R. and Silva, M.A., *Creating Excellence,* New York: The Penguin Group, 1984.

Hinton, T. and Schaeffer, W., *Customer-Focused Quality: What to Do on Monday Morning,* New York: Prentice Hall, 1994.

Hodgetts, R., *Blueprints for Continuous Improvement,* New York: AMA Membership Publications Division, American Management Association, 1993.

Hoerr, J., "Sharpening Minds for a Competitive Edge," *Business Week,* Dec. 17, 1990.

Kraar, L., "Your Rivals Can Be Your Allies," *Fortune,* Mar. 27, 1989, pp. 66-72.

Krass, P., "Outsourcing Twice Removed," *Information Week,* Nov. 4, 1991, p. 25.

Mattimore, B.W., *99% Inspiration, Tips Tales & Techniques for Liberating Your Business Creativity,* New York: AMACOM, 1994.

Miller, J.B., *The Corporate Coach,* New York: HarperCollins, 1993.

Mills, D.Q., *Rebirth of the Corporations,* New York: Wiley, 1991.

Morris, T., *True Success: A New Philosophy of Excellence,* New York: G.P. Putnam's Sons, 1994.

Nayak, R., "Productivity and the White Collar," *The New York Times,* July 7, 1991.

Peters, T., *Thriving on Chaos,* New York: Knopf, 1987.

Peterson, D.E. and Hillkirk, J., *A Better Idea: Redefining the Way Americans Work,* Boston: Houghton Mifflin, 1991.

Russo, J.E. and Shoemaker, P.J.H., *10 Barriers to Brilliant Decision Making & How to Overcome Them,* New York: Simon & Shuster, 1989.

Sashkin, M. and Sashkin, M.G., *The New Teamwork,* New York: AMA Membership Publications Division, 1994.

Schwartz, P., *The Art of the Long View,* New York: Doubleday, 1991.

Selznik, P., *Leadership in Administration,* New York: Harper & Row, 1957.

Stewart, T.A., "The Search for the Organization of Tomorrow," *Fortune,* May 18, 1992.

Stewart, T.A., "Re-Engineering—The Hot New Managing Tool," *Fortune,* August 23, 1993, pp. 41-45.

Tomasko, R.M., *Rethinking the Corporation: The Architecture of Change,* New York: AMACOM, 1993.

Walton, M., *The Deming Management Method,* New York: Perigee Books/G.P. Putnam, 1986.

Whiteley, R.C., *The Customer-Driven Company: Moving from Talk to Action,* Reading, MA: Addison-Wesley, 1991.

Zaleznik, A., *The Managerial Mystique,* New York: Harper & Row, 1989.

Ziglar, Z., *Top Performance,* New York: Berkley, 1986.

Ziglar, Z., *Secrets of Closing the Sale,* New York: Berkley, 1984.

Suggested Reading for Women Managers

Bernstein, P., *Family Ties, Corporate Bonds,* Doubleday, 1985.

Briles, J., *The Confidence Factor,* Master Media Limited, 1990.

Dowling, C., *Perfect Women,* Summit Books, 1988.

Duff, C.S., *When Women Work Together,* Conari Press, 1993.

Faludi, S., *Backlash: The Undeclared War Against American Women,* Crown Publishers, 1991.

Fierman, J., "Do Women Manage Differently?" *Fortune,* December 17, 1990.

Fisher, A.B., "When Will Women Get to the Top?" *Fortune,* September 21, 1992.

Hardesty, S. and Jacobs, N., *Success and Betrayal: The Crisis of Women in Corporate America,* Franklin Watts, 1986.

Helgesen, S., *The Female Advantage: Women's Ways of Leadership,* Doubleday, 1990.

Hennig, M. and Jardin, A., *The Managerial Woman,* New York: John Wiley & Sons, 1977.

Jongeward, D. and Scott, D., *Women as Winners,* Addison-Wesley Publishing Co., 1983.

Loden, M., *Feminine Leadership or How to Succeed in Business Without Being One of the Boys,* Random House, 1985.

Molloy, J.T., *The Woman's Dress for Success Book,* New York: Warner Books, 1977.

Morrison, A.M., White, R.P. and Van Velsorand, E., *Breaking the Glass Ceiling,* Addison-Wesley Publishing Co., 1987.

Rosener, J., "How Women Lead," *Harvard Business Review,* November-December, 1990.

Scheele, Dr. A., "You're Jealous. What Career Envy Really Means," *Working Woman,* September 1991.

Steinem, Gloria, *Moving Beyond Words,* New York: Simon & Schuster, 1994.

Thomson, A. McKay and Wood, M.D., *Management Strategies for Women,* Simon & Schuster, 1980.

Weiss, D.E., *The Great Divide: How Women and Men Really Differ,* Poseidon Press, 1991.

Index